Embracing Our Selves

The Voice Dialogue Manual

Hal Stone, Ph.D.
Sidra Stone, Ph.D.

New World Library
Novato, CA

Nataraj Publishing
a division of

New World Library
14 Pamaron Way
Novato, CA 94949

Editorial collaborator: Kimberley Peterson
Production coordination: Merrill Peterson
Cover design: Kathleen Vande Kieft
Cover Photo: Hella Hammid
Text Design: Abigail Johnston
Typography: Harrington-Young, Albany, CA

The authors of this book do not dispense medical advice or prescribe the use of any technique as a form of treatment for physical or mental problems without the advice of a physician, either directly or indirectly. In the event you use any of the information in this book, neither the authors nor the publisher can assume any responsibility for your actions. The intent of the authors is only to offer information of a general nature to help you in your quest for personal growth.

This book was originally published as *Embracing Our Selves: Voice Dialogue Manual*, by De Vorss & Co., Marina Del Rey, CA, in 1985.

First Printing, January 1989
Printed in Canada on acid-free paper
ISBN 1-57731-082-9
Distributed to the trade by Publishers Group West

02 01 00 98 97 15 14 13 12 11 10 9 8

To
Belle and Herman Levi
and
Ethel and Sam Stone

Contents

Introduction
by Shakti Gawain

There is a powerful, tingling sensation I feel throughout my body when I hear or read something that I know is profoundly true and important. I call that sensation my "truth bell," and I experienced it quite dramatically the first time I read Hal and Sidra Stone's material on the Voice Dialogue process.

A friend of mine had been seeing a therapist who used Voice Dialogue and had been telling me about it. She sent me a pamphlet written by Hal and Sidra describing Voice Dialogue and that is when my truth bell started ringing. I nearly devoured the pamphlet, excited because it touched on so many things that I'd been discovering and experiencing.

The idea that we have many different "voices" or subpersonalities within us was not new to me. Since childhood I had been fascinated with the story *The Three Faces of Eve*, sensing, perhaps, that it had more relevance to all of us than we might realize. As an adult I had done considerable work with gestalt, transactional analysis, Jungian therapy, and other forms of consciousness work which involve the awareness of many different aspects within the self. But I had never seen or heard it described so clearly and accurately with such insight and understanding.

Eager to learn more, I read the first edition of this book, took an introductory seminar, and began using Voice Dialogue in my own personal process and in my work with others. The more I learned and worked with it, the more excited I felt. The process was fascinating and the results were powerful and dramatic.

Within a short time I met and got to know Hal and Sidra themselves. I have sometimes had the experience of reading a book that moved me deeply, subsequently meeting the author, and feeling somewhat disappointed that the personality did not seem to match the material that came through it. My experience with Hal and Sidra was the opposite. In person they match their material beautifully—down-to-earth and unassuming, intelligent and creative, deeply wise and loving. They have become dear friends and teachers to me and have strongly influenced my personal life and my work. I feel blessed to have them in my life, and I'm excited about sharing their work with others.

I consider the Voice Dialogue process to be one of the most powerful tools for personal growth that I've ever discovered. It has made a significant difference in my life and in the lives of many others I know. I feel that understanding and integrating this work can facilitate a major expansion of consciousness not only for each of us individually but for the entire planet as well.

With love,
Shakti Gawain

Preface

We are delighted that Shakti Gawain and Nataraj Publishing have enabled us to present you with this edition of *Embracing Our Selves.* Many years have passed since the original edition was published and during this period of time we have traveled and taught widely through the United States, Europe, Israel, and Australia. We have watched the Voice Dialogue process emerge around the world, often in places we have never been, taught by teachers that we have never met. This has certainly been a source of gratification for us, primarily because the real spirit of the work has thus far continued to be present during this emergence.

We have continued our own explorations with the Voice Dialogue process and some of our new thinking has been incorporated into this edition. In particular, we have found ourselves more and more interested in the role of the primary selves and their place in the overall development of personality. In our clinical work, we now spend much more time working with the primary selves. We feel it is important for each of us to develop a complete understanding of, and a real appreciation for, the primary selves and how they have operated in each of our lives. Thus you will find here a new emphasis on the role of these selves. We have also added sections on the complementary energies of personal/impersonal and being/doing because these, too, have proven very useful.

As we have become more aware of the impact of this work, we have increasingly realized that certain safeguards should be kept in mind when using it. Therefore, we have expanded the section on safeguards in the Voice Dialogue process and we suggest that you read it carefully. Above all, please be aware that Voice Dialogue is a communications tool as well as a method that can be used for getting to know ourselves better. It is neither a psychotherapeutic system nor a substitute for appropriate psychotherapy when this is indicated.

In our travels, teachings, and writings we have steadfastly refused to provide any kind of certification process for training in Voice Dialogue. There is no such thing as a Voice Dialogue therapy. It is impossible to separate Voice Dialogue from an understanding of dream work, symbolic visualization, a knowledge of energetics, training in interpersonal processes, or a multitude of other approaches to understanding the evolution of consciousness. The richer the background of the facilitator in all of these approaches, the richer will be the quality of facilitation. This is one of the reasons why the Voice Dialogue process can be integrated into any theoretical approach or any way of working with issues of personal growth. It supplements and enriches them rather than polarizing against them. It is for this reason that you will find the work being used by an amazingly wide range of therapists, consciousness teachers, and nonprofessionals of different orientations.

We must keep in mind that Voice Dialogue is not a thing unto itself but rather a means to an end. As a tool for communication and for the exploration of consciousness, it helps to being to our awareness the inner knowing and deeper intuitions that lie dormant in each of us. It is one among a multitude of approaches that are concerned with the process of personal growth and transformation. However positive a tool Voice Dialogue may be, we must always keep the process primary—in this way the tool will remain in its proper perspective.

In the first edition of this book, we presented our early thinking about how the many selves interact in relationships, and we developed the theory of bonding patterns. Since then our own thinking has deepened and has evolved to a considerable extent on matters of personal relationships in general and primary relationships in particular. On the recommendation of our editor, we have removed the relationship chapter from this book. A new book fully devoted to issues of relationship, *Embracing Each Other*, is now available from Nataraj Publishing.

We feel that the new format for *Embracing Our Selves* makes this work more accessible and enjoyable, that it will lead you, the reader, along the path of discovery in a most delightful and effortless fashion. We wish you a happy journey.

Hal and Sidra Stone
Albion, CA

Acknowledgments

We are extremely grateful to the many friends, colleagues, clients, and program participants around the world who have given us so much. In addition to the basic dialogue and dream material that we used in creating this book and our theories, they have contributed their insights, their wisdom, their support, and their love. For these, too, we are extremely grateful.

We cannot thank everyone individually, but we would like to give specific thanks to some people who have been especially helpful throughout the years. First, we wish to thank Herb and Beverly Gelfand for their truly generous support and love. Without them, life would have been far more difficult.

Our thanks, too, to Carolyn Conger for being a part of our lives and bringing to us all the gifts, both personal and professional, that are so naturally a part of her. She has been a trailbreaker, a support, and a guiding force in the development of many of the centers around the world.

Zahina Ayeroff has been more than an administrator. Her genius and grace in dealing with the myriad details of our lives have simplified matters greatly and made it possible for us to concentrate on our professional work and growth.

Shaki Gawain has thrown her marvelous energy and her love behind our work and behind us, personally, and supported us unstintingly. For this, we are truly grateful.

When we think of the early years of the first edition of *Embracing Our Selves*, two people stand out. Marilyn Reardon, who spent untold hours typing the very first drafts of our manuscript while cheerfully and competently attending to all the other business aspects of our professional and personal lives, still merits our thanks. We also wish to thank Hedda Lark, who helped with the editing, gave us much valuable advice, and coordinated all the details of the original publication with DeVorss & Co.

We wish to acknowledge the following people who helped to bring our work to other cities and countries and who have continued to support our work and programs in recent years: In Los Angels, we wish to thank Paul Abell, Hillary Anderson, Carol Bardin, Yvonne de Miranda, Liza Hughes, Larry Novick, John Rhone, Diana Russell, Alice Scully, Marsha Sheldon, Elizabeth Shuck, Ronna Siegel, Patricial Spangler, and Marion Young. We would also like to thank Gina Thompson for her ongoing personal and professional support as director of the Center for the Healing Arts and, later, the Hermes Project.

We would like to thank Richard Lamm for initially introducing our work to Holland, and arranging the first workshop in The Hague. Richard is now in Los Angeles. The work in Holland has been continued beautifully by Robert Stamboliev and Jerien Koolbergen who conduct ongoing teaching and training programs. They have gathered around them a wonderful group of teachers and have contributed much to the further evolution of Voice Dialogue. In Holland, too, we would like to thank Jan Leewis, David Grabjian, and Chaitzen Doustra of the Mesa Verde Uitgivers for arranging the translation and publication of

Embracing Our Selves in Dutch. Our first foreign language edition was a very exciting event for us.

Special thanks go to Lydia Duncan who has supported us professionally and personally throughout the years. A tireless worker and a woman of many gifts, she introduced Voice Dialogue to England and to Australia. She arranged for the first English workshop and it was her work in Australia which was largely responsible for the success of our two-month tour of that country. We would also like to thank Christopher Sanderson and Christobel Munson for sponsoring our tour of Australia, for the many hours they spent in planning and making arrangements and for their delicious hospitality. In addition to Lydia, we would like to thank Gabriella Pinto who has continued coordinating the work in England and has been a strong loving support, both professionally and personally. Thanks, too, to Don Ball and Sheila Borges who played a major role in coordinating Voice Dialogue activities there during the early years.

In Israel, we would like to thank Yael Haft-Pomrock both for her initial vision and for her unceasing efforts on behalf of Voice Dialogue over the past years. We also wish to thank Gusty Dreyfuss for his hard work and support, particularly in the first, most difficult, years.

From the very beginning, Joseph Heller has supported our work. We thank him for his support and for his introduction of Voice Dialogue into many areas of the world that we have not yet reached personally. Joseph was the first to recognize the synergistic effects of combining Voice Dialogue with bodywork and he incorporated Voice Dialogue into his Hellerwork trainings in the '70s.

The following people have supported our work over the years with love and enthusiasm and we would like to offer them our special thanks: Lucia Bettler and Phil Bohnert of Houston; Betty Bosdell of Chicago (now in Southern California); Anna Ivara and Arthur Levy of New York; Lynn Lumbard of San Francisco; Jennifer and Ed Moffatt of Sun

Valley; Susan Sims Smith of Little Rock; Susan Scwartz of Oslo; Fr. Bill Whittier of Minneapolis; Eberhard Winkler of Zurich; and Martha Lou Wolff (now in Southern California) and Diana Smith in Paris.

To our children—Joshua, Judith, Elizabeth, Claudia, and Recha—we wish to say a very special thank you for all the gifts you've given us and for how much you have taught us about life!

In closing, we would like to thank Marc Allen and Kimberley Peterson for their roles in bringing forth this edition of *Embracing Our Selves.* Marc was most helpful and remained personally involved in all stages of production. Kimberley, as our editor, was intelligent, sensitive and skillful, as she gently and tactfully guided us through this revision.

Last, but not least, we would like to express our delight with our new publisher, Nataraj Publishing. It is both an honor and a pleasure to be members of the exciting and creative Nataraj family.

Prologue

The Awakening

Once upon a time there was a tigress who was about to give birth. One day when she was out hunting she came upon a herd of goats. She gave chase and, even in her condition, managed to kill one of them. But the stress of the chase forced her into labor, and she died as she gave birth to a male cub. The goats, who had run away, returned when they sensed that the danger was over. Approaching the dead tigress, they discovered her newborn cub and adopted him into their herd.

The tiger cub grew up among the goats believing he, too, was a goat. He bleated as well as he could, he smelled like a goat, and ate only vegetation; in every respect he behaved like a goat. Yet within him, as we are well aware, beat the heart of a tiger.

All went well until the day that an older tiger approached the goat herd and attacked and killed one of the goats. The rest of the goats ran away as soon as they saw the old tiger, but our tiger/goat saw no reason to run away, of course, for he sensed no danger.

Although the old tiger was a veteran of many hunts, he had never in his life been as shocked as he was when he confronted the young tiger. He did not know what to make of this full-grown tiger who smelled like a goat, bleated like a goat, and in every other way acted like a goat. Being a rather gruff old duffer, and not particularly sympathetic, the old tiger grabbed the young one by the scruff of the neck, dragged him to a nearby creek, and showed him his reflection in the water. But the young tiger was unimpressed with his own reflection; it meant nothing to him and he failed to see his similarity to the old tiger.

Frustrated by this lack of comprehension, the old tiger dragged the young one back to the place where he had made his kill. There he ripped a piece of meat from the dead goat and shoved it into the mouth of our young friend.

We can well imagine the young tiger's shock and consternation. At first he gagged and tried spitting out the raw flesh, but the old tiger was determined to show the young one who he really was, so he made sure the cub swallowed this new food. When he was sure the cub had swallowed it all, the old tiger shoved another piece of meat into him, and this time there was a change.

Our young tiger now allowed himself to taste the raw flesh and the warm blood, and he ate this piece with gusto. When he finished chewing, the young tiger stretched, and then, for the first time in his young life, he let out a powerful roar—the roar of the jungle cat. Then the two tigers disappeared together into the forest.

Heinrich Zimmer tells this story in the opening of his book, *The Philosophy of India*, and calls the young tiger's roar the "roar of awakening." What is this "roar of awakening?" It is the discovery that we are more than we think we are. It is the discovery that we have taken on identities that incorrectly or inadequately express our essential being. It is as though we have been dreaming and suddenly we awaken from the dream, look around, and become aware of a totally different reality.

Let us reconsider the story of the tiger/goat: Until he meets the old tiger, he believes he is a goat and he experiences the world as a goat would experience it. The young tiger's reality is that of a goat, but we can see that his goat-like perception of reality allows him to experience only a fraction of his total being. We know he is capable of many other perceptions, emotions, and activities. We might paraphrase the story and say that he only manifested his goat "self" until the old tiger awakened him to his essential being—the tiger he really was.

Symbolically, we are all raised as goats; we are all raised in cultures and families where we are trained to think, feel, and see in specific, predetermined ways. Because our learned perceptions are all that we know, we naturally assume that the world around us actually exists as we perceive it, and the self we know is the only one there is. This is our reality.

Consider a man who is raised in a family that worships the mind: If this man believes his mind is his primary source of information regarding the world, then he is in the same situation as our tiger/goat. This man will know nothing of his "other" nature. He will know nothing of his imagination, his deeper intuitions, the reality and validity of his feelings. He will not have access to the information available from these other sources. Furthermore, he will be denied the richness and pleasure that this "other" nature could bring to him.

It is this "other" nature—these "lost" parts of ourselves—that this book and the Voice Dialogue method seek to restore. It is hoped that through using the techniques and understanding the processes described in *Embracing Our Selves*, you, too, may give voice to your own deep "roar of awakening" and discover the wealth of your unexplored selves.

PART I

The Voice Dialogue Method

1

A New Vision of Consciousness

The Introduction to Our Selves

The moment of awakening is a very special time in our lives. It may happen while we are awake, it may be the result of a dream, or it may occur during meditation. It is always accompanied by a heightened awareness—our perceptions and feelings are intensified and we experience a sense of new perspectives. The moment of awakening is well-illustrated by the case of Marilyn, a woman in her thirties who had a strong sense of identification with the role of "mother." Throughout her life, she treated everyone she encountered as a mother would treat a child. She had taken it upon herself to care for the world; this attitude was her "goat nature." After she entered therapy she had the following dream. It appeared at that moment of awakening when Marilyn began to separate from her maternal nature, when she began to awaken from the "sleep" she had mistaken for reality.

> Sounds have become acute. There is so much noise and confusion I cannot rest. I finally become fully awake and I look

> about me. It is as if I were in a strange house and yet I know it is my house and I have lived in it for a long time. There is a mirror across from my bed and I glance at it. I am horrified to see that I have grown old while I slept. The noise is deafening and I go out to try to find where it is coming from. As I reach the kitchen door, I realize it comes from there. Around the kitchen table are many people, some young, some far older than I am. They are all dressed in children's clothes and are waiting to be fed. They see me and begin to pound their bowls on the table and call me "mother." I see my priest across the room with his back to me, and I think he can surely explain this to me, but as I approach him he turns around and I see that he is wearing a bib and holding a bowl, too! I run back to the door to leave and, as I pass the table, I see my parents there, wearing bibs like all the rest. I reach the door as a man comes in. I know him to be my husband, although he is not the husband I had when I went to sleep. He makes a pass at me and I feel relieved, thinking at least he doesn't think I'm his mother. When I look at him, however, he is wearing knickers and his face is the face of a child. I think that this is a nightmare and I run and shut myself in my room in order to wake up more fully, but I know I am not asleep. I ask myself over and over again: "What have I done while I slept?" Ray comes into the room [Ray is a therapist in the city where she lived]. I think that surely he can help me to understand this, but he is crying because he has hurt his knee and wants me to bandage it.

This dream clearly shows Marilyn's moment of awakening. Until now, the only reality that she has known has been this self-programmed "mother" identity (her goat nature) that she has been locked into since early childhood. The dream image is so poignant—during the time she has been asleep she has grown old while everyone around her has become a child needing nurturing. But now Marilyn is awake and separating from her identification with her mother nature. She is looking at herself and her surroundings through newly opened eyes and thus is beginning to ask questions and search for something different. She is curious.

She wants to discover what exists within her, other than this mother, and to move toward the fullness of her being. Much as our tiger/goat discovered his tiger self, Marilyn, too, will discover parts of her true nature that she has not known before.

The "roar of awakening" is not always a roar. We may experience it as a roar when it applies to our "tiger" selves—our sexuality or intense feelings—but many other facets of our true nature also await discovery. Ralph, a successful, hardworking, rational sixty-two-year-old man, had the following dream of discovery:

> I am walking on a country road. Suddenly I hear a noise; it sounds like a cry. I look down and, to the side of the road, I see a hand sticking up from the earth. I am shocked and I run to the hand and start digging there. I dig deeper until I unearth the body of a child who is about three or four years of age. He is barely alive. I start to clean him off and I hold him to me.

In this dream, awakening comes as an unearthing of something that was buried long ago—the inner child. Ralph had spent his life identified with those traits that pushed him toward great financial and political success, yet something was missing from his life. He had never known a real intimacy with others. In this dream he began to deal with that intimacy as he made the remarkable discovery that a very important part of himself had been buried—his vulnerability, his fear of the world, his feelings of isolation, and his fear of abandonment. These qualities were embodied in the child who was "buried," one of Ralph's selves that had been fully repressed by the time he was four.

Sometimes the process of awakening to what lies within us is presented to us as a journey. This is a very common motif in dream symbolism. A fifty-year-old woman at the beginning of her voyage of personal discovery dreamed she had to go on a journey by herself, with no assistance from her husband or anyone else. The journey stretched ahead of her; it was a long and difficult process to find her way home. Her unconscious was portraying her evolving consciousness as a journey, a journey that each one of us must take alone. It is a long and often difficult way home, for in order to embrace our "tiger nature" and experience our roar of awakening, we must first meet and embrace the multitude of selves that make up the rich totality of our entire being. As we uncover each new self and learn to honor it, it becomes a source of information for us in our continuing journey.

After becoming aware of her strong maternal identification Marilyn (the woman who had dreamed of being a mother to everyone) realized she had also strongly identified with her rational self. She took up meditation, and this practice precipitated experiences far different from anything that she had known before. For example, one night she had a dream with a very religious flavor. It upset her because spirituality was not a legitimate part of her "goat nature" (rationality). The following experience resulted:

> I awakened from a dream feeling very disturbed. I could not go back to sleep so I went down to the living room and lit a cigarette. The kitchen light was on, throwing a shaft of light into the living room, so I did not turn on any other light. Our living room rug is sand-colored and the path of light from the kitchen door illuminated it. I was idly looking at this portion of the rug when it suddenly seemed filled with writing. We have a clear plate glass top on the coffee table and I thought that perhaps a letter was lying on it and the light had somehow projected the writing onto the rug, but there was no letter on the coffee table. I even moved the coffee table but the writing remained. I then tried to rub it out with my foot, thinking that the children had been writing in the nap of the rug with their fingers. Still it persisted, so I sat down to try to read it but was unable to. I thought: Whoever you are, please show me what you are trying to say. The words then appeared on the rug one at a time and I was able to read them. If I couldn't read one of them and felt confused, the word reappeared on the rug at

once. This occurred each time I felt confusion. It no longer seemed like a sand-colored rug but more like sand itself with words etched deeply into it. These are the words I can recall:

You meet yourself not yet. You must love your life. Find a mind whose hope is a light to light the way for your soul. I gave you Mary [a figure in the dream from which she had awakened and from which her disturbance arose]. Why have you not hoped? Now you have begun again. Put love next to hope and follow them to your self. The voyage has begun.

I closed my eyes and thought, this is crazy. I am imagining this. Writing cannot appear on a carpet. Something said to me: "Can you throw stones at those who will not see?"

I opened my eyes and the writing was gone. I got up and looked closely at the space where it had been. I felt it must have left some mark because it had not been written on the surface but with depth, as if it were actually written in sand. There was not a trace. I was angry with myself because I had not accepted it at once and thus had lost some of the words.

In the tiger story, the roar of awakening represents the discovery of our basic instinctual nature. It tells us we must fully become what we are. Ralph discovered the lost little boy of his childhood who would be reclaimed through this process. In Marilyn's case, we discover a radically different kind of energy—what we would call spiritual or transpersonal energy. Her vision initiated her into a different reality. She was asked to find a new mind—a mind of hope that could light the way for her soul. The voice of her spiritual nature offered such a different teaching from what she had known until now! In effect, she was being asked to develop new ways of thinking that were more compatible with the realities of these emergent spiritual energies. The evolution of consciousness is filled with such surprises.

In contrast to Marilyn, Jane was working on the issue of empowerment. Her roar of awakening happened during psychotherapy. She had learned how to be powerful in the world, but at the expense of her inner child and her basic instinctual reactions. She was introduced to her inner child during a Voice Dialogue session (the Voice Dialogue method will be discussed in detail in Chapter Three) when the child was allowed to speak and become real for one of the first times in Jane's adulthood. As a result of this process, Jane became aware of the child, and thus successfully separated from it. A few nights later she encountered her lost instinctual energies in the following dream:

> I am in a room with a small lion. I rush to the door, quite terrified, and open it and push the lion out. I come back into the room, breathing a sigh of relief, when I see another, much larger lion. I am terrified and I rush to the door to open it, but the lion gets there first, preventing me from opening the door to either get it out or leave it behind.

This dream is very much like our tiger story. This time, however, it is a lion that our dreamer must face. She cannot escape her lion, and it grows and becomes more powerful. In fact, the lion is an aspect of herself that can no longer be ignored. By facing this lion and learning to use its energies, she will make the power of her instincts available. With this power, she can successfully care for herself and, in particular, for her inner child. This is true empowerment: Our vulnerability is available in relationships in a conscious way, and our instinctual energies are also available to function protectively. Thus, our energies are balanced; we do not need to behave in a particularly assertive fashion for we are quite naturally in a position of power.

How We Develop

We have referred to the fact that we are made up of many selves. These selves have been referred to in many different ways by many different people. They have been known as the many I's, selves or partial selves, complexes, multiple personalities, and, more recently, as energy patterns. We use the terms *selves*, *subpersonalities*, and *energy patterns* interchangeably throughout this book.

The concept that we are made up of different selves is sometimes difficult to understand. Some people object to this idea, arguing that such a theory fragments the personality. We feel that it is already "fragmented," and our task is to become aware of this fragmentation or multiplicity of selves so that we can make valid choices in our lives.

These contradictory feelings are apparent in all of us at one time or another. The higher the emotional stakes, the more likely we are to experience a variety of feelings in any given situation. Consider a woman whose only child is leaving home—on one side, we can see her feelings of relief: "I wish she'd hurry up and move out. I'm so eager to have the house to myself." On the other side, we see her feelings of loss: "I wish she wouldn't go. I wish she would stay and keep me company forever. She's such fun." Or think of a man who is offered a promotion to a key leadership position. Needless to say, one part of him is overjoyed and looks forward to the challenge, the authority, and the excitement that come with the position. Another part regrets the loss of camaraderie that necessarily accompanies this move up from the ranks.

How do these selves develop? A newborn infant is a unique human being who comes into the world with its own genetic make-up that determines its physiology (and some of its behavior) and with a specific quality of "being" unique to the infant. We call this unique quality of being the infant's "psychic fingerprint." Any woman who has had more than one child will readily acknowledge how different each child was, even in utero. After birth this difference is even more apparent.

The newborn infant is quite defenseless, totally vulnerable, and dependent upon the adult world for its survival. However, along with its basic, unique psychic fingerprint, the infant also has the potential to develop an infinite array of energy patterns or selves, the sum total of which will constitute the individual personality. At this point in life, the armoring of our vulnerability and the development of our personality begin.

The infant learns that he or she must establish some measure of control over the environment to avoid unpleasantness. This development of control is actually the evolution of the personality. Personality develops as a way of dealing with vulnerability. The stronger the developing personality, the farther away the child moves from vulnerability, from its psychic fingerprint. It loses contact with its unique being as it learns to be powerful.

How does this process work? How does the child become more powerful? The child learns, for example, that the mother is very happy when baby smiles. Now baby may enjoy smiling, but soon enjoyment will be overridden by the knowledge that smiling brings about certain consequences. Similarly, going to the toilet soon becomes a *cause célèbre* as a system of rewards and punishments is established in relation to the acts of urination and defecation. Aggression is also either rewarded or punished. It may be seen as a means of mastering the world or it may be treated as negative or antisocial behavior.

In some instances, the child might try to establish some measure of control over the environment by retreating into fantasy. Daydreams may then become a key factor in shaping the personality. For example, a young boy whose parents separated developed a fantasy that he was in a submarine deep under the sea. He spent increasing amounts of time in his fantasy submarine in an effort to make himself feel better. Objectively speaking, he was obviously retreating from pain. On another level, he had found a way of dealing with his extreme vulnerability. In contrast, another child realized that success in school was the key to mastering his environment and protecting his vulnerable selves, so he developed his ambitious side and his pleasing characteristics.

In our developmental process we are rewarded for certain behaviors and punished for others; thus, some selves are strengthened and others are weakened. We learn our lessons well and consequently develop "personalities." It is strange to think that a personality is actually a system of subpersonalities (selves) that eradicates our psychic fingerprint as it brings us control—and thereby power—in the world.

In fact, one of the earliest aspects of our personality to develop is the self that watches over us. It is like a bodyguard—constantly searching for dangers that may lurk around us and determining how it can best protect us from them. It incorporates parental and societal injunctions and controls our behavior, to a large extent, by establishing a set of rules that it feels will ensure our safety and our acceptance by others. It decides how emotional we can be. It makes sure we do not act foolishly or in ways in which we might embarrass ourselves. We call this self the protector/controller.

The protector/controller is the primary energy pattern behind many other selves. For example, it will utilize the energies of the rational self and the responsible parent as a way of maintaining control over our environment. When most people use the word "I," they are in fact referring to their protector/controller. For the vast majority of us, protector/controller energy is the directing agent of personality. It is what many people think of as an ego.

We see then how, in the development of personality, different energy patterns serve to make our sojourn on earth a more successful one. The problem is, of course, that we gradually begin to lose track of our psychic fingerprint. This is a sad state of affairs, for our whole system of relationships is affected by this loss. If we are no longer in touch with those qualities that make up our unique psychic fingerprint, then it is *not* our deepest and most vulnerable self that is involved in relationships. Instead, it is a group of subpersonalities, watched over by the protector/controller, that determines our feelings and behavior. Thus, we always have a vague fear that if the other person *really* knew what we were like, he or she would abandon us (even though we ourselves do not know what this mysterious "real" person is actually like).

We can see, therefore, how important it is to learn about the subpersonalities that operate within us. Without this understanding, we are in the powerless position of watching different subpersonalities drive our psychological car while we sit in the back seat or, worse yet, hide in the trunk. It becomes a matter of great importance to discover what these selves are and how they operate within us. This journey of discovery is the evolution of consciousness.

It may seem strange to think of our car being driven by different selves, each demanding its turn, yet this is exactly the situation. We have usually been so well-conditioned that by the time we reach adulthood, and generally long before, we have lost all connection to our psychic fingerprint—to our true being. As has been suggested, we no longer know who we are or what we feel. Our tigers and lions have long been buried, and we only glimpse them in momentary lapses. We may fall into rages periodically and not know why. It is easy to forget about such outbursts, to believe that "that really wasn't me that felt like killing, it was just an aberration."

Our lions and tigers often emerge when we drink and the protector/controller's control begins to dissolve in the alcohol. For example, a very quiet, controlled man flew into rages and used terrible language to his wife whenever he drank. This went on for years. The therapist suggested to the wife that she record her husband's remarks during one of his inebriated diatribes. She did this and played it back to him when he was sober. He was in a state of shock when he heard the tape. He couldn't believe he had really said those things!

Let us examine how these lions and tigers get buried in the first place. Consider the hypothetical case of Kevin, a young four-year-old child. He was playing outdoors when, suddenly, he ran into the house because another child had hit him. His mother responded very protectively, and said, "Johnnie is a mean boy. Why don't you stay with me and keep me company." In doing this, she failed to help her son deal with his instinctual life. She had most likely never dealt with hers and did not know how to support Kevin's natural aggressions.

That night, Kevin had a nightmare. He woke up screaming about a lion in his room. His mother came in and comforted him and assured him that there was no lion, that it was "just a dream." So he went back to bed and soon dreamed the same nightmare. He awoke screaming once again. This time his mother turned on the lights and, together, they looked under the bed and in the closet. Thus, she demonstrated fully that there was no lion. After a few more repetitions of this scenario, there really was no more lion for Kevin.

What has actually happened here? First, Kevin was protected from dealing with his natural aggression. Then, the natural aggression appeared in a dream in the form of a lion. Because he had denied the lion in his waking life, and his mother supported his denial, the lion in his dream became his enemy. Next, the reality of the symbolic life was denied. Kevin's mother had never learned to honor the dream, to honor the symbolic life, so how could she do otherwise? So it is that early in Kevin's life the protector/controller grew stronger and became a directing agent that made sure Kevin would avoid aggressive children. Because he did not know how to deal with aggression, Kevin either became a victim to such children or played only with children who posed no threat to him.

Kevin grew up to become a trial attorney, yet he was always filled with anxiety in the courtroom. What filled him with such dread whenever he faced an unscrupulous attorney on the opposing side of the case? It was his lion, stirring deep inside his loins. He did not realize this, however. Instead, he felt discomfort as this part of him (that his mother disowned in herself and taught him to disown in himself) was activated deep in his unconscious.

Without his lion available to him as an ally, Kevin felt vulnerable, and the child within him felt endangered. He was also unaware of this inner child; he had lost contact with it a long time ago as well, for, unlike Peter Pan, Kevin grew up. His "psychological car" was driven at various times by his inner pusher, his pleaser, his frightened child, and his inner critic, who was always willing to let him know how inadequate he really was. At night Kevin often dreamed of great violence but, after all, to him these were "only" dreams.

From our perspective, Kevin's evolution is a perfectly normal and natural one. He has no awareness operating, so no aware ego can drive his car in accordance with the rules that would suit his essential being. Instead, it is driven by his subpersonalities (an amazing array of characters). This is exactly the case with the vast majority of us before we experience our own roar of awakening.

As we have said before, one of the primary issues in the evolution of consciousness is the discovery of these subpersonalities and how they operate within us. Before we discuss the discovery of these selves and how we go about learning more about them, we must first define a conceptual structure that will be referred to over and over again in this book. Our approach to the exploration of selves is based on this conceptual structure or definition of consciousness and related terms.

The Nature of Consciousness

In approaching the definition of consciousness, we start with the basic idea that consciousness is not an *entity*—it is a *process*. What we will be defining, therefore, is not consciousness but the evolution of consciousness. We call it consciousness, but we are not talking about a static condition of being. As far as we are concerned, people do not become conscious; consciousness is not a state that people strive to attain. Consciousness is a process that must be lived out—an evolutionary process that continually changes from one moment to the next. As we refer to consciousness in the coming pages, it will be important to keep this kinetic aspect of the process in mind.

Consciousness evolves on three distinctly different levels. The first is the level of awareness. The second level is the *experience* of the different selves, subpersonalities, or energy patterns. The third level is the development of an aware ego.

Awareness

Awareness is the capacity to witness life in all its aspects without evaluating or judging the energy patterns being witnessed, and without needing to control the outcome of an event. It is often referred to in spiritual and esoteric writings as the "witness state" or "consciousness." In these writings, it is seen as a position of nonattachment. It is neither rational nor, conversely, emotional. It is simply a point of reference that objectively witnesses what is.

This awareness level of consciousness must be clearly differentiated from the energy pattern that we call the protector/controller. The protector/controller is subjective in its observations. It is always deeply concerned about our impact on others. It always has a specific goal in mind. It is generally quite rational and very much determines what we perceive and the way we think and behave. In contrast, the awareness level is simply the silent witness, observing in an objective fashion. Most meditative systems seek to develop the awareness level of consciousness. It is a nonaction reference point. It does not do anything except witness. In traditional psychological systems, this awareness would be related to the concept of pure insight.

The Experience of the Selves

The second aspect of the evolution of consciousness is the experience of the energy patterns. We see everything in life as an energy pattern of one kind or another. These patterns relate to our internal states—be they physical, emotional, mental, or spiritual. The energy patterns may vary from a vague feeling or barely discernible sensation to a fully developed subpersonality. The next examples will illustrate this phase of the process.

A man is angry and is either raging inside or expressing his rage for all to see. We would say that he is overcome by his enraged self. His consciousness is not participating because his awareness is not available. Once he becomes aware of his rage, two of our basic conditions for consciousness will have been met: He will experience his rage, and, on another level, his awareness will dispassionately inform him of this fact.

In another example, a woman experiences powerful energies during a meditation and identifies them as spiritual energies. Again, if she has an awareness level that witnesses this spiritual experience, then two conditions of consciousness have been met, and we would say that here, too, consciousness is evolving.

Let us consider yet a third example, taken from an actual case we encountered in our work with Voice Dialogue. Susan was at a party with her husband, and she was feeling very jealous because he was showing a great deal of attention to another woman there. Susan's strong spiritual training, however, had taught her that feelings such as anger and jealousy can and *should* be transmuted. She had learned how to do this by meditating, so she meditated until she felt detached from the situation. Soon, she was no longer feeling jealousy; she was feeling love.

From our perspective, Susan actually controlled her emotional reaction with the help of her protector/controller, and then, through her meditative capabilities, tapped into a love energy from her spiritual side. She, however, believed she had transmuted the jealousy into love. From our perspective, neither transmutation nor awareness are at play here; Susan has simply buried her jealousy. Had she been aware, she would have felt the jealousy within her, and she would also have been aware of this feeling and its significance.

It is important to remember that perfection is thankfully beyond the grasp of most of us. Therefore, we do not expect awareness and experience to occur simultaneously. We do not need to "wait" for our awareness to develop—we can live our lives fully, as we are, for our awareness will eventually enter into the picture.

So far in our system we have described awareness and the experience of the energy patterns. As we have stated before, we view the experiencing of the energy patterns from a holistic perspective. This means simply that it is all-inclusive—it incorporates experiences deriving from physical, emotional, mental, and spiritual dimensions. Our perceptions and experience of the world in which we live take place within this holistic spectrum of energies. We must yet incorporate the third level to complete our definition of the evolution of consciousness.

The Aware Ego

In its traditional definition, and we agree with this view, the ego has been referred to as the *executive function* of the psyche, or the choice maker. Someone has to run the operation and the ego does the job. According to our system, the ego receives its information from both the awareness level and the experience of the different energy patterns. As our consciousness evolves, the ego becomes a more aware ego. As a more aware ego, it is in a better position to make real choices.

However, very early in this work it becomes clear that the ego has succumbed to a combination of different subpersonalities that have taken over its executive function. Thus, what is functioning as the ego may, in fact, be a combination of the protector/controller, pusher, pleaser, perfectionist, and inner critic. This unique combination of subpersonalities, or energy systems, perceives the world in which we live, processes this information, and then directs our lives. When this happens, our ego has *identified* with these particular patterns. Most people believe that they have free will because *they* choose to do a particular thing and they think that this is really choosing. We have discovered, however, that there is remarkably little choice in the world. Unless we awaken to the consciousness process, the vast majority of us are run by the energy patterns with which we are identified or by those which we have disowned.

Let us contrast an ego identified with a particular set of subpersonalities with an aware ego. A physician, John, wished to go to Mexico to practice medicine in order to help the poor people there. He considered himself very altruistic and spiritual, and he wished to do some kind of planetary service. Shortly after he made his decision he dreamed he was sitting on a throne somewhere in Mexico, being honored with respect and gifts by the local peasants.

According to our system, John's ego has been identified with a spiritual self-sacrificing energy pattern. He had always been a very responsible man and service was a part of the way the responsible father within him acted in the world. The dream revealed a new energy pattern that John was not aware of before the dream—his power broker—that part of him that selfishly sought aggrandizement. This does not indicate a wrong choice; it simply means that when John chose, no aware ego was present. The spiritual service-oriented responsible father made the choice.

It is now possible for John to step back from this self and witness, from the level of awareness, the spiritually oriented self-sacrificing self with which he has been identified. Furthermore, he can witness this new self—his need for self-aggrandizement. His ego receives the information made available by the awareness level *and* by the experience of his two selves. His ego is now more aware, and he is now in a position to make a *real* choice about going to Mexico. He may choose to go, not go, or to defer the decision—the actual decision is inconsequential. What matters is which self makes the decision. It can readily be seen that as our consciousness evolves, decision-making becomes somewhat more complex!

Thus far, we have described the three aspects of the evolution of consciousness and their interrelationships. The consequences of this definition are far-reaching, for if we accept this hypothesis, there will be no reason to feel bad or guilty about the way we are. Each self will be fully honored; our awareness will simply witness what is.

However, most of us have a surgeon's mentality when it comes to those selves we dislike. We try so hard to get rid of our temper, our rage, jealousy, pettiness, shyness, feelings of inadequacy...the list is endless. In an attempt to eradicate these rejected selves, we make them much stronger by driving them into the unconscious where they are free to operate beyond our control. If we can learn to step back and allow our awareness to operate, we will not only encounter these selves, we will also realize that our wish to eradicate these patterns is actually the voice of yet another self. We have within us a subpersonality that labels these unwanted selves as detestable and makes us feel absolutely dreadful for having them in the first place. But when our awareness is allowed to operate and we rise above this surgical mentality, we will rejoice at our newfound sense of freedom.

The rejection of unacceptable energy patterns brings up the question of transmutation and how it applies to the evolution of consciousness. This is an important concept today because so many people are trying to transmute instinctual energies as they adhere to spiritual traditions. The idea of *transmutation* is quite different from *transformation*. We have defined transmutation in the alchemical sense—changing energies from one form to another. We have described consciousness as a continually changing evolutionary process. The evolution of consciousness is also a process of ever-increasing expansion of the awareness level, ever-increasing awareness of the ego, and ever-increasing experience of the vast multitude of energy patterns that are available to be experienced. Transformation, a change in composition and character, can occur at any of these three levels. Let us now examine the issues of transmutation through an example.

George was strongly identified with a spiritual, loving part of himself. He believed he had no reason to express negative feelings when he could just as easily express positive ones. He had always believed he was successfully transmuting his negative energies by learning to control them and act in a loving and kind way. He truly believed that experiencing negativity would add to the negative energies in the world and was committed to transmuting negative energies into gold, much as the alchemists of old did. Difficulties in business—he had become involved with dishonest people who endangered his business—led him to seek therapy. Because he had rejected his own dishonesty, power, and negativity, he was blind to these qualities in other people. During this period he had the following dream:

> I am walking on a path and I come to a tree. There is a snake in the tree and it is angry at me. It jumps to bite me and I have a sword and I cut it in half. Then the part with the head jumps again and I cut it in half again. I keep doing this until there is only a small piece of the head left. This small piece leaps at me and I feel the fangs sink deeply into my hand.

What George considered to be transmutation we recognize as the repression of his instinctual life. The snake was angry with him—and for good reason. George was raised in a family setting where control was the key word. No awareness guided this family's interactions; hence, no aware ego had developed in any of its members. George's ego was identified with a system of spiritual values. Thus, his natural protector/controller had simply taken on these spiritual values because they served his purpose. Instead of transmuting his rage, dishonesty, and negativity, George was, in fact, unconsciously *empowering* these feelings in the very act of repressing them. The snake, a classic symbol of our basic instinctual life, will not go away and it will have its revenge—of that we may be sure.

Sam, on the other hand, identified with power and had always rejected his vulnerability. In the course of therapy he became aware of his power and the degree to which he had been identified with it. He also became aware of the vulnerable child within him. His older brother, Jack, had also been a power person and a lot of Sam's need for power originated in this relationship. He had the following dream shortly after the discovery of his inner child:

> I'm at a party and my brother Jack is there. He goes someplace in the room and when he returns to me, he is crying. I hold him in my arms and he tells me that someone hurt his feelings and he wonders why anyone would hurt him like that.

This dream shows that Sam has developed awareness in his waking life. He is now aware of his opposing energy patterns of vulnerability and power. This is transformation—an awareness of the opposites and the ability of the aware ego to honor both patterns and tolerate the tension that exists between them. Out of this separation from the power (the self with which he has been identified) and the honoring of the child (the self he has repressed), an organic transformation of the energy patterns themselves occurs. In the dream, Jack—the brother who symbolizes the power side—becomes more vulnerable and Sam is now holding him. This is a symbolic portrayal of the transformational process as it occurs in a specific energy pattern.

You may have already noticed in your reading of this chapter that there is a dictum underlying our ideas, a basic premise for our work. It is simple: We must learn to honor all our selves. The selves we do not honor grow inside of us in unconscious ways, gaining power and authority. The snake that George tries so hard to kill lives inside him, growing in power, waiting to have its revenge. We must develop both awareness and an aware ego that can exist separately from the selves we have identified with and acknowledge those selves from which we flee. Honoring all the selves in this way will provide us with a greater degree of choice in our actions.

But who, you may ask, are "we?" We have seen from our discussion of consciousness thus far that who "we" are can be rather problematical. In the context of our system, the word "we" refers to the ego that is involved in the evolution of consciousness. It is an ego that is becoming more and more aware as it processes the information received from our awareness and the experience of the different energy patterns.

In this chapter we have traced the development of the personality—the group of selves that has evolved to protect our initial vulnerability and has gradually obscured the psychic fingerprint present at our birth. This original set of selves, the primary selves, serves as a functioning ego until such time as we embark on our journey of consciousness. This first step in this journey is to contact our disowned selves, to reclaim our lost heritage.

2

Disowned Selves: Our Lost Heritage

We humans are a most delightful mélange of energy patterns or selves. Some of these energies are familiar and comfortable, some are curious or unfamiliar, and some are downright distasteful. In this chapter we will examine the development of the latter energies—our disowned selves—and their effect on our lives. Disowned selves are energy patterns that have been partially or totally excluded from our lives. They can range from being angelically spiritual, creative, and mystical to being lustful, selfish, and even demonic.

To better understand this process, we must examine more closely how we disown some of our selves. What is a disowned self? Pause for a moment and think of someone whom you dislike intensely, someone who possesses, in your opinion, totally reprehensible character traits. What is it that makes this individual so worthy of your contempt? Be specific about the qualities that repel you. If you are glad that you are in no way similar to this despicable person, you have discovered your first disowned self. The traits in this person that irritate you reflect an energy pattern within you that you do not wish to integrate into your life under any circumstances.

Our disowned selves can be detected by the intense, often uncharacteristic emotional reaction we have to others. The following examples will illustrate this:

> —a man who was an honest, sincere, and faithful husband for thirty years was outraged by a woman he encountered who "had no sense of loyalty or commitment, whose idea of a relationship was a two-day sexual involvement with someone whom she would never see again."
>
> —a dreamy, spiritually oriented young man perceived his financially successful older brother as "almost demonic in his pursuit of money, power, and women."
>
> —a thoughtful, gentle, and kind woman couldn't bear her boss who was "cruel, selfish, and only interested in results."
>
> —a tough self-made man couldn't "stand wimps or victims. They make me want to puke!"

These examples clearly convey the intense emotions attached to the disowned self. These emotions are the result of the tremendous energy in the disowned energy pattern itself, as well as the energy utilized in keeping it disowned. It is no wonder that intense feelings come into play whenever we see a disowned self reflected in someone else.

Before we explore our disowned selves further, one important distinction needs to be made: In general, the term for a self that is not conscious is an *unconscious* self, but *not all unconscious selves are necessarily disowned.* An unconscious self is simply unconscious—no energy is holding it down or maintaining its unconscious status. However, every disowned self has an opposite energy with which the ego and the protector/controller are identified. For example, a woman who has buried a disowned self associated with uninhibited sexuality may, in fact, consider herself to be a morally upright, highly disciplined person. This opposite, morally upright energy, in conjunction with the protector/controller, is constantly holding the disowned self at bay. Ultimately, however, we have no way of knowing that a self is disowned until we become aware of it.

The Development of the Disowned Selves

The disowned self is an energy pattern that has been punished every time it has emerged. These punishments might have been subtle—a raised eyebrow, the withdrawal of attention, a "that's rather unattractive, don't you think?" — or they may have been powerful punishments such as beatings or public humiliation. Whatever the nature of these repressive environmental forces, the result is the same: A set of energy patterns is deemed totally unacceptable and is, therefore, repressed but not totally destroyed. These energy patterns live on in our unconscious.

In Jungian terms, our disowned selves are a part of our shadow. When we see them reflected in others—when we see someone unashamedly living out an energy pattern similar to one we have disowned—we feel this disowned pattern resonate within ourselves. However, this pattern has been associated with pain and punishment in the past, so we want it to go away as soon as possible. In order to quiet our internal discomfort we must rid ourselves of the corresponding external stimulus. We must kill off the person who is so audaciously living out *our* disowned self, whether we do it literally—as in a Jack-the-Ripper-style murder—or symbolically—such as sitting in judgment of someone. Hester Prynne in *The Scarlet Letter* painfully but clearly illustrated the price paid for living out the adulterous disowned self belonging to the Puritan community in which she lived.

One woman we worked with, Jane, had been taught to disown her sexuality: From an early age, she was punished for any evidence of flirtatiousness or sexuality. She learned to bury her sexuality, and this energy pattern then became a disowned self. By the time she reached adulthood she had learned to dress soberly; value her objectivity, rationality, and independence; and perceive her sexuality as an incidental part of life. Nevertheless, her sexuality did exist someplace in her unconscious.

One evening Jane went to a party where she encountered a woman—flirting outrageously, dressed in a very revealing décolletage, and surrounded by men—who personified Jane's disowned self. An interesting thing happened: Jane's disowned self began to vibrate sympathetically with this woman's. Jane had always been punished for behaving like this woman, so she became acutely uncomfortable as their two energy patterns vibrated with one another—the one unashamed and flamboyant, the other a hidden and unrecognized echo of what it might have been.

To remove the source of her discomfort Jane judged "the other woman": "I've never seen such a disgusting, vulgar exhibition in my entire life! Isn't she ashamed to walk around like that? I'd think her husband would be embarrassed to death!" Just as Jane expressed herself with great vehemence and self-righteousness, so do we use judgment to eliminate the vibrating energy of our disowned selves.

Anger and irritability are also usually disowned fairly early in life. Very few parents can resist the temptation to do away with these "negative" energies in their offspring. Therefore, most of us were taught not to express these feelings directly. People often recall their terrible childhood tempers, but these emotions rarely persist into adult life. It can be quite revealing to track the initial disowning of such selves. When talking to one client's anger voice we heard the following story of its disowning:

> ANGER: I had to go underground when she was very young because whenever I came out, her mother got upset and her father withdrew. He'd just walk out of the room if she said anything negative. So she learned to hide me. She learned how to please everyone and make everyone happy, but she never let me out. She never said anything negative or angry or selfish.

A disowned self accumulates energy much as water will slowly accumulate behind a dam—and we have built a different dam for each disowned self. These disowned selves are constantly coming through to us in our dreams. Some of these buried instinctual energies are illustrated by the following dreams:

—Someone is trying to break into my house.

—I'm being chased by wild animals.

—I'm driving my car and Mexican teenagers in the car next to me are leering at me.

—I'm with some bad teenage boys and I'm very perturbed with them. They are trying to molest me sexually. I'm trying to lecture to them. One of the boys touches me on the vagina and I am inflamed sexually.

Each of these dreams symbolizes repressed instinctual energy that is using the dream to make itself known to us. In fact, one of our greatest allies in the evolution of our consciousness is our dream process. By observing our dreams and learning their symbolic language we can recognize both disowned energy patterns and energy patterns with which we are identified. Our disowned selves constantly call out to us in our dreams to come and pay attention to them.

Our Disowned Selves in Relation to Others

The parts with which we identify usually determine our choice of relationships. For instance, if we are identified with a rational self, that self will want us to relate to rational people. Although our basic tendency is to be repelled by our disowned selves, they *do* hold a certain fascination for us. The highly indignant sober citizen who wants to do away with pornography yet spends months at a time evaluating pornographic material is a fine example of this type of behavior.

Although attraction to a disowned self perceived in another can often lead to the integration of these energies, unfortunately, we are more likely to see individuals lock into destructive relationships with those who reflect a disowned self. Thus, a woman who negates her sexuality and her physical being will be fascinated by a "he-man" and marry him. She will then do all she can to tame his sexuality and keep him from pursuing his outdoor life. He, in turn, may have been attracted to her timid, nonphysical way of life and intrigued by her sexual inaccessibility. Once married, he, too, is likely to object to these behaviors. Instead of learning from one another, instead of integrating these disowned selves, they live with the reflection of them in their mates, judging them and continually being angered by them.

We can be helpless victims to the multitude of relationships in our lives that reflect our disowned selves, or we can accept the challenge of these relationships and ask: "How is this person, or this situation, my teacher?" Asking this question in itself represents a major shift in consciousness. A great deal of the stress in our lives results from our tendency to attract reflections of our disowned selves in our relationships, and we continue to suffer as the same patterns are repeated in our lives. Unfortunately, for most of us there is no support to learn the lesson inherent in this process. Without this support the energy of our disowned selves grows stronger and more twisted.

When natural instinctual energies such as the need for survival, sexuality, and aggression are disowned over time, they cycle back into the unconscious and go through a significant change. Energy cannot be destroyed; thus, these disowned instincts begin to operate unconsciously and attract additional energy to themselves. They soon lose their natural qualities and become malevolent. At this point we give them a new name—demonic energies. When the energy of a disowned self becomes demonic, natural aggression is often transformed into killing rage, jealousy becomes uncontrollable passion, and natural sexual impulses turn into fearsome experiences. These demonic energies may break through into our daily lives as destructive and vicious behaviors, both on a personal and on a social level.

Cultural Aspects of the Disowning Process: The Birth of the Demonic

Certain energy patterns are culturally disowned. Western civilization, for example, has created the seven deadly sins. Who among us has not been encouraged at one time or another to do away with pride, covetousness, lust, anger, gluttony, envy, and sloth?

Since the Age of Enlightenment humanity has disowned all the "darker" energies—the passionate, the irrational, the mystical, the unclear, and the paradoxical—and admired, almost worshipped, rationality, detachment, scientific objectivity, and clarity. In this way, we have negated much of the information available to us as human beings. We have also negated our anger, irritability, insecurities, and confusions in favor of balance, good humor, certainty, and self-confidence.

The disowning of "the seven deadly sins" results in a particular build-up of instinctual energies in the unconscious that we call demonic energies. They are among the major disowned energy patterns, and as a society we pay a particularly heavy price for their negation.

Traits associated with "the seven deadly sins"—sexuality, sensuality, and emotionality—are natural energy patterns. If, for a variety of reasons, these energies are considered unacceptable they become demonic. Further, it takes tremendous energy to keep our instinctual life buried, and the longer and more deeply it is buried, the more demonic it becomes and the more energy is required to keep it buried. Much of the physical illness and exhaustion that plagues us today can be attributed to disowning these energies.

Many of us harbor the profound fear that if we let these energies out, total chaos will prevail in the world. We wish to make it absolutely clear that we are *not* recommending that people "let these energies out." Voice Dialogue provides us with a way to become aware of these powerful energies and learn how to gradually allow them to emerge in a safe environment. Demonic energies do not have to take over in this process. If, however, we do not allow these selves to speak to us, if we continue to disown them, they will build in intensity, they will be projected, and eventually they will break through into our lives and we will be forced to dance to *their* tune.

The word *demonic* is frightening to many; it conjures up visions of monsters, malevolent creatures, and images of Satan. Nevertheless, we use the word because it clearly distinguishes between a natural instinctual life and a disowned instinctual life that has become distorted. We work with the energies and voices of the demonic in order to help restore them to their natural, undistorted state. In this way, these energies can be used to support us in life as they were meant to do.

Working with demonic energies is one of the most difficult aspects of the Voice Dialogue process. Most of us—whether subject or facilitator—fear these energies and are reluctant to confront them. Our unconscious, therefore, is often our best means of confronting and dealing with the demonic. As we mentioned earlier, our disowned selves constantly communicate to us through our dreams and this is equally true of our demonic energy.

If we carefully study our dreams, it becomes abundantly clear that the intelligence behind the dream process wants these instinctual energies honored and embraced. The case of one woman, Agnes, clearly reveals this process at work. Agnes had done a great deal of psychological work and was aware of energy patterns—demonic energies in particular. She decided to learn more about her own demonic energies and what they represented in her life. Soon after making this decision she had the following dream:

> It was early morning at the beach and I was with Tom. We went into the ocean and it was dark. We were embracing and rolling sensually in the water. Then the tide brought us back to shore. It was daylight again and we left the water. I went back to my hotel room. I knew he would follow. When I closed the door behind me I got frightened about what would happen next.
>
> At that point, I called on an actress to help me. She went into the shower. I walked in so I could watch the shower on all three sides. She then told me that she was frightened and couldn't finish this love scene with Tom.
>
> Then we both decided to view an image of her completing it. After we visualized the lovemaking, Tom entered the shower and, as he closed the door behind him, he became a wild beast. He had a serpent's tail, clawed bird's feet, a beak with teeth, and claws on the ends of his wings. He devoured the actress, tearing and shredding her. He had cloven feet, like Satan, and after he consumed her they both disappeared.

This dream provides us with a clear example of how our energy becomes demonic. At first, Agnes experienced Tom sensually, but her control side feared this sensuality and gradually disowned it. So she called in the actress—that part of her that acts rather than experiences. But even the actress was afraid, so together they used their powers of imagination to distance themselves still further from the primary energy pattern of sensuality.

At this point in the process a remarkable transformation occurred: Tom became a monster. A few seconds earlier he was merely the embodiment of ordinary sensuality. However, as this energy pattern was more strongly denied, he changed from a naturally sexual being to a vicious Satan-like beast who shredded and devoured the actress.

This is how our energies become demonic: Our natural instincts, disowned over time, become distorted and threatening. Agnes's dream was telling her that these energies needed to be examined and embraced, and if they were ignored they might well do her harm. Such dreams are compelling warnings from the unconscious that it is time to embrace a self that has been disowned.

It is possible to learn to honor an energy pattern without being required to *live* it. The Voice Dialogue process can allow Agnes to experience the total sensual continuum within her before it is able to sour and turn against her. Embracing her sensuality does not mean that Agnes must become sexually promiscuous. If Agnes had learned to embrace her sensuality in the first place, it would not have become demonic. Embracing our demonic selves does not mean releasing them in the world and living them out; quite the contrary, we have a better chance of controlling them when they are allowed expression in a balanced way.

But to express our demonic energy, we must learn to recognize it operating in our conscious lives, as well as in our dreams. As long as it remains unconscious, it is projected; thus, we believe our enemies are outside us. We do not know what is unconscious, because the unconscious *is* unconscious, so it is hard to recognize our projections. Thus, our "reality" is that we are good people living in an evil and chaotic world.

We cannot resolve this dilemma for you any more than we can resolve it for ourselves. We can, however, show you a process, together with a theoretical structure, for embracing our totality as human beings. We can try to create for you the sense of excitement we experience in the adventure of discovery when we begin to embrace our selves. It is easy to embrace the "goodies," but it is not so easy to embrace the "baddies." Demonic energy patterns are among the most difficult to embrace. Here, particularly for people with a spiritual orientation, the medicine is generally bitter.

Encountering the Demonic: Embracing Our Disowned Selves

Sally, a very loving, caring woman, provided us with a beautiful example of how demonic energies develop and how, at a certain point in the evolution of consciousness, the disowned energy pattern presents itself to us, insisting that we look at it however repugnant it may be. She had the following dream:

> I dreamt I was the emissary of some emperor, making contact and hopefully arranging an alliance with the sultan of a large country in the Middle East. It was about 800 A.D. I was with the sultan and he decided to take me for a tour of his palace. After seeing all the beautiful aspects of it—fountains, gardens, and so on—he took me to the dungeons and prisons to show me how he dealt with people who were criminals or wrongdoers. He was very impersonal about his treatment of these people and felt he was fair and equitable in his handling of their punishment. He showed me people being punished in the mildest manner, such as whipping for some minor infraction, to tortures and deaths by torture that ran the range from awful to revolting and ghastly! I, the messenger/emissary, was horrified and appalled at the sultan's cold-blooded indifference to the suffering of the tortured and dying people. He was proud of his system of punishments, feeling he was fairly assigning punishments. When I asked him how he could not be affected by the pain of his victims, he was surprised I should ask and just answered that human life was of small importance, and very expendable; that the lives of these people just didn't

> matter. I was shaken and revolted by his callous indifference to the incredibly horrible way he was torturing people to death. Then I woke up, feeling revolted, shaken, and appalled at the scenes of torture and dying, and terrified of the cold-blooded sultan I had just witnessed in my dream.

Sally was raised in a patriarchal family that was highly impersonal and rejected feelings. She made up her mind early in life that she would not be that way, and so she became the opposite—a totally loving and caring human being. Her impersonal qualities and negative feelings were buried. Throughout her life she encountered situations in which individuals embodying demonic energies attacked her. As we said earlier, what we disown, life brings to us, over and over again, until we can recognize the teaching within these repetitive, unpleasant life experiences.

In the dream, Sally's unconscious brought this negated energy to her. She met the cruelty of the sultan—a man not merely cruel, but impersonally cruel. He was everything she had chosen not to be by identifying with her loving self. There is nothing wrong with being loving, but Sally was identified with this pattern to the exclusion of her instinctual heritage; she was trying to be a certain way at the expense of other feelings. This is like building a beautiful home on top of a rattlesnake pit: We are unaware of the snakes writhing beneath us until one day someone gets bitten, or we ourselves are poisoned.

Marvin was another person we worked with who had disowned his negativity for many years. He also had within him a very caring and loving side and a self that was a real searcher. An illness forced him to look in at himself in new ways, and during this period he had the following dream:

> I'm with a man who is a killer. I don't want to be with him, but I have no choice. He commits a robbery and kills people in the process. I am an accessory. We spend time with many of my

> friends and they see me with this killer and I realize that I'm going to be tainted by him.
>
> In the last scene, he comes toward me to kill me. I have a shotgun. He taunts me; dares me to kill him. I shoot and the gun misfires. He laughs and again comes toward me. This time I fire and blow his head off. Then I hear police sirens. I think that they will never believe me when I tell them what happened. I am a killer now and they won't know why.

When an energy pattern is ready to be integrated, it appears in dreams in various ways, but basically it demands entrance; it demands submission. Phone calls in our dreams, dreams of people chasing us, or people trying to break into our homes—these are all energy patterns of different kinds trying to make contact with us.

The killer in Marvin, a symbolic expression of his demonic nature, wanted recognition. It insisted on recognition and was quite persistent, even giving Marvin a second chance to be a murderer. Marvin could not maintain the disowning process through the authority of his more loving nature and found he had to learn to embrace both patterns—his demonic as well as his loving selves.

In the next few weeks following this dream Marvin began to appreciate its implications; he realized how much he had disowned this energy. He then had the following dream:

> I am at a racetrack and a race is going on. A very large horse is in the lead. Suddenly he leaves the track and comes racing after me. I am very much afraid and I start running. The horse is breathing down my neck as I awaken.

In this dream, a transformation of energy had already occurred—the killer energy had been honored to some extent. It was now a powerful horse; although it was chasing him, it was, nonetheless, a horse rather than a killer. Demonic energy was gradually being transformed into the powerful, natural instinct that it was before it became demonic. This transformation is the goal of working with demonic energies.

As you can see, it is quite difficult to overcome the intense effect of our demonic energies. How much easier it would be if we could recognize and embrace our disowned selves before these energy patterns are subverted into the demonic. Yet, as we have seen, our disowned selves were often established long ago, before we were old enough to comprehend what was happening. Further, until now, as you read this book, chances are no one has even pointed out this problem, much less offered you guidance in resolving it. So how, then, can you begin to embrace *your* disowned selves?

First, it is important to recognize that a disowned self is operating. Notice your irritation with someone—does it feel good? Do you feel self-righteous? Isn't that other person *so* dreadful? Unfortunately, having read about disowned selves, you cannot bask in the sunshine of moral superiority for too long. You now know you cannot reform the other person. It is time to look at those qualities with which you are over-identified (you know—the ones that make you proud) and recognize how they limit you.

Perhaps you are excessively neat, relentlessly hardworking, compulsively kind and thoughtful, always caring and giving, always right, or never complaining or angry. Many of these qualities make us feel special, and we really do not want to give them up. So think about how these qualities can limit you, can make you intolerant, inflexible, unable to relax and accept yourself and others as full, complex human beings. It is nice to try to live a perfect life, but what if that means never trying anything new because you are afraid to make a mistake?

Now comes the fun. Although at first it may seem awkward, talk to the disowned self directly. See what it thinks; ask it how it would run things if it were in control. Feel its new energy, and allow yourself to see the world through a new perspective. Your disowned self is bound to be a source of new ideas, new inspirations, new solutions to previously unsolvable problems. After all, its views have never been available before. You will be surprised at the new energy that will become available. It is important to keep in mind that we are not suggesting you *become* the disowned self—simply allow its energy to speak.

In the past couple of decades, we have heard a few horror stories about people who were given permission to identify with previously disowned selves. One high-ranking well-mannered business executive learned to express anger and assert himself in an encounter group. When he returned to work, his formerly disowned anger dominated his behavior. He started an argument with his formerly feared boss and told him to "fuck off." He was promptly fired and had a great deal of trouble getting another job once the circumstances of his dismissal became known.

This is a perfect example of over-identifying with first one extreme (the obedient son) and then the other (the angry father) without benefit of an intervening aware ego. When anger is first released, there may be an increase in overall irritability and reactivity but it is important not to over-identify with these feelings, as the executive did.

The release of primitive earth energies such as sex and aggression is followed by extremely favorable consequences when monitored by an aware ego. For instance, Alex, a highly spiritual man who had spent years practicing self-discipline and self-denial, was involved in a legal action with some rather unscrupulous characters. He experienced a lot of anxiety about this as a substantial sum of money was involved.

During a Voice Dialogue session his disowned primitive energies emerged in the form of a howling wolf who had been caged for years. The wolf itself was afraid to be released because it felt so destructive. The wolf explained that whenever it had previously threatened to break out of its cage, Alex would meditate or do yoga for a couple of hours and thus weaken the wolf's power so that it was no longer a threat.

After having the opportunity to be expressed, the wolf gradually stopped howling and became a most attractive masculine energy of amazing power. Alex was finally able to step into his wolf self and utilize these wolf energies on his own behalf. When he encountered his legal opponents armed with his wolf-power, he was able to resolve the problem quickly and in his favor.

A disowned self can be very persistent. Mary's business partner, Jack, represented a disowned self but Mary did not use him as a teacher. Their relationship ended bitterly, and for many years thereafter Mary dreamt disturbing dreams about Jack. According to Mary, he was "a self-centered man whose primary concern was his own well-being, both financial and emotional." In her dreams he invariably appeared irritated by her lack of self-assertion and he was always trying to tell her how to run her life. She, in turn, became defensive and angry and tried to argue with him and make him go away. She always woke up angry and frustrated, thinking of how manipulative, controlling, and selfish he was and how angry she was that she had dreamt about him again.

This is a perfect example of how a self, disowned by day, might try to get through to us at night. Night after night this subpersonality came to Mary, trying to talk to her, and night after night he was sent away. Although Mary perceived her "dream-Jack" as an intruder, he was actually trying to balance her, to show her that she need not be a helpless victim to the world around her. But such was the strength of her combined cultural and personal history of disowning that she could not listen to him.

In a Voice Dialogue session one day Mary's hopeless-little-girl subpersonality was talking when Jack suddenly slipped in for a moment.

JACK (with irritation): Mary needs to get her life organized.

FACILITATOR: You sound like a totally different voice from that little girl. How about moving here and telling us what you have to say about Mary's situation? (Mary changes chairs but looks uncomfortable. She doesn't really want to hear this voice.) I can see that she doesn't want you to talk, but let's give it a try. I hear that you've been trying to give her advice for some time.

JACK: Yes, I have. She doesn't like me though, and I don't like her at all. She's a wimp. I know what she has to do to make money. I'm very good at making money. And I'm not ashamed of it either. She's ashamed of wanting to make money.

FACILITATOR: And you're not?

JACK: You bet I'm not. I need money to enjoy life. I like nice things. I like comfort and I like power. You need money for all of that. She's too worried about whether or not people are going to like her.

FACILITATOR: Don't you worry about that?

JACK: Not at all. People like me. I'm happy with myself. I like being the center of attention and people love to be with me. I think they're lucky to get a chance to be with me. I give them a chance to bask in my warmth and they love it. You know, like in the sun. As I said before, I think *they're* lucky to get to be with me, not vice versa. (Smiling, very self-satisfied.) People don't like it when you try to please them. Besides, if I don't go out of my way for them, I don't resent them. So I don't get angry with them.

FACILITATOR: But what about people not liking you? Mary worries about that.

JACK: As I said, I just don't care. She thinks I'm selfish but I don't care. And because I don't really care, I can be very persuasive and charming, too. I'm not worried about being genuine, you see. She is. And as far as I'm concerned, that kind of worry doesn't work. I like to figure out what works and then I go ahead and do it. I don't waste time worrying about other things.

FACILITATOR: Speaking of figuring out what works, what would you suggest to Mary in terms of her business?

"Jack" then proceeded to give detailed suggestions, some of which he had already given in dreams, but now Mary, along with the facilitator, was able to listen to them. When Mary returned to her aware ego she had a great deal more color in her face and strength in her voice. She was excited about these ideas and eager to try them out. Mary radiated a totally new sense of self-containment and self-sufficiency.

When a disowned self breaks through like this, other selves may object and try to push it back down. In Mary's case, this objection came from a witch-like subpersonality who emerged briefly two days later and destroyed the sense of self-sufficiency that "Jack" had provided for Mary. Mary was aware of the loss of the "Jack" energies and the re-emergence of the despondent child, but the witch was so fast in her attack on the previously disowned "Jack" energies that she remained almost invisible. It is very important, when uncovering disowned subpersonalities, to talk to the other subpersonalities, such as this witch or the protector/controller, who want them to stay disowned.

> WITCH (with venom): I have to teach her (Mary) the Awful Truth. I had to put her back in her place. She was taking too much attention for herself. She needed to be punished for that! To be pushed back there and over there (gesturing to a corner).
>
> FACILITATOR: Why?
>
> WITCH: Because that's where she belongs! In the background, not up front. I get very irritated when she pushes her way out in front like that!!

This is a fascinating introject! We can imagine how Mary's mother might have felt when she had to teach Mary to disown her power and her desire for attention. We can surmise that when Mary's "Jack" subpersonality came through in Mary as a child, it resonated with her mother's disowned "Jack" voice, which craved attention. Mary's mother most likely punished this voice with all the bitterness and judgment that we feel when we see our disowned self in another. Thus, the subpersonality in Mary that echoed her mother's admonishments to be a second-class citizen was like a destructive witch who carried with her many generations of hatred.

With this hypothesis in mind, the facilitator continued the questioning.

> FACILITATOR: Why does she belong in the background like that?
>
> WITCH: I don't know. Just because she does.
>
> FACILITATOR: Tell me, do you feel the same way about Mary's brother?
>
> WITCH: No.
>
> FACILITATOR: Would you feel the same way if Mary were a man?
>
> WITCH (hesitating): I'm not sure. (Gaining power again.) I don't care. All I know is I have to remind her about the Awful Truth, to slap her down and keep her back there (pointing), out of the way. And I don't like it when she doesn't stay there!
>
> FACILITATOR: But why do you have to slap her down and keep her there?
>
> WITCH: Because if I don't, her father will kill her! It's better that I push her out of the way.

The last was such a surprise that the witch disappeared and Mary's aware ego took over again. As we have said before, there has usually been a very good reason to disown a subpersonality. By working with the subpersonality that enforces the disowning, the aware ego discovers this reason and can then deal with the disowned subpersonality in a conscious and constructive fashion. We might expect that the witch will no longer have unquestioned authority and will no longer be able to push the "Jack" subpersonality down automatically without any resistance from Mary. The aware ego will know what is happening and, we hope, will intervene.

Conclusion

It is important to understand the concept of disowned selves and to actively accept the challenge of the multitude of life situations that bring our disowned selves to us. The challenge to embrace these selves in a creative fashion is, perhaps, the most difficult task in the evolution of consciousness.

Previously we spoke of the roar of awakening, the first realization that you are more than you think you are. In this chapter we have introduced you to the concept that many selves live in the shadows, far away from the primary selves that usually dominate our lives. In the next chapter we will discuss the Voice Dialogue method and how to use it to become acquainted with all the selves—the familiar and the unfamiliar—that make up the sum total of who you are.

3

Voice Dialogue

Exploring the Selves

We can experience our roar of awakening in many different ways, but once this has happened, it is usually impossible to go back.

The evolution of consciousness beckons to us to explore the full range of our selves, and we are compelled to accept this challenge.

A thirty-five-year-old woman, Sylvia, who had been identified with her rational mind all her life, was introduced to the process of guided imagery, a procedure that directly taps into symbolic energies. After undergoing this technique, she found all of her nonrational subpersonalities—both feeling and spiritual—had been activated, and she had the following dream:

> I am in a round building. It is perfectly planned and beautifully maintained, but I find myself walking out of it. As I leave, I turn to look behind me and while I am looking, the sliding exit door closes noiselessly and disappears. The building is

> perfectly round and completely smooth and I know that I'll never be able to re-enter it. I turn and look around me. I am in a freshly tilled garden. The soil is black and moist and nothing is planted in it but a row of magnificent rose bushes around its borders.

Sylvia has lived a well-ordered rational life. In her dream she is leaving the perfection, predictability, and safety of this life. She finds herself in a new setting, a garden where things grow organically and now she must learn to cultivate this garden; it is, in fact, a symbol of herself. This is really a beautiful image because when we experience our roar of awakening, we become gardeners of the soul.

Just as there are many ways of awakening, many doors through which one can leave one's initial state of consciousness, there are also many ways to proceed in the evolution of consciousness. We would like to introduce you now to an approach that is very useful to us, both for initially igniting the evolution of consciousness and for facilitating its expansion. This method is called Voice Dialogue. We developed it as a means of working with one another psychologically when we first met in the early 1970s. It provided us with a new tool to help us in our own transformational processes, one that proved to be inclusive and flexible and fun. It helped us to move beyond our own rational, intuitive, and psychologically sophisticated protector/controllers and encouraged an ever-widening expansion of consciousness. Over the years, Voice Dialogue has proven to be a dramatically effective and frequently humorous tool for igniting and expanding the evolution of consciousness by helping us to explore our subpersonalities, expand our awareness, and clarify the role of our egos in maintaining psychological health.

The Basic Components of Voice Dialogue

An Exploration of Our Subpersonalities

Voice Dialogue provides direct access to the subpersonalities we discussed in the first chapter. It offers the opportunity to separate them from the total personality and deal with them as independent, interacting psychic units or energy systems. In using Voice Dialogue, we directly engage these subpersonalities or voices in a dialogue without the interference of a critical, embarrassed, or repressive protector/controller. Each subpersonality is addressed directly, both as an individual entity and as a part of the total personality. Each of these subpersonalities experiences life differently, occupying its own portion of the energy system.

Each subpersonality is a distinct energy pattern and animates our physical body with its particular energies. Although we may sense these energies within ourselves as a thrill of fear or the queasiness of anxiety, when observed externally these energies are awesome, and the changes they bring about in the body are remarkable. A captain of industry, a man with a taut jaw, dull eyes, and furrowed brow, may suddenly transform himself, appearing to us as a young child. His eyes will widen and sparkle, his furrowed brow will smooth miraculously, his jaw will relax, and his smile will turn from a grimace to an infectious grin. His shoulders will relax and the persistent headache that is like background music in his daily life will disappear. All this will happen as a different energy takes over his body.

The Role of the Ego

Voice Dialogue definitively separates the ego from the protector/controller and the primary subpersonalities that work alongside it. The ego occupies a central physical space, and the subpersonalities play out their conflicts around it. When a subpersonality begins to take over the ego, the alert Voice Dialogue facilitator will point out this takeover, ask the subject to move to another space, and engage the subpersonality directly. In this way the ego becomes more and more clearly differentiated; that is to say, it becomes a more aware ego.

Enhancement of Awareness

Voice Dialogue introduces awareness into our psychological make-up. Physical spaces exist for each subpersonality, for the ego who coordinates and executes, and, separate from all the others, for our awareness. From its still point, nonjudgmentally, and with no decisions to make, the awareness can witness and review all that is going on. From this still point, everything is noted and accepted; nothing needs to be changed. From this still point, the drama played out by the subpersonalities and the ego is clearly visible.

Guidelines for the Use of Voice Dialogue

Subpersonalities, or voices, are constantly operating within everyone. As we have stated earlier, they are the energy systems that experience life. Voice Dialogue gives us a chance to objectify them, recognize them, name them, understand them, and work with them creatively. When we use Voice Dialogue, we are sensitizing ourselves and others to the drama played out by these subpersonalities.

Identification of Subpersonalities: Creating a Psychic Map

The first step in facilitating Voice Dialogue is the identification of the subpersonalities. The procedure for doing this will vary from one individual to another. Ideally, the facilitator first gets centered, quieting the inner pushers and critics, and then conducts the session in a relaxed yet alert fashion. In this way, all the facilitator's attention will be concentrated on the subject, on the subject's energy patterns, and on physiological and linguistic cues.

The facilitator begins by encouraging the subject to talk either about life in general or about a specific experience that seems important. The conversation between them serves several functions: it establishes or enhances rapport, it conveys information, and, most importantly for the Voice Dialogue process, it gives the facilitator the opportunity to create a "psychic map" of the territory. This "map" can either exist solely in the facilitator's mind, or it can actually be written down.

As in the exploration of any new territory, it is helpful to have the orientation a psychic map provides to gain a sense of what we as facilitators are moving into. This is an important safeguard in the work because it means that as facilitators we are not going to jump into working with any one particular area before we have at least some idea of how it relates to the whole person.

At this point in the process, the facilitator is particularly interested in differentiating the primary selves the subject has identified with from the disowned selves. The psychic map serves as a reference so the facilitator can easily track the interacting patterns of these selves. Throughout the process, but most particularly at first, the facilitator will be very interested in talking with the primary selves in order to find out as much as possible about them and their reasons for existence. The following hypothetical example illustrates how this works:

FACILITATOR: What seems to be on your mind these days?

HANK (Hank is a little slumped over, a little tired looking, speaks without much enthusiasm): I'm getting into arguments

> with my wife because she wants me to take a vacation. She says I'm too caught up in my work. But I like my work! (As he speaks the following words, he seems to gain some strength, his eyes light up, and he sits up straighter.) You know I *do* work at a very important job and this is a particularly important time, especially with all the tax laws changing. People depend upon me to be sure that everything is done correctly and they know that when I do a job, I do it well. I must say (here he looks proud of himself) I don't disappoint them, I do take care of everything just as they expect me to. I don't know what to do about her—I mean my wife. She doesn't understand the importance of all this. All she knows is that I need to relax (here Hank's lips tighten and he begins to look irritated).

The facilitator notes how rapidly Hank is speaking, the tightness about his lips, his furrowed brow, and his narrowed eyes. The entire effect is one of contraction, concentration, and tension. At this point the facilitator will begin to fill in the psychic map, noting that a group of responsible, achievement-oriented, primary selves are speaking—not an aware ego. The psychic map is conjectural and open to continuing correction and modification, but it constitutes a useful beginning to the Voice Dialogue process and the initial identification of the subpersonalities.

On this "map," the facilitator might well suppose that Hank's primary selves include a responsible self ("I must say I don't disappoint them, I do take care of everything just as they expect me to."), a pusher ("I work at a very important job and this is a particularly important time."), a perfectionist ("People depend upon me to be sure that everything is done correctly and they know that when I do a job, I do it well."), and a judgmental self ("She doesn't understand the importance of all this. All she knows is that I need to relax.").

Hank's first sentences ("I'm getting into arguments with my wife because she wants me to take a vacation. She says I'm too caught up in my work.") and his generally depressed air suggest that a part of him is a victim son to his wife's demanding mother. The facilitator hypothesizes that the disowned selves would probably be Hank's irresponsible self, his lazy self, his fun-lover, his relaxed self, and his self-accepting, loving, nonjudgmental, gentle self—they might encompass all the selves that know how to enjoy life.

With some ideas as to the nature of Hank's primary selves, and some hypotheses as to the nature of his disowned selves, the facilitator will continue his exploration.

> FACILITATOR: You look as though her insistence on relaxation irritates you.
>
> HANK (looking irritated): It does. I don't really enjoy vacations. It takes me too long to relax and by the time I'm relaxed, it's time to go home and I have to gear up again. It's a total waste of time and money.

The facilitator notes that this is probably a combination of Hank's pusher ("It takes me too long to relax and by the time I'm relaxed, it's time to go home and I have to gear up again.") and his judgmental self ("It's a total waste of time and money.") talking. Does Hank have any access to a self that can relax? The facilitator continues.

> FACILITATOR: What was it like the last time you relaxed?
>
> HANK: It was nice. We went to Hawaii about five years ago for our anniversary and I slept a lot, I drank Mai Tais because I didn't always need my head to be clear, looked at rainbows, and walked on the beach. I didn't even bother to swim or exercise. I liked it. (As he talks and remembers this, he visibly relaxes—his throat seems less constricted and his eyes even twinkle from time to time. The lines in his forehead become less pronounced and his shoulders seem to relax.)

As the facilitator encourages Hank to talk more about this vacation, he notices a relaxed self who might be called "Hawaiian Hank," a self that is in distinct contrast to the primary selves. The facilitator puts this self on the psychic map opposite the primary selves.

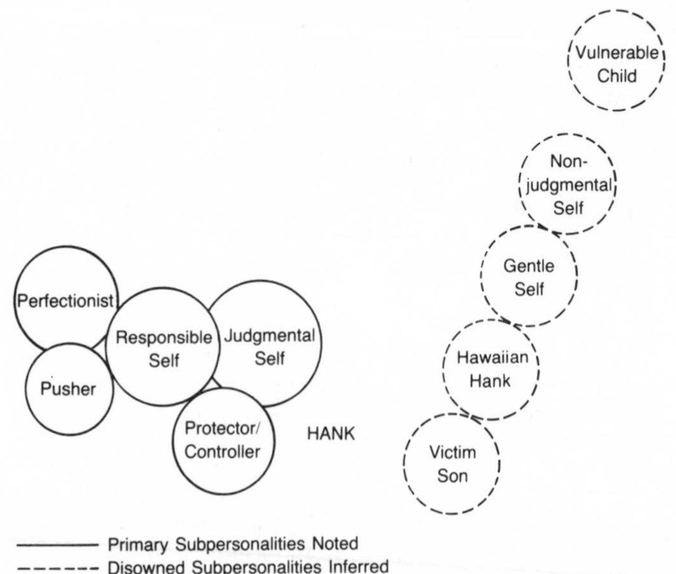

The facilitator may continue the conversation or may decide that enough information has already been gathered. Basically, a psychic map has been created that contains the primary selves represented by a pusher, a perfectionist, a responsible self, and a judgmental self. Evidence of a "Hawaiian Hank" contrasts with these primary selves and suggests a balancing energy. There is also a suggestion of a victim-son self who bonds with Hank's wife's demanding mother. In addition to this specific information, the facilitator knows that there is *always* a vulnerable child somewhere opposite (or behind) the primary selves, a child who, in Hank's life, was probably disowned.

The facilitator is now ready to discuss some of these observations with Hank and start the process of Voice Dialogue with some of Hank's primary selves. We recommend that the protector/controller or any of the other primary selves be addressed first. In Hank's case, it would be quite natural to start with the perfectionist. The facilitator might lead in with an observation such as: "A part of you is very proud of how efficient you are and how well you work. I'd like to talk with it."

As the facilitator and the subject find themselves becoming comfortable with one another, the facilitator might begin to alert the subject to the subtle psychological and physiological changes that signal the activation of a new subpersonality. For instance, the facilitator might point out to Hank as he perks up while talking about his work, "You started to look a lot perkier when you were just talking about your work. It seems as though a big part of you really enjoys working."

As the facilitator alerts Hank to these subtle changes, Hank's awareness is being trained to recognize shifts in Hank's energy patterns. As his awareness expands, Hank gradually learns to make these distinctions independently of a facilitator through his aware ego. Further, the facilitator will find his own sensitivity to changing energy patterns increasing because his awareness is in a constant state of expansion as well.

Physically Separating Subpersonalities

When the facilitator decides (with the consent of the subject) to talk to a specific subpersonality, the subject should be asked to move to a different space in the room. This can mean changing seats or simply moving the chair. The subject should, whenever possible, choose this new position. Different subpersonalities like different places. A vulnerable child invariably chooses a corner of a couch (often with a pillow clutched to the chest). The inner critic usually wants an imposing space or chair. A judgmental voice might want to stand, or to sit on a window seat; it usually likes some location that is higher than the others. An angry voice might want to pace about. As the subpersonalities stake out their territories, one may find the extroverted power voices on one side of the room and the sensitive voices on the other, or perhaps the vulnerable child will be surrounded by protecting, defensive subpersonalities. Some subpersonalities like to sit close to the facilitator and some prefer distance. For some, the placement of subpersonalities reflects the psychic map. For others, it is of little importance and will change from session to session.

If the subject is too uncomfortable to choose a new placement for the voice, the facilitator might unobtrusively suggest a move to a particular spot. Especially in the beginning, the task of choosing "the proper position" can be very threatening to someone who is self-conscious. Thus, to allay anxiety and get the process started the facilitator can lend a gentle hand. If the facilitator is feeling frisky and it looks as though the subject is ready for an adventure, the facilitator might suggest (with humor): "Instead of talking to the voice we were planning to talk to, let's talk to the part of you that has to make the 'right' decision on where to sit."

Facilitating the Subpersonalities

From this point on, the facilitator simply talks to the subpersonality as he or she would to a real person. This becomes easier as time passes and the voice takes on the full dimension of a real person. The facilitator can be empathetic and nonjudgmental, asking questions when appropriate, or simply listening if a voice happens to be particularly garrulous. A basic principle of Voice Dialogue work is: Whatever progress is made is acceptable—specific problems do not need to be resolved in a single session. The aware ego is responsible for any problem solving.

Voice Dialogue, when done properly, is a relaxed but alert exploration. It does not require great effort. If the facilitator is feeling pressured or tense, it might be safe to assume that the facilitator's pusher and/or problem solver is at work. This psychological pusher may have some specific agenda, and the Voice Dialogue may soon become a power struggle between two subpersonalities.

If the facilitator's awareness is alerted to this situation it is often possible to step back and conduct a quick interior dialogue that might sound like the following:

> EGO: There's something wrong. I'm pushing too hard. What's the matter?
>
> INNER THERAPIST (taking advantage of awareness level): You're trying too hard. You're trying to do an "important" piece of work and do it too quickly because you want to make a good impression. Just relax.
>
> EGO: It's hard to do that with the pusher operating.
>
> INNER THERAPIST: Just let go. The subject's anger voice can't come out right now because the protector/controller is stopping it. How about dropping it and checking with the protector/controller to find out why he's blocking and what his rules are.

At this point, the facilitator might tell the subject: "Some part of you isn't happy about our talking to the anger voice. Let's move over and see what it has to say." The focus then switches to the new voice, and the facilitator (with the help of the awareness level), freed from the need to do a brilliant piece of work uncovering the anger voice, starts to move in a different direction.

As we have said before, Voice Dialogue is a transformational process for facilitator, subject, and observers. Ideally, we do not invest too much energy in bringing forth a particular voice. During birthing, the doctor does not grab at the head of the baby in order to deliver it from the mother; likewise, the facilitator should act as a good midwife and simply assist gently as needed.

But ideals are ideals. And as humans we *do* occasionally fall a bit short of perfection! So, if, when you are acting as a facilitator, you identify a particular pattern, and your pusher starts pushing too hard, merely treat it as part of your process. Step back and consult your awareness, as suggested above. If that does not free you from the need to push the voice out perfectly and immediately, you might return the subject to the ego position and discuss this interchange. This, too, requires a certain amount of awareness and objectivity.

If you remain stuck in the power struggle in spite of trying these suggestions, accept the fact that you *are* stuck. Do not blame yourself; simply end the work as quickly as possible and use the experience to learn about yourself. You might find someone to work with the voices in you that get stuck in the interchange.

If you are working with a spouse or close friend, you might explain what happened and try reversing roles. Let the other person be the facilitator and work with the voice that has been activated in you. We would suggest that this role reversal be done when it is safe and appropriate—when both people are feeling pretty good about one another and are engaged in a mutual exploration. If a power struggle is a core issue, get a third person to help break the deadlock.

The exciting aspect of all this is that there are no mistakes! Every hook-in, every difficult facilitation, every wrong turn is a possible source of growth. Each one has something to teach us—each one can add to our awareness of how we function in this world.

Separating the Subpersonality from the Aware Ego

In order to separate a subpersonality from the aware ego, encourage each voice to speak of the subject as a separate entity. This is particularly important in the early stages of dialogue work when the voice will invariably say "I" when speaking of an event in the subject's life. The voice might say, "I went to a party last night and met an interesting woman and I suddenly felt very inadequate." The facilitator then separates the subject's actions from the voice's reaction: "You mean, *he* went to a party and met an interesting woman . . . and *you* started to feel inadequate, right?"

Sometimes a separation is not possible, even after many

such interventions. If all else is going well and the subject seems to be making the differentiation between the subpersonalities and the aware ego, it is not necessary to insist on this separation. The facilitator simply relaxes and continues the process, being careful to differentiate between the subject's subpersonality and aware ego. This distinction can be strengthened by pointing to the positions around the room occupied by the various parts (including the aware ego) as they speak.

The aware ego has its own position, clearly differentiated from the subpersonalities. After each session, we return to the aware ego in its particular position, and the facilitator and subject discuss the session in whatever fashion they choose. This further differentiates between the aware ego and the voices and ensures that the subject has been returned to ordinary ego functioning.

Remaining Nonjudgmental

It is important to remain nonjudgmental when doing Voice Dialogue. The voices are like people: If the facilitator is truly open and interested, they will blossom. If they sense a lack of acceptance or disapproval, they will withdraw or even attack. In fact, the voices may be more sensitive to our judgments than we are ourselves!

Again, because we are human, it is likely that at some time or another, we will judge a voice. Should this happen, try to be aware of it and explore your judgment later. If your judgment is strong and you cannot separate from it, stop and return to the ego position. If at all possible, do not criticize a voice. This may well put an end to any communication and cause the subject to terminate the work.

In the Voice Dialogue process, voices are sometimes discovered that do harm the individual or those around him or her. When talking to such a voice, it is helpful to discuss this damage objectively and determine how the voice feels about it. Such a discussion is delicate, so be sure that there is no judgment—just curiosity. An interaction like this can bring about some surprising insights.

Let us see what happens when a facilitator is questioning a critic.

> FACILITATOR: I was wondering about how you feel toward Janet. You criticize her all the time about her looks and her lack of accomplishment, and every time you say something, she freezes up and can't get anything done.
>
> CRITIC (with real venom): I don't care. She's better off dead than living in that half-assed fashion. I despise her and, frankly, I don't care if I kill her. She deserves to die, the creep!

Here, the facilitator has given Janet's critic a chance to reveal the depth of its hatred and the extent of its destructive potential—important information for Janet's awareness. Had the facilitator been judgmental, the critic would have seen the question as an attack and most probably would have withheld the information.

Sometimes we are surprised at the motivations and feelings revealed by a voice when we withhold judgments and keep questioning. Another virulent critic was asked pretty much the same question asked of Janet's critic.

> FACILITATOR: Tell me how you feel about Frances. You've been pretty irritated with her over just about everything and it looks as though you paralyze her so that she can't get anything done.
>
> CRITIC: Well, she deserves everything I say. (Pause . . . long silence . . . bursts into tears.) I just don't want anybody to pick on her. I figure that if I criticize her first, I'll keep her from making mistakes and nobody else will pick on her. I really don't hate her. I didn't know that I hurt her so much. When I criticize her, I never think of how it might hurt her.

Here we have one of those great surprises that occur so often in this work. Time and again we have found that when we are open to all possibilities, there is no predicting what will happen.

It is quite difficult to remain impartial in the face of a conflict between the energy of the protector/controller and freedom and expressive energies. People in the human potential movement, in particular, have a tendency to identify with the voices that want freedom, emotional and creative expressiveness, and new frontiers. The energy of the protector/controller is seen as resistant, negative, and unsupportive to the development of consciousness. In fact, the protector/controller energy has practically become a disowned self. Many of these people try mightily to grow and expand and change—in the process they deny their controller energy. Thus they lose the balance this energy can provide them.

In Voice Dialogue, it is important to honor both sides. If the facilitator has identified with freedom and expression, this part will be supported and the protector/controller axis will be denied, or at least not honored. This causes the protector/controller in turn to shrink back and begin to operate unconsciously. Thus a split takes place between control and freedom, with the protector/controller feeling maligned, rejected, and quite angry. On the other hand, if the protector/controller feels honored, then it will trust the facilitator and the process, and it will gradually open, quite like a flower, and transform in a natural and organic way.

Relax and Take Your Time

Subpersonalities, as we have said, are like people: They like to feel that they have our undivided attention as well as plenty of time to express themselves. So whenever possible allow plenty of time for them to emerge. A facilitator may have to sit in silence for quite some time before a vulnerable child will even speak. Often, the voice that takes forty minutes to be fully uncovered is a most important part of the personality. So, push the pusher aside and be patient.

Nevertheless, be observant; some voices really do not want to stay around too long. They will probably tell you that they are finished and will promptly vanish. A vulnerable child may say, "It hurts too much to stay here any longer. I want to go now." A pusher may say briskly, "That's it. I've said what I had to say. Now go talk to someone else."

Observing Changes in Energy Patterns

Each subpersonality is a distinct energy pattern—each has a distinct facial expression, posture, and tone of voice, and each creates a different set of energetic vibrations in its surroundings. As we participate in Voice Dialogue, either as a facilitator or a subject, we become increasingly aware of the nature of these energy patterns. An experienced practitioner of this method soon becomes an expert in the detection of shifts in energy patterns, even when the words remain the same.

We are fond of saying, "It's not what is said, it's who says it." This was illustrated dramatically in the following incident: A nineteen-year-old friend was visiting from New York. We took her out to dinner and we all ordered drinks. The waiter asked our young friend for I.D. and she said, with great assurance, "I don't have any I.D. with me, but I'm nineteen so you can give me a drink." When he left, we laughingly told her that the drinking age in California was twenty-one, not eighteen as in New York, and we assumed that she would not get her drink. Amazingly enough, he brought her the drink—the energy pattern had such authority that it was stronger than the actual words she had spoken.

When acting as facilitators in Voice Dialogue, we become more aware of these changing patterns. We alert the subject to changes as other subpersonalities take over. We ask the subject to change position and address ourselves to each new voice. In this way, our awareness can learn to recognize the different voices. It can also learn about the flow of subpersonalities—it sees how anger is replaced by the hurt child, which is replaced by the withdrawn father, and so on.

Oftentimes a group of subpersonalities with similar energy patterns presents itself as one voice—perhaps a critic-pusher-perfectionist may appear. For the sake of simplicity, the facilitator might choose not to separate them, particularly in the early sessions. This is a personal choice that varies from one situation to the next. Should this grouping arise again, an effort might then be made to separate the individual energies.

Thus, both the facilitator and the subject experience a marked expansion of their awareness levels as they become more and more sensitive to the shadowplay of subpersonalities in a person. And it *is* like the play of shadows that change the appearance of a landscape as the clouds pass overhead.

Voice Dialogue as an Altered State of Consciousness

Voice Dialogue puts the subject into an altered or nonordinary state of consciousness. The aware ego and the protector/controller, who usually dominate consciousness, are set aside temporarily as other energy patterns are given the opportunity to express themselves fully. The subject's condition when in a subpersonality is very similar to someone under hypnosis. Therefore, the facilitator must remain alert and not let his or her attention wander.

With this in mind, the facilitator will automatically be careful when dealing with a voice. Interruptions should be avoided whenever possible. The subject is in a vulnerable state and intrusions such as phone calls or conversations among others are jarring and quite unpleasant.

The facilitator should also take care not to leave a subject alone while in a voice, for it is much like leaving someone in a hypnotic trance. If an emergency arises, take the time to return the subject to the aware ego. Explain the circumstances in as much detail as appropriate, in order to ensure the subject is grounded in the ego before you leave. Tell the subject how long you will be gone and make arrangements to continue your exploration when you return.

Because a subject has been in an altered state of consciousness during Voice Dialogue, the way a session ends is critical. It is important to return the subject to an ordinary state of consciousness. We have provided a number of guidelines below regarding the termination of individual sessions.

1. Whenever possible, before returning to the ego place end the work with one of the primary selves. Always keep in mind that the protector/controller and the primary selves have been responsible for running the subject's life, and will continue to do so, until an aware ego emerges that can do the job. The continuity of working with the primary selves grounds the process of Voice Dialogue and keeps it safe. In an altered state of consciousness the primary selves are not operative for a period of time; they relinquish their hold on the subject's consciousness when the subject enters a different state of consciousness. To facilitate the return of the subject to a normal state of consciousness, return to the primary self and ask it how it felt about the work, review what took place in the session, and help it to re-establish its equilibrium.

2. Working with the awareness (as opposed to the ego) also grounds and balances the subject. To do this, the subject is asked to stand next to the facilitator and face the different selves. (With people who are used to meditation, this can be done by suggesting that the subject go into a meditative space to witness the different selves.) You can do this either after working with many different selves or after each encounter with a separate self. This second approach does have an advantage—it helps both the subject and the facilitator to differentiate more clearly between the various selves that are encountered. Then, when the last actual dialogue has taken place, the facilitator can summarize all the work that has been done.

The awareness level is the level of insight, where people

more clearly see the process that is going on within them and separate from the different selves. Having the person stand and face the different selves and then summarizing the work helps bring things together and provides a solid ground for the work. It is important to allow plenty of time for this process.

3. Having summarized the work for the awareness level, we may then choose to provide a direct experience of the selves to the aware ego. The subject returns to the seat where the ego was originally sitting. Here the facilitator suggests that the subject *feel* the different selves, as well as being aware of them. For example, let us say that the facilitator has worked with an aggressive power self and a sensitive feeling self in a man. After the work is over and the subject is back in the aware ego, the facilitator might say the following:

> FACILITATOR: Now I would like to give you an experience of these different selves while you are in the place of the aware ego. Can you feel these two selves on each side of you?
>
> SUBJECT: Yes I can (if he says no, then the separation is not yet sufficient to continue this particular step).
>
> FACILITATOR: Okay, now I want you to allow your power self to emerge—as though you were channelling it—but you're in charge of it rather than it being in charge of you.

At this point the facilitator would call on his or her own power to support the emerging power energy, although it usually does not require much effort when dealing with a primary self with which the ego has been identified. After a minute or so, once the facilitator feels the subject is really feeling and expressing this energy, the subject is asked to leave the power energy and return to the aware ego. This space is held for a moment, and then the facilitator suggests that the subject allow the more sensitive self to emerge. Because the subject has disowned this energy, it may be necessary for the facilitator to help it to come through. The facilitator does this by getting in touch with his or her own sensitive energy. This helps induce the energy in the subject; hence, it is called *energetic induction*. This process is necessary until the subject is able to access the disowned energy directly. After the subject holds the sensitive energy for a minute or so, the facilitator asks that it be released and that the subject return to the aware ego. The process is then repeated a second time.

This process should not necessarily be done with every subject or every time with the same subject. It requires a subject who has had a clear experience of different selves and is beginning to sense that each of these selves is a real energy configuration. The advantage of this process is that it strengthens the aware ego and enables it to gain some measure of control over the different selves.

We are always dealing with a two-step process with every self: First, there is recognition; the aware ego has begun to separate and thus recognizes a particular energy. Eventually this recognition leads to the next step: The subject develops the ability to choose how to use the energy. This is exactly why we work with the energies in the aware ego.

4. Finally, there must be enough time for the facilitator and the subject to ensure they are in good contact and review any general issues or reactions that need to be shared. Sometimes a subject may experience a particularly intense altered state of consciousness. In such a case, in addition to the basic steps we have described for terminating a session, the facilitator might suggest that the subject not enter immediately into the daily routine. An experience of this kind is best followed by a time of quiet, a cup of tea or coffee, or a walk. It is a time to savor the experience and, for safety's sake, to avoid driving or other activities requiring concentration until the subject is fully grounded.

Please keep in mind that these procedures are not meant to be slavishly followed. They are available as guidelines; as facilitators, we can keep them in mind while making our own choices about how to proceed. Different facilitators have amazingly different styles and approaches to the work—this is one of the reasons why the Voice Dialogue process has thus far remained alive and vital.

Working with Demonic Energies

Working with demonic energies represents a special case that requires the greatest awareness and skill on the part of the facilitator. Demonic energies are instinctual energies that have been disowned over time and have become destructive. This destructiveness can either operate against the individual or, through the individual, against others. In the process of working with demonic energies, and gaining an understanding of why they have become so negative and destructive, we will have the opportunity to transform them back into the original instinctual powers they were before they were repressed.

A basic principle applies to working with demonic energies: The aware ego must be operating, and a clear separation must exist between it and the primary selves that have been responsible for repressing the energies in question. The facilitator must clearly understand, and help the subject to understand, the reasons the primary selves want to repress the demonic energies. Further, once these reasons have been uncovered, they must be respected.

It is quite difficult to resist individuals who want to work with their demonic energies. The facilitator may easily be carried along by demonic energies that are ready to break out in a subject. However, if no aware ego is available, who will handle these energies once they break out? They were repressed in the first place because they were dangerous and they still *are* dangerous.

The presence of an aware ego can lessen the danger—an aware ego is separate from, and has respect for, the primary self system. An aware ego is also prepared to deal with disowned instinctual energies while continuing to embrace the primary selves. It is this approach that grounds the process and keeps demonic energies under control.

The other safeguard we recommend most strongly is that demonic energies should not be facilitated by a facilitator who has not explored this area in himself or herself. This advice is true in working with other selves as well, but it has particular significance and relevance when working with the demonic.

Voice Dialogue Is Not a Substitute for Personal Reactions

Voice Dialogue is a technique for the exploration of subpersonalities and the expansion of consciousness. Although we encourage its use in primary relationships and among friends, it is not intended as a substitute for interpersonal interactions. If strong feelings exist between subject and facilitator—particularly negative or judgmental ones—do not try to "solve" them by doing Voice Dialogue. Talk directly with one another about them to "clear" these negative feelings or work with a third person if the negative interaction cannot be overcome.

Voice Dialogue should only be carried out in an atmosphere of mutual trust and respect. Subjects need assurance that the process will be objective and free of hidden agendas or manipulations. It is not a good idea to do Voice Dialogue to prove a point as the various selves are very sensitive to being manipulated.

Taping Sessions

Many people who work in Voice Dialogue like to tape their sessions. This can be quite valuable because a subject may not recall much after a dialogue session. We are not specifically recommending this; we are simply reporting that it is frequently done and with good results.

Video taping is also effective because it clearly reveals major shifts that can take place as different selves emerge. Viewing the differences between major energy systems as they come into operation can be a very powerful experience in itself.

The Awareness Level of Consciousness

Earlier we discussed the awareness level of consciousness and its importance. Now we will examine ways to expand this level. In addition to Voice Dialogue itself, meditation can be a very effective way to expand awareness. As we meditate, we witness thoughts and feelings as they flow through and an awareness gradually develops.

It is important to clearly differentiate between awareness and the protector/controller—a self that simply loves to masquerade as an objective awareness. Our awareness, whether expanded through meditation or Voice Dialogue, is a pure witness state. It is nonjudgmental and therefore capable of looking at all aspects of our selves with equanimity. It is separate from our thoughts, feelings, and values and from our subpersonalities and the energies they represent.

Voice Dialogue presents us with a tangible way of expanding the awareness level and clearly differentiating it from other components of consciousness—it is given a space all its own. As we described in our "guidelines" section, after the facilitator has finished a session, the subject stands next to the facilitator and faces the different selves that have just had the chance to speak. This gives the subject essentially the same objective viewpoint as the facilitator. This placement is called the *position of awareness.*

While the subject is standing in the position of awareness, the facilitator sums up the work that has been done. An experienced facilitator with a clear understanding of psychodynamics may give a fairly detailed analysis of the interaction between the different selves and the ego. A less experienced facilitator might summarize in a much more limited way. As awareness and experience of the selves expands, the ability to understand and communicate the dynamic interactions within the psyche will also expand. The important thing is not to feel attached to the statements that are made.

We also prefer that the subject remain silent in the awareness level. This will help differentiate the awareness level from the aware ego. Only in the aware ego do we talk, for the moment we use language, it is difficult to remain in the awareness level.

The Aware Ego

Often we are asked, "If you have awareness, how can you have an ego? We must remember that awareness is not an action state; it is not a place where we make choices. Awareness bestows the gift of being able to step back from any experience, thought, or behavior and witness it, but it is not an active influence. Someone or something has to receive this information and decide what to do with it; therefore, we require an ego that is constantly in the process of becoming more aware.

Some part of us must make the choices in life, and, as Voice Dialogue quickly teaches us, the choices are generally made by those primary selves with which the ego is identified. As the ego separates from the different selves, it becomes more experienced with, aware of, and separate from them. This ever-expanding combination of awareness and experience creates what we call the aware ego—the only part of consciousness that may possibly become aware of, and embrace, all our selves. Thus, over time, the aware ego develops a real choice about what actions (or inaction) it wishes to take.

In Voice Dialogue we honor the difference between awareness and the aware ego by giving each a separate place and treating them quite differently. If the subject has had meditative experience, he or she may be asked, while in the place of the ego, to go into a meditative space. In this place the review for the awareness is done. Even with meditators, however, we have found that standing in the place of awareness is valuable. Physical separation of the awareness from the selves and the aware ego is very valuable. Yet even here we must be careful not to cast the Voice Dialogue process in concrete. If, as facilitator, you feel required to have the individual stand every time, even when it does not seem appropriate, the work can easily become stilted and boring. We must emphasize again that the experienced facilitator develops his or her unique style so that the work stays alive and vital.

The most difficult differentiation to make in Voice Dialogue is the one between the awareness level, the aware ego, and the protector/controller or other primary self. For example, suppose the protector/controller operates primarily through a subject's mind. The mind readily assumes the guise of awareness and purports to witness whatever is happening. In such a case, it would be essential to talk to the mind so that awareness can truly separate from this primary self system. Without this separation, the aware ego would remain essentially rational because its experience of awareness would have been the rational mind, not true awareness.

Oftentimes the protector/controller is a combination of the mind and a self concerned with control. An "observer" is present in some form in each of us—it watches over us and protects our vulnerability. The awareness level does not protect anything; it is not rational or emotional; it is simply separate from all the selves, a nonjudgmental vantage point from which to view all life. When this vantage point begins to exclude selves or judge them, we know that the protector/controller or another primary self has taken over in some way.

Each Voice Dialogue session, whether done as subject or facilitator, adds some information to our awareness level and thereby expands our consciousness. Each "wrong turn," each power struggle, each dream that we work on also contributes to our understanding and growth. And the more we develop our awareness, the more adept we become at calling this awareness into our everyday life. We can learn to put ourselves into our awareness level when we feel a voice is too strong or too weak, and, in this way, step back and consider a voice objectively. From this perspective we can determine its valid points and decide how to best separate from it. For example, our pusher may be nagging us to get to work on a project, and it may be right—we may need to motivate ourselves—but we need not identify with it. We need not become tense and miserable while taking time to relax before starting on the project.

Each foray into awareness strengthens and expands it, and it can be pleasant, too. Stepping into awareness is like putting a cool hand on a fevered brow—it is soothing, calming, and refreshing. If it is not, if we experience feelings of blame or tension, then we can safely assume we are dealing with the protector/controller again.

Built-in Protection in Voice Dialogue: Respecting the Primary Selves

The most effective protection for individuals using Voice Dialogue is the facilitator's commitment to respect the individual subject and his or her primary selves. The facilitator should make it clear at the outset that nobody is expected to do anything that causes discomfort. It can be extremely helpful to say something like: "If at any point you find yourself uncomfortable with anything that we do, please let me know and we will stop. It is important that you do not force yourself to go beyond your own level of comfort. It is particularly helpful if you can make this decision consciously, instead of having things stop automatically when another self interferes for your protection."

This commitment, in addition to the emphasis it places on working with the primary selves, effectively grounds the Voice Dialogue work. It focuses the work within the comfort zone of the primary selves and honors the role they have played in the past. It allows them to explain the reasons for their development and encourages them to describe the services they perform, services that may still be necessary. This work with the primary selves enables both facilitators and subjects to witness the roles they have played, to witness the need for these selves, and to appreciate their importance, both in the past and the present.

Working with the primary selves in this way allows them to continue their protective and adaptive functions as they gradually separate from the operating ego. As this separation occurs, the aware ego becomes increasingly aware of these primary selves and their automatic functions, and it begins to assume greater responsibility in the subject's life. Last, but certainly not least, the work with the primary selves enables them to change.

For example, if Mary (from Chapter One) has been identified with her good mother all her life, and if this is her primary self, the facilitator will spend much time with this self, exploring its developmental history and its views on life. In working repeatedly with this self, the facilitator will reassure this good mother that its views will be respected as Mary introduces changes into her life. Because Mary already has children and manages a large therapy practice, her good mother wants to be sure that Mary does not change too abruptly, that she moves gently in untangling from the commitments that the good mother has made.

The facilitator, in honoring the primary good mother

self, allows change to come naturally into Mary's life. The actual form of these changes will be based, at least in part, on the good mother's input, for this self had time to think about the changes, consider their importance, and decide how to make the necessary transitions as smoothly as possible. Many of these changes will reflect changes in the good mother itself, as new information is presented and it updates its evaluation of Mary's life situation.

As an additional safeguard, the facilitator may want to check back at the end of each session with the primary self to allow it to express its reactions to the session. This is particularly important when new selves have been introduced whose viewpoints oppose those of the primary selves. For instance, as the facilitator moves into new areas with Mary, he or she might work with a selfish voice, a nonnurturing voice, a wanderer voice, an irritable voice, or an impersonal or even withdrawn male voice. These selves would obviously express very different perspectives. The facilitator would then give Mary's good mother a chance to express its views at the session's end so that this input could be considered alongside input from these newer selves. This return to the primary self is an excellent safeguard, particularly when disowned material is introduced. It helps to keep the psychological system balanced and coherent and helps to keep the subject in charge of his or her own life.

The Subpersonalities Protect Themselves

It has been suggested that Voice Dialogue is almost tamperproof, in part because each subpersonality automatically protects itself. If it feels judged, manipulated, seduced, or in any way mistreated or dishonored, a subpersonality will react. It may withdraw, or it may even verbally attack the facilitator. Subpersonalities are extremely sensitive—they can detect issues unknown to the facilitator.

The individual subpersonality's self-protectiveness is clearly illustrated by an incident observed at a beginning

Voice Dialogue workshop. One of the participants, Lani, was strongly identified with her pleasing daughter self. Lani's pleasing daughter had been activated in the workshop, and its job was to please the workshop leader by facilitating the anger voice in another participant, Jeri. Although Lani's pleasing daughter did not approve of anger and was even a little afraid of it, Lani dutifully went ahead with the facilitation. When Jeri's anger voice was elicited, it reacted to Lani: "I don't like you and I won't talk to you. I'll talk to her (pointing to a group member who was clearly comfortable with anger). You just make me mad. I feel like hurting you. That's all I have to say. I'm leaving now."

Lani had no idea she was identified with her pleasing daughter, and her judgments of Jeri's anger voice were totally unconscious. The anger voice, however, knew about these judgments and protected itself accordingly—it left. This is often what a subpersonality will do when it feels judged—it will react and then, if it feels it is not properly appreciated, it will leave. An incident of this type can be a useful learning experience. In this instance, the workshop leader intervened and directed the next piece of work, the facilitation of Lani's pleasing daughter self. Up until this time Lani's pleasing daughter *was* Lani; no selves other than this particularly strong primary self were available. The work with her pleasing daughter gave Lani the chance to see how that particular primary self operated and to begin to separate her aware ego from it.

The protector/controller is another major safeguard in this work. Because its purpose is to protect the subject, it often steps in to correct some action it fears might be detrimental. It may, for instance, take over a dialogue process if a subject's vulnerability is threatened. When the protector/controller intervenes, either the quality and spontaneity of the communication will suddenly change, or the protector/controller itself may take over and begin to speak. For example, the protector/controller might say, "That's enough! Nancy has spent her entire life being frightened and it's taken the rest of us a long time to learn to take risks. Now she needs to practice speaking up and taking care of herself. She needs to tell her husband how she feels and she can't act like a scared rabbit at work. I don't think it's a good idea to give much more time to her frightened child. It will set her back. She has had to fight long and hard to overcome the child's fears and find some protection for it." Thus the protector/controller helps the facilitator to keep the session in balance.

Occasionally, those who have had a great deal of therapy or consciousness work have learned to push aside, or perhaps even disown, the protector/controller, and they are left without protection. What we call a "New Age protector /controller" may then take over; this New Age version encourages a variety of new experiences and urges the subject to ever greater psychological feats of daring. If a more conservative protector/controller does not seem evident, it is a good idea for the facilitator to resurrect one or induce some other protective self to perform this natural regulatory function.

The subpersonalities also protect themselves by revealing themselves only to a facilitator who has access to a similar energy. Thus, the facilitator must be aware of and able to locate the energy pattern within himself or herself that resonates with the subject's energy pattern. For example, the facilitator must be able to connect with his or her own inner child before the subject's inner child will be trusting enough to emerge. An inner child will not respond to lots of words and rational energy, it will remain hidden until someone who understands approaches it with a warm energy that resonates with its own. Conversely, a rational subpersonality will not talk with a facilitator who has no access to mental energies but is, instead, identified with feelings—whose communications are primarily energetic, fairly nonverbal, and vague. Ultimately the best and most natural safeguard is that the facilitator can facilitate only what has already been experienced within.

The Subject's Responsibility

The Voice Dialogue method encourages empowerment in both the facilitator and the subject. It is a *joint* exploration, and care is taken to acknowledge that the ultimate expert is the subject's awareness. This stance most definitely discourages child-parent bondings and encourages the subject to avoid giving up power to the facilitator. As we become more skilled in Voice Dialogue, we become more sensitive subjects. With expanded awareness, a subject can detect the shift in energies as one voice goes in to replace another. Experienced subjects will often say, "I feel as though this voice is leaving and a new one is coming in." The facilitator can then decide whether to explore the new voice or try to continue to clarify the current one.

Because Voice Dialogue is a joint exploration, it is the subject's responsibility to react to the facilitator. The aim here is the expansion of consciousness, not the validation of the facilitator's view of life. Thus, if anything feels wrong or uncomfortable, the subject is responsible for stopping the facilitation, returning to the ego, and discussing the interaction. It is not always possible to do this; sometimes a dialogue must be completed first. But once back in the ego state, by all means react! The facilitator is striving to become conscious, too, and your reactions will only help matters.

For example, one subject complained after a very intense piece of work, "I didn't like it when you handed me the tissues, it broke my flow." Another might express anger: "I felt that you were judging the voice that just spoke. It felt unfair and I don't feel as though I can trust you." Another reaction might be: "I sensed that you were afraid of that voice." Sometimes the subject says, "You ask too many questions. You keep interrupting me when I stop to think."

All of these reactions give the facilitator the opportunity to study his or her own voices. In the first instance, a hovering mother may have been activated; in the second, a judge; in the third, a frightened child; and in the fourth, a pusher.

There is always something new to learn and to experience.

So, when you facilitate this work, remember to relax—you are only half the team. You will come up against your own areas of unconsciousness, your disowned selves, your projections, and the subjects with whom you are working will become your teachers.

As facilitator, you must be willing to become the subject (or at least to have your actions closely scrutinized), and as subject, you must accept some responsibility for what goes on. This is one of the most important safeguards of the system, for the subject is encouraged to remain in a state of empowerment at all times and accept a major share of the responsibility for what happens. As we mentioned before, the more expanded the subject's awareness, the more finely the subject will attune to the subtleties of his or her own voices and the more responsibility he or she will take. Sooner or later, the subject takes almost full responsibility, knowing which voices need facilitation at what time, essentially using the facilitator as a helper.

Voice Dialogue Is Not Psychotherapy

Voice Dialogue is not a school of psychotherapy, it is not a substitute for psychotherapy, and it is not a profession in and of itself. It is a technique for psychological exploration and for the expansion of awareness. Although it can be a highly effective tool for any psychotherapist it should be clearly understood that it is not a complete and autonomous therapeutic system.

In instances of severe mental or emotional disturbance, a qualified professional should always be consulted. We cannot provide accurate guidelines for determining when psychotherapy is needed, but, briefly, these are the times when one is not functioning as well as might be expected, when a person feels unhappy, suicidal, out of control, or "stuck" in persistent patterns of behavior that seem counterproductive or unreasonably resistant to change. In addition to this, we have found that ongoing psychotherapy is usually the only way to repair the damage done by a dysfunctional (perhaps alcoholic or abusive) family. In such instances, we urge the reader to contact an appropriate psychotherapist because there may well be a need for ongoing work.

Voice Dialogue can be viewed as a tool similar to meditation. It can provide amazingly powerful experiences and a good deal of personal information. It can transform us and heal us. This is why we support its use by professional and nonprofessional alike. For anyone facilitating Voice Dialogue, the wider the training, the more effective the work. The reader must keep in mind, therefore, that Voice Dialogue, when used by a nonprofessional, does not necessarily provide the guidance and understanding possible in an ongoing process with a trained therapist or counselor.

When Voice Dialogue Is Not Useful

The study of multiple personalities is becoming increasingly popular in the field of psychiatry. By and large, these multiple selves are still viewed as a pathological condition. The practice of Voice Dialogue teaches us very quickly that multiple personalities are perfectly natural and belong to all of us. What is it then that determines pathology? If there is no ego capable of reflecting on the voices that are elicited, then we have a condition of pathology. There must be a reflecting ego, an ego that can say, "This is a voice." Voice Dialogue cannot be done without this ego.

The occurrence of true multiple personalities is rare and the reader is unlikely to encounter it. However, in a true multiple personality each personality behaves completely autonomously and has no awareness of the existence of any other personality. No operating ego is keeping track of what happens when any one of these personalities takes over. For instance, a therapist received a number of telephone messages from several apparently different "people" but the same telephone number was given for all of these "people." When she returned these calls, the therapist realized that the messages were actually from the same individual but had been made by several of this individual's personalities. None of these personalities had any knowledge that any of the other personalities had telephoned the therapist. No operating ego was aware of the actions of these different selves.

The reader is asked to remember that Voice Dialogue is not for everybody. If someone does not feel comfortable with this work, do not force it. If there is severe emotional disturbance, do not attempt to engage in Voice Dialogue except under the supervision of a qualified therapist who is directly responsible for the individual concerned.

With the exception of these limiting considerations, the way in which Voice Dialogue is used reflects the degree of comfort of the facilitator. The greater the skill and experience, and the more highly evolved the personal process of the facilitator, the wider the range of people with whom she or he can work using this method.

In Summary

Voice Dialogue is a tool for transformation. It is one among a multitude of approaches that can be used in the evolution of consciousness. It can be used in relation to any other approach to growth, healing, and transformation. It lends itself beautifully to being used with visual imagery and combines with a multitude of gestalt, psychosynthesis, and dramatic techniques. It can dramatically enhance the analytic therapies.

To practice Voice Dialogue, a subject needs to be ready to acknowledge the existence of different selves. This is not acceptable to many people, so do not force the method. A rich array of approaches to the evolution of consciousness is available, and different people need very different things at different times in their process.

As a general rule, we would say to facilitators: Do only what is comfortable. Remember that Voice Dialogue is basically a communication tool. It certainly has therapeutic implications, but fundamentally it is a way of gradually learning to experience, to live, and to communicate the totality of our being. In this framework it is significant to note that learning to facilitate Voice Dialogue is as important as experiencing it.

PART II

The Voices

Introduction

In this section we will explore a wide range of energy patterns—the voices. Of course, we cannot introduce you to all of them, but we will include some of the most common ones. We will listen as they come to life in the dialogues that follow, and we will experience their depth and the way they interact with one another. In listening to these voices—their complaints, their desires—you will gain a sense of how real they are.

To more easily discuss these energy patterns with you, we have given them names. Once a self is discussed and named, we will illustrate how it works using Voice Dialogue transcripts. Listing subpersonalities by name is a mixed blessing because the adventure in Voice Dialogue comes from learning how to tune into an unfamiliar energy pattern and pursue it without preconceptions. The names we have chosen are simply convenient labels to help you recognize the patterns we are describing. They are not sacred and you do not need to marry yourselves to them—see them only as "temporary relationships."

In the interest of clarity and simplicity, we will be listing the different voices as separate entities. We will try to convey a sense of how they are constantly interacting with each other inside us and, to some extent, how they behave in relationships with others.

At this time we would like to re-emphasize the contrast between the primary and the disowned selves. The primary selves are the ones that we are identified with. In this culture, they are likely to be the protector/controller and the heavyweights. For each of these primary selves, there is an equal and opposite disowned or less developed self. It is helpful to think of the psyche in terms of the dynamic balance between these two systems. Please keep this balance in mind as you read the transcripts that follow.

4

The Protector/Controller: Meeting "The Boss"

The Development of Personality

We are born into this world in a condition of extreme vulnerability: We have no armor, no defenses; in fact, we do not yet even have a personality. However, we each have a special vibration, a uniqueness of being—our psychic fingerprint. For a brief time, we are without guilt, without the need to build a wall of protection around ourselves.

This situation soon changes, for we discover fairly early in the game of life that we must obey certain rules of conduct. Even as infants, we learn that some behaviors please and some displease those in our environment. Thus, we develop a consciousness that pays attention to these environmental cues. The birth of personality is coincident with the birth of this consciousness—the protector/controller energy pattern.*

* We are grateful to our friend and colleague, Mackie Ramsey of Carmel, California, for her use of the term *protector* to describe this vital energy pattern.

The protector/controller observes our environment and determines which of our behaviors will work best and please the most people. Under its direction, even the simplest behaviors such as smiling and cooing soon lose their spontaneity and become automatic reactions to our environment. We become "less natural" because our protector/controller is now monitoring and evaluating all the "dangers" we encounter.

As we mature, the protector/controller functions increasingly as a master computer network. It utilizes some of our other selves—our primary selves—to accomplish its ends. These selves define us and how we will behave and interact. For example, the protector/controller may decide it is important for us to please others. Our pleasing self will then be incorporated into the primary self system because it gets results—the approval of parents and others. The drive to be a success in school can be the beginning of another primary self system—the inner drive for achievement, success, and money. These primary selves simply describe what the ego is identified with and what is primary to the personality at any particular time. These selves may well change over time.

In working with Voice Dialogue, it is crucial to understand these primary selves for they are the gateway into the process. The facilitator needs to know how the primary selves developed, how they protect the subject's vulnerability, and what they fear will happen to the subject if they are not in control. They are the determining factors of personality, always screening, protecting, observing, and controlling. The facilitator must develop a sympathetic and caring relationship with the protector/controller and the primary selves before other selves can be explored.

These primary selves, then, develop and coalesce into what ultimately becomes known as our personality. Some may be related to genetic predispositions, others to purely environmental factors. For example, one child may be predisposed to introverted behavior patterns, so, as blockages are encountered in the environment, this child may tend to retreat within by engaging in fantasy. Another child may develop into an extrovert and interact with the environment in assertive, or even aggressive, ways. These behavioral responses may be determined by genetic considerations, sibling placement, and the particular relationship which exists between child and parents.

The personality is fundamentally a system of energy patterns that helps to protect our vulnerability. As this system evolves, we become powerful and strong. Vulnerability, as we have said, is generally not rewarded; power and strength are. So we go to good schools and get a good education and thus become more powerful. We learn how to study and work. We learn how to get what we want. We learn to please and to drive ourselves unmercifully in our quest for success. And we become even more powerful.

One day we awaken to find ourselves fully grown, and in possession of a fully developed personality. We have learned how to be successful on the planet and we are powerful. This is not a judgment; this kind of power is an absolute requirement for survival. If we have not mastered these skills already, we must learn to develop them after we have become adults. Many therapeutic approaches in the consciousness movement help people learn to move from helplessness and vulnerability to power. It is a most significant step, but the tragedy of this move to power is that we lose our connection to vulnerability. We lose our connection to the unique vibration of our psychic fingerprint.

A wonderful fairy tale called *The Snow Queen* provides a metaphor for this process. The story begins with two small children, Hans and Gerda. They spend hours listening to Gerda's grandmother spin stories about life and the mysterious and magical things of the world. They love the flowers and the sunshine but most of all they love each other. Together they manifest beautifully the psychic fingerprint that is so much a part of childhood.

While Hans and Gerda live happily, another drama is

unfolding: A goblin has built a special mirror with a most peculiar property. Whenever someone looks into it, everything that once looked beautiful begins to look ugly. He flies up to heaven, holding the mirror so that when he reaches God, God will look into it. The higher he flies, the more violently the mirror vibrates, and soon it shatters into millions of pieces which scatter across the earth.

One piece of the mirror flies into Hans's eye and another into his heart. Suddenly, Gerda is a big bore to him, and his grandmother becomes an old fool. Even the roses that grow on the window ledge, he notices, are now covered with worms. We would say that Hans has become a fully rational young man. Matters of the heart and soul which used to be all important now repel him.

When the Snow Queen comes to visit that evening, as she has on many previous evenings, he suddenly finds her irresistible. Although, in the past, she could not tempt him to leave, now his home looks ugly and foolish to Hans and he readily goes with her. She kisses him on the mouth, and his heart freezes totally. He is taken to the far north, to her home, where he spends his days working on puzzles. He sees the frozen world around him as a place of great beauty and no longer remembers anything about warmth, love, and feelings. He has totally identified with his cold, rational self and disowns all others. He is freezing to death, but he does not know it.

Now Gerda must find Hans and redeem him from the power of the Snow Queen. This task is a metaphor of Gerda's consciousness process and her ability to remain in contact with her psychic fingerprint—a task that will ultimately redeem Hans.

Sad as it may seem, Hans's fate is the fate of many of us. The development of personality generally requires the disowning of our more sensitive feeling selves. Their resurrection is one of the goals of the evolution of consciousness.

One of the first steps toward this end is to discover which selves are in charge of our personality. Who and what are *really* in charge of this entity we call the ego? We begin our journey to redemption by examining the phenomenology of the protector/controller. We shall see how it operates, how the protector/controller and its many friends determine which parts of us are rejected in our growing-up years.

The Protector/Controller

The protector/controller is somewhat similar to the Freudian "superego" or the transactional analysis "parent." This self ensures that the disowned selves remain disowned. It arises early in life and, after determining which behaviors are socially acceptable, creates a persona which can face the world. Its function is protection: It protects our vulnerability and can even save our lives by ensuring that we act appropriately. The protector/controller is both culturally and familially influenced, and each has its own basic inviolable principles.

In Voice Dialogue, work with the protector/controller is significant because this self is the basic energy pattern protecting each human being. However, this self is generally afraid of psychological work—it does not necessarily seek expansion and growth. It tends to be conservative in outlook and distrustful of new ideas.

Regardless of who is participating, one of the first steps in Voice Dialogue is to discover the wishes and desires of the protector/controller. The protector/controller must feel safe with the work and the facilitator. It must feel it has the right to control the work to a considerable extent. If it becomes too fearful or threatened by the work, it must have the right to stop the work or slow it down. This, more than anything else, creates the safe circumstances so essential for real trust to develop in the process.

It is fascinating to examine typical protector/controllers and realize their overall similarity. All are basically rational, all want to maintain an appearance of appropriate behavior (which may vary greatly from Los Angeles to New York to London), all want to maintain control over interpersonal situations, and they all want to protect the individual—however this may be done—at any price! The following dialogue is a good example of a typical Californian protector/controller:

FACILITATOR: Since you seem to be the one who runs Fred's life, I'd like to find out some more about you.

PROTECTOR/CONTROLLER: (stretching his arms across the back of the couch and adopting an expansive pose): Fine, ask me anything, fire away!

FACILITATOR: OK. Let's get down to basics. How do you want Fred to appear to others?

PROTECTOR/CONTROLLER: Oh, that's an easy one (with a charming and comfortable smile). I want everyone to like him. He should be at ease with people, very empathetic, helpful, understanding, and enthusiastic. You know—a fine person. I want everyone to be able to say, "Now, there's a *really* good person."

FACILITATOR: You seem to do a great job. Everyone *does* like him.

PROTECTOR/CONTROLLER: You bet! His family likes him, his friends like him, his ex-wife and ex-girlfriends like him. I'm great in groups. Groups like him, his therapists like him. I've studied a lot of psychology and I know just what to say and do to charm everybody. I do a good job with you, don't I?

FACILITATOR (smiling): You certainly do.

PROTECTOR/CONTROLLER: I'm really pleased with myself. I've got things just the way I want them and I don't want them disturbed. Not at all!

FACILITATOR: Tell me, what is it that you really wouldn't want Fred to do?

PROTECTOR/CONTROLLER: That's simple. I don't want him

to be selfish or inconsiderate. I never want him to disregard others or hurt their feelings. I also want to be very sure that nobody dislikes him or can say a bad word about him. I don't want him to lose his reputation as a real nice guy, no matter what!

FACILITATOR: Even if it makes him unhappy?

PROTECTOR/CONTROLLER: I really don't care about his happiness. *I just want everyone else to be happy with him* [emphasis ours]. And everyone *is* happy with him.

FACILITATOR: But he came to see me because he's not very happy with his life. He feels alienated and unfulfilled.

PROTECTOR/CONTROLLER: As I said, that's none of my concern.

This particular protector/controller had a history of familial as well as cultural influences. It chose to make Fred the "good boy" in contrast to his brother who was more self-involved and had been quite successful in everything he tried. Here the protector/controller was combined with pleaser, good son, and good father. In later work, these other voices would be brought up and dealt with separately.

No attempt was made to change Fred's protector/controller. Our aim was to help Fred's awareness level witness this pattern so that his ego would become more aware and stop identifying with the protector/controller. Any attempt to weaken Fred's protector/controller would have eroded Fred's image and threatened his particular niche in the family. Many families divide up personality attributes and encourage the various protector/controllers to develop along specific lines that give an individual a particular role in the family.

A protector/controller from New York presents another picture. This protector/controller was very interested in achievement, although Judy, herself, was more concerned about her social life.

FACILITATOR: Judy has talked about her inability to be as spontaneous as some of her friends in California, so I thought I'd like to ask you how you feel about spontaneity—about trying new things.

PROTECTOR/CONTROLLER: It looks pretty immature to me. I don't want her doing anything that she hasn't really thought through . . . nothing that she'll have to repudiate later . . . . These Californians and their spontaneity . . . just give them something new and they'll go after it with a passion. Then, two years later, there they are . . . another fad and they've made fools of themselves by giving in to it. I don't want her to look foolish! That's my biggest fear—looking foolish or, worse yet, acting immature. You have to maintain a certain maturity, a dignity, even a little cynicism in this life or people won't respect you. You know, one year they're all eating vegetables and another year they're all doing TM and another year it's aerobics. As far as I'm concerned, they all look like a bunch of children running after some magical prescription for the good life. There *is* none. And knowing that fact is maturity. *I* know.

My job is to keep Judy mature and wise and to never, never let her look foolish. That includes falling in love. If she misses a little fun, that's fine. Fun is for children anyway. Life is serious and Judy should stay serious and responsible.

I make sure that Judy is a person that people will respect and trust. They can depend upon her to be rational, like I am, and careful in all her decisions and actions. I've done wonders for her professional life.

An Israeli protector/controller voiced grave concerns for safety, both physical and psychological.

PROTECTOR/CONTROLLER: As far as I'm concerned the most important thing is to keep his vulnerability covered. He must never show his fears, or his needs or feelings . . . someone might use them against him. He should always look as though he's in charge of the situation. That's why I don't like him talking to you. He is—actually, *I* am—not always in charge. And if he isn't in charge, it could be dangerous for him. He needs me to protect him so he doesn't react impulsively. He's got to think things through or he could get in trouble. That would be the worst thing as far as I'm concerned—acting impulsively and not being in control of things.

Many Israeli protector/controllers share this concern. Confusion, vulnerability, lack of direction, "uncontrollable" anger, sexuality, fear—any of these are considered potentially dangerous by protector/controllers who view the need for rationality and absolute control as a matter of life and death.

As you may have noticed, protector/controllers tend to support a national or regional stereotype. They are usually eager to keep people as close to the local or familial norm as possible in order to prevent the difficulties that can arise from behaving too individually. It is important to be aware of their rules when doing Voice Dialogue with protector/controllers. This was brought to our attention quite strongly in London.

British protector/controllers, as a group, objected to uncovering unpleasant, earthy, or foolish subpersonalities. However, they would never allow anyone to be impolite or refuse to cooperate. They superficially "cooperated." We did not actually discover much about them until we asked the protector/controllers about their rules for disowning subpersonalities.

FACILITATOR: Norma's adventurous subpersonality has talked about her desire to travel and to create an exciting new job for her. She's feeling very constricted here in London. What do you have to say about that?

PROTECTOR/CONTROLLER: That's all very well for her to say, but Norma is getting along in years and it's most embarrassing for me to hear her talking with such enthusiasm and lack of sense. I'm just happy that none of her friends could hear her. As far as I'm concerned, it's all rubbish. I will *not* have her going off chasing rainbows. I don't find enthusiasm and excitement attractive and I do my best to keep them subdued. If she comes up with a good solid plan, presented soberly, I might listen to her, but basically I agreed with that other voice you talked to—the one that said she should face the fact that nothing much will ever happen in her life. And the sooner she faces that fact the better off she'll be.

I might also mention that I don't like the way you stir her up. I don't like her excitement and hope. She'll only be disappointed. I'll save her that trouble. By the way, I don't want her to start dressing colorfully like she used to; I prefer sober, unobtrusive colors.

And, speaking of colors (as the protector/controller gets even more emphatic), I *don't* want her showing off, flirting, wearing makeup, and making a sexual spectacle of herself. I want her to be sensible and sober as is appropriate for someone who'll be thirty-four next year! She's too old to act like she's twenty, even though people often think she is. She should act her age.

FACILITATOR: But you see how unhappy she is and how that other sober voice that you like wants to die. Do you have any room to negotiate? We won't encourage her to do anything without your approval.

PROTECTOR/CONTROLLER: Well, it *is* true that the sober voice makes Norma want to die. Perhaps if we can work out a way that she won't look too foolish, I might, I just *might*, be willing to compromise a little. At least in terms of how she dresses. She *has* been looking a little drab lately.

The facilitator was then able to enter into an alliance with the protector/controller, to respect its cultural demands for being sensible, tasteful, appropriate, and reserved. The British protector/controller must be assured of respect and cooperation in order to permit any real investigation into disowned selves. If not, it will reappear to undermine and negate the subpersonalities it has disowned or controlled in the past. In addition, it may well try to block further forays into these forbidden areas.

If, while working with an energy pattern, the facilitator feels a contraction in the subject, it is generally safe to assume that the protector/controller is reacting to the work. In the following example, the facilitator was talking to a voice which the subject, Calvin, had identified as a freedom voice. It wanted Calvin to be more adventurous, to take more risks. In the midst of this dialogue, the facilitator felt a contraction in Calvin and a different presence appeared.

FACILITATOR: It seems like a different part is here now. Could you move over so we could talk to this new part? (Calvin moves over.) Well, hello—who are you?

PROTECTOR/CONTROLLER: I don't know who I am, but I don't like what's going on. I don't like what this other voice is saying. I've worked hard and long to stabilize Calvin's life, and I'm not about to see it go down the drain.

FACILITATOR: What worries you the most?

PROTECTOR/CONTROLLER: He's going to end up taking risks and giving up his job and losing all of his financial security. I've seen too many people do that. It frightens me. I need stability. He's not a millionaire. He needs that weekly check.

FACILITATOR: You do understand that I'm not encouraging Calvin to give up his job or follow the advice of the freedom voice, don't you? My job is to help him to hear all the parts. It certainly sounds like you would help him avoid doing things too rashly or precipitously.

PROTECTOR/CONTROLLER: You bet your ass I would—and I'm glad you have some sense of how important I am.

The facilitator now has the option of going back to the freedom voice or staying with the protector/controller. The direction is not important; what matters is that Calvin's awareness level should now witness the conflict of opposites. It will be difficult now for Calvin to identify with either the freedom voice or the protector/controller. The purpose of the process is to learn how to drive your "psychological car." Then you can receive advice from different energy patterns while *you* drive—you make the choices and decisions with greater awareness.

Conservative and *liberal* are not simply words that describe peoples' politics, they are energy patterns that exist within each of us, our conservative and liberal natures. The conservative is connected to traditional values. It is fearful of change and it shrinks away from possibilities of greater freedom.

Our liberal nature encourages us to take greater risks. It is an energy that moves us to break with tradition, take chances, move toward alternative forms of behavior, and thus gain more choices over what we do. The protector/controller energy is our inner conservative nature. It tends to be more cautious where our liberal nature encourages more risk taking. If we honor both, we do not have to project either our liberal or conservative nature onto our environment, and our decisions in life will be more balanced.

From this general description of the protector/controller we can get some feeling of the significant place it occupies in our lives. This energy is also quite important in the evolution of consciousness. A new phenomenon has appeared in many individuals today who have been involved in the evolution of their consciousness: In their pursuit of freedom they have disowned their protector/controllers. They have struggled for years to become free emotionally and sexually. They meditate, visualize, and expand in many directions. Very commonly, in the course of all this, they literally negate the protector/controller. They see no reason for its existence. In the following dialogue the facilitator is responding to the fact that the protector/controller has been rejected by the subject's freedom voice:

FACILITATOR: I have the real sense that Drew hasn't been listening to you for many years.

PROTECTOR/CONTROLLER: It's true. She always tries so hard to be free, to act free. She does so many things that I hate.

FACILITATOR: Like what, for example?

PROTECTOR/CONTROLLER (quite distressed): I don't like it when she sleeps with so many men. I hate a lot of them. They're not nice. Some of them are downright creepy! And she's always ready to "grow"—always ready for another workshop. And she never has any money. That other voice says, "Spend it, the universe will take care of you—it's worth it." Well, it's *not* worth it to me. If she would listen to me she wouldn't be anxious all the time. She wouldn't need all those workshops to reduce her anxiety!

Drew's rejection of her protector/controller energy is amazingly common in parts of the world where people have been involved in consciousness work for extended periods of time. Conversely, in those parts of the world where psychological work is relatively new, protector/controllers are usually very strong.

As mentioned earlier, when we do Voice Dialogue in different cities around the world, the protector/controller is the first order of business. It has been functioning as the operating ego for many years. It is not about to be displaced by any upstart facilitator or any form of consciousness work. It must be honored, and the job it has done must be honored. Its viewpoint must be considered and respected whenever any other work is being done.

5

The Heavyweights

The Powerful Selves

In this chapter we will introduce you to the heavies in Voice Dialogue: your pusher, critic, perfectionist, power broker, and pleaser. Any of these subpersonalities might be part of your own general protector/controller pattern. They also might operate independently. This will vary from one person to another, but in mainstream America these particular selves usually represent our primary selves, those selves selected by the protector/controller to ensure that we are protected and successful in our lives. Let us look first at the pusher and how it operates.

The Pusher

A strong pusher will certainly help you achieve success in the world. It might also give you migraines, backaches, heart attacks, and a generally bilious attitude toward life. The pusher is one of the easiest voices to hear. Most of us are able to tune in at almost any time to this subpersonality who—whip in one hand, a list of unfinished business in the other—urges us on: "Your journals are unread, the beds are unmade, the dissertation unwritten, your exercise schedule awaits you, the garden needs weeding, the faucet is leaking . . . ." The list is endless. Our hours of work go unappreciated, and we can definitely count on one thing: As soon as we cross an item off the top of the list, the pusher will add one more to the bottom.

The pusher pushes us all. It may seem that the successful "type A" professional who is well organized and constantly on the go has the strongest pusher, but we've spoken with even stronger pushers in housewives who sit around all day in their bathrobes, leaving the dishes undone and the beds unmade. These pushers have lists so long and unattainable that the women have just given up and fallen into a depressive subpersonality who believes any attempt to get anything done is futile.

How to Experience Your Pusher

Before any further theoretical discussion, we would like to give you the opportunity to experience your pusher. In order to move into this particular system, start to think about all the things you have to do. Continue to compile this mental list until you experience a change of mood. A few leading questions might help, such as: What needs to be done around the house? For your spouse? For your children, your parents? What about work, savings, career planning, investment planning, keeping abreast of inflation, retirement planning? What reading material have you left unread? What projects are unfinished? What needs repair? Who do you need to call? What needs cleaning or organizing? What growth potential—physical, psychological, or spiritual—is as yet unrealized?

Hopefully, by now you have activated this specific subpersonality. How do you feel as your list of "things to do" grows? Until now, you have been focused on reading this book; now a subpersonality has taken over. You, yourself, are no longer in control. Feel the physical sensations that belong to this subpersonality. Do they differ from those you experience when you are peaceful and relaxed? Where does the tension focus? Is it in your jaws, face, hands, shoulders, head, or stomach? Is this feeling with you most of the time, or is it intermittent?

If you find the feeling fading, you can get back into this subpersonality by thinking of additional things to do. Or the subpersonality may be so strong that you feel the urge to drop this book and get something else done. Do you notice any feelings becoming stronger, such as: "I don't have enough time," "there's so much to do," "it never ends," "better just get going and get some of this done . . . ?"

You have just met your pusher. This energy seems to occur throughout our society. It does not like us to rest, relax, or waste time. It is particularly fond of interrupting our moments of relaxation with reminders of what must be done. It will try to keep us from enjoying a second cup of coffee before starting work, and it may totally disrupt any attempts to lie out in the yard and enjoy the sunshine on a Sunday afternoon. It can be a rather harsh taskmaster, but it does get its job done. Success in the Western world is usually dependent upon the pusher.

The pusher develops early in life, encouraged by parents, teachers, and employers. In very ambitious families, this subpersonality is so valued that it clearly overshadows all the rest. We all know at least one man who brags of not having taken a vacation in years—such a man has no aware ego, his life is completely run by this particular subpersonality, his pusher. Our pushers are generally rewarded by everyone around us. After all, isn't it great to have somebody else who is willing to work constantly?

It is easy to physically feel the pusher take over. We tense up. Our jaws may lock, our teeth may clench, our neck or shoulder muscles may tighten, and we might even feel a sick, panicky feeling in our stomachs. We can see the pusher in the mirror, as well. Our faces do not look relaxed and glowing, and we tend to look tight and perhaps a bit haggard.

Please keep in mind that we do not view the pusher as a negative energy. No energy pattern is inherently positive or negative. Everything is relative to our awareness and our ability to direct energy through an aware ego so that we can make real choices about what we do. When the pusher is in charge, we are being driven down the freeway of life at a high speed. This pusher may be mildly amusing or an active demon whose demands can easily destroy us. It certainly destroys the job of living for many people.

Sylvester, a man in his early forties, dreamt repeatedly over a ten-year period that he was driving to work on the freeway at high speeds, and each time his car crashed into something. This image of driving at high speed on the freeway is a perfect metaphor of the pusher energy. Sylvester's unconscious was delivering a clear warning, and sure enough, at the end of ten years, he had a heart attack. Our physical bodies often pay the price of supporting an overly endowed pusher. Yet it is this breakdown that oftentimes gives us our first real opportunity to develop an awareness level that can see that our car has, in fact, been driven by the pusher rather than ourselves.

The pusher, the critic, and the perfectionist make an awesome trio when they run our lives—as they often do. We now introduce you to some of our favorite pushers.

Reading Lists for Professionals (and Nonprofessionals)

One of the cooperative ventures the critic and pusher engage in entails making people feel bad because they do not know enough (critic) and then providing them with reading lists to help them improve (pusher). The following dialogue between a therapist and his client, a therapist himself, will help illustrate this remarkable partnership:

THERAPIST: From what you're saying, you're not sure of yourself when you're doing therapy.

JOHN: That's right. I always feel that I don't know enough. I think of therapists I know and they all seem so well read—like they know what they're doing all the time.

THERAPIST: Could we talk to the part of you that feels like you don't know enough?

JOHN: That would be easy. It's our old friend again. (John has done dialogue work before and he readily moves over to make room for his critic.)

CRITIC: Hello again. I'm glad to be back—not that I'm ever really gone.

THERAPIST: Are you there most of the time?

CRITIC: Well, to tell you the truth, the real issue is whether he is ever there. Me, I'm always here.

THERAPIST: You're pretty sure of yourself.

CRITIC: I love working with therapists, especially younger ones. It's so easy to make them feel bad about themselves.

THERAPIST: How do you do that with John?

CRITIC: Just the way he said—I make him feel bad about how little he knows. Once I've got that going it's just a question of suggesting things to read.

THERAPIST: Do *you* make these suggestions?

CRITIC: I think so—I never thought about it. I guess someone else does that.

THERAPIST: Could I talk to the part that suggests the readings? (John shifts chairs again.)

THERAPIST: Are you the part of John that suggests his readings?

PUSHER: Yes, that's me. I work with the critic. Once John starts listening to the critic, he's ripe for me.

THERAPIST: What is the reading list you have for him?

PUSHER: Well, first of all there are the journals.

THERAPIST: Could you list some that you require?

PUSHER: Well, let's start with the basic psychoanalytic journals. Because this is a main interest of his, I expect him to read the basic journals concerned with psychoanalysis. He needs to keep up with current trends in psychology, so I expect him to read the *American Psychologist*. I also expect him to read some of the basic Jungian journals. I also like him to keep on top of what is happening in medicine, so I like him to read *The New England Journal of Medicine* as well.

THERAPIST: That's a good list already. How about books?

PUSHER: Books I have a-plenty. The whole basic series on psychoanalysis is an absolute must. The complete Jungian series is a must.

THERAPIST: Does that include the Alchemy and Mysterium?

PUSHER: Absolutely. Everything. It's all a must.

THERAPIST: Is there anything else?

PUSHER: Of course. I like the image of knowing something about everything, so I'm asking him to read the Fritz Perls and Polster books for Gestalt, the basic Reichian literature, and then there is the philosophy.

THERAPIST: Hold it. Do you mean that he listens to this and actually plans to read all these books?

PUSHER: He has the journals and books piled up in his bedroom. They're always there for him to see. When he goes into a bookstore I remind him of all the other things he needs to know about. It's really fun.

THERAPIST: It sounds like a real gas. Doesn't he ever wise up to what you're doing?

PUSHER: What do you mean, wise up? These books are all important. Would you deny that?

THERAPIST: Well, let's say that many are interesting but I haven't found reading all of them essential for the work I do.

PUSHER: Well, don't tell him that. He might start balking.

THERAPIST: What if he did?

PUSHER: I don't know. It's never happened . . . I couldn't even imagine it.

After doing dialogue work with a large number of pushers, one wonders what percentage of books in the world are purchased by pushers, rather than by the choice of an aware ego. We can only admire the supreme confidence of the pusher in these times, when so many of us doubt ourselves. Listen to the following dialogue between a therapist and a female client's pusher who is planning her leisure time:

THERAPIST (speaking to pusher): Sally tells me that she has one day a week free when she can do absolutely anything she wants to do, and that you really don't have any power over her on that day.

PUSHER (innocently): That's true. Anything she wants she can do.

THERAPIST (suspiciously): How could she have a whole day free when she has her child to take care of? What time does this free day start?

PUSHER: Oh, well it doesn't start until she drops her daughter off at school at 9:00 AM and she has to be home in time to pick her up at 2:30 PM.

THERAPIST: Oh, I see. It's not *quite* a full day, is it? I bet you have lots of plans for her between nine and 2:30.

PUSHER: No, she just does what she likes to do. She gets her nails done and goes to the hairdresser. Then she gets her shopping done. Then she has lunch with her girlfriends so she's sure to see them once a week because that's the only day she can see them. You realize these all are things for her own good—things just for her. She's just spending the day taking care of herself.

THERAPIST: I see you've learned that Sally has to take care of herself and it seems to me that you've set up a pretty busy schedule for her to do this. But, tell me, even though you sound so accepting of her need to take care of herself, what if she decided she needed to spend the day in her bathrobe reading a novel or doing nothing?

PUSHER (totally incredulous): Never, *absolutely* never!

How much of our lives do we live under the domination of such voices, thinking all the time that we are doing exactly what we choose to do? How little we understand the lack of freedom that characterizes most of our lives.

The New Age Pusher

Nothing in recent history has been more exciting for pushers (at least on the West Coast) than this current period of New Age expansionism. The possibilities for tormenting us are limitless, and our pushers delight in the unfolding of a myriad of "shoulds." Marilyn's pusher had been satisfied with a career, a home, a husband, children, travel, and a few extra frills. After Marilyn read a few books on consciousness expansion in the New Age, she began to experience a tightness in her shoulders.

THERAPIST: Let's talk to the voice that's making your shoulders tight—do you know which one that is? (Marilyn moves over to the pusher's chair. The pusher has appeared in previous dialogues and is familiar with the process.)

PUSHER: You bet we do; it's me again.

THERAPIST: I'll be darned! I thought you'd decided to take a vacation. You sure had me fooled.

PUSHER: Well, I did let her go to Hawaii, but I brought a couple of books for her to read. I let her take it easy for a couple of days and then I got her again.

THERAPIST: Amazing. How did you do it?

PUSHER: I got her to read *The Aquarian Conspiracy* and now there's so much to do.

THERAPIST: Hold it—what do you mean, there's so much to do?

PUSHER: Well, first of all, we got a chance to visit a Kahuna while we were in Hawaii. I think she should study about Kahunas and psychic surgery, too. To back up to the beginning: This New Age consciousness is fascinating, just fascinating. First, we have to get her diet under control. Then she has to join a health club and start working out regularly. And I want her to do yoga. We need to refine her energies. There's a lot to read—dozens of books. Next, she needs to study about energies. Energy fields, balancing, clearing—you know, all that.

The pusher became increasingly excited. One idea led to the next; no encouragement was necessary. A seductive enthusiasm lit its eyes as it went on.

PUSHER: Of course, she'll have to start some form of meditation and I'd also like her to study with someone who will sharpen her psychic powers and teach her to read auras. She should do some reading—it's OK with me if it's in popularized form—on the new discoveries in quantum physics that are paralleling mystical beliefs and also in brain research that supports the existence of ESP and other levels of awareness.

THERAPIST: And she's supposed to do all this while she works and runs a household? You're kidding me.

PUSHER (with great enthusiasm and urgency): No, I'm not. She'll be left behind if she doesn't.

THERAPIST (laughing): No wonder she came back from Hawaii with tense shoulders!

This pusher was a sly one. It was excited and positive most of the time, and if Marilyn had allowed herself to get carried away by the excitement, she would have been exhausted pretty quickly. But here, too, we have a hint of the vulnerable child underneath—the one who is afraid of getting left behind when everybody else is out greeting the New Age. A further exploration of the child's fears gave Marilyn's aware ego more perspective on the situation and allowed her to make conscious choices about what to do and what not to do.

The Pusher's Nemesis: The Do-nothing

In order to balance the pusher, who plays a major role in our lives, it is fun to talk to its opposite. The opposite subpersonality might be a beach bum, a hippie, a bag lady, a sloth, or a spoiled princess. This voice is a repository of wonderfully relaxing self-indulgent suggestions, much to the pusher's dismay.

The subpersonality that will permit and even encourage us to do nothing provides an important balancing energy to the pusher, particularly in our generally pusher-oriented society. This voice permits us to slow down, take care of ourselves, and enjoy life. If this energy is not incorporated into our own lives, we will most definitely draw someone into our orbit (a husband, a child, an employer) who will carry this energy for us.

Remember Sally? (see p. 36.) Her pusher ran her life totally. Sally had a husband who carried her disowned self—a hippie. As long as Sally identified with her pusher—worrying, working, and full of responsibility twenty-four, no, thirty-eight hours a day—her husband was locked into his hippie subpersonality. He chided her about worrying too much, he refused to take any serious responsibility for their finances, and he talked about selling everything and going off somewhere to live a simple and undemanding life. The more Sally's pusher heard this, the harder it pushed, and Sally became ever more judgmental about her husband's lack of responsibility. In the following dialogue, we talked to Sally's hippie:

HIPPIE: You know (stretching back lazily and talking slowly), I just can't believe Sally.

THERAPIST: What do you mean, you can't believe her?

HIPPIE (smiling): She's always worried, always has a ten-foot list of things to do, always busy. Do you really think that it gets her anywhere?

THERAPIST: She certainly thinks it does. What do you think would happen if she didn't work so hard?

HIPPIE (lazily grinning): Nothing! So things would take a little longer to do. Nobody's going to die from that.

THERAPIST: What will happen to the business?

HIPPIE: Somebody else will take care of things if she doesn't jump up and do everything immediately. You know, she's so efficient she doesn't even give anyone else a chance.

This last observation is so true. Well-developed pushers have a tendency to rush in and do things before ordinary mortals even see that something needs to be done.

HIPPIE: I'd like to show her that the world won't come to an end if she lets herself relax a little.

THERAPIST: What would you suggest?

HIPPIE: First, I'd have her leave all her bookkeeping at the store. What she doesn't do one day, she'll do the next. When she brings it home, she gets tense. I'd suggest she relax at night, watch TV, make love, ignore anything that isn't done by dinner time. Just leave it until the next day. And don't worry. Just don't worry. Especially about money. She should just relax. It'll all be OK. It always has been. She's forgotten how to trust (smiling easily). The important thing is that she loves her husband and he loves her, so they should enjoy one another.

It was amazing to see how Sally's physical appearance changed as this hippie voice talked. Her face relaxed and the worry lines disappeared, her shoulders—which were always tense—relaxed, and she smiled easily. She twinkled.

As Sally listened to her hippie, her consciousness separated from the pusher. She decided to try to relax and follow some of the hippie's suggestions. The change was nothing short of miraculous. As her pusher backed off, her husband's hippie pulled out of his relationship with Sally—it happened in perfect balance. Sally's husband began to worry and accept some responsibility for finances and the burden was suddenly an equally shared set of concerns. Together, they handled everything beautifully, and together they were able to relax and feel mutually supported, and to move ahead in ways neither felt were possible before. Their relationship was deeper, stronger, and solidly balanced. They also had much more fun.

As we said earlier, we are born into the world quite vulnerable, and fairly early in life we discover that being vulnerable is not the best way to be. We develop a personality made up of our primary selves that is, in effect, a defense against vulnerability. The pusher is one of the *cornerstones* of that personality for most people. Working hand-in-hand with the protector/controller, it incorporates all the parental and societal injunctions, all the things we should and should not do, into our personalities. We never realize that our life is being lived *for* us by an energy pattern that dominates us.

The answer to this dilemma is consciousness: being aware of these energy patterns. This awareness does not attempt to eradicate or judge anything. As in Sally's case, consciousness is simply an awareness and an experience, and these bring with them the possibility of choice. Sally heard her pusher and her hippie. In the Voice Dialogue session, we were helping her awareness separate from the system of ideas and attitudes and feelings that had dominated her way of being in the world. She began to "drive her own car" for the first time. She continued to listen to the pusher, but it was no longer dominant, she no longer automatically believed what it told her. She was developing a more aware ego.

There is no way to demonstrate the full effect the critic and pusher have had on our society, but our personal estimate is that if we suddenly neutralized the critic and pusher in our country, seventy-five percent of the hospital beds would be emptied, and ninety percent of the clients in psychotherapy would be finished. Surprisingly enough, the ability to say no to these energies changes them. Listen to the following dialogue that occurred at the time of such a change. The subject was a hard-driven businessman who had just begun to discover his vulnerability.

FACILITATOR: How do you feel now that Don is saying no to you (pusher)?

PUSHER: I'll tell you the truth—I don't mind. I'm tired.

FACILITATOR: I never thought I'd hear you say that.

PUSHER: I've been at it for a long time.

FACILITATOR: Aren't you afraid he'll stop doing things?

PUSHER: I don't know; he seems able to handle things. I don't know—my steam is gone.

The awareness and the experience of an energy pattern (pusher, critic, or any other one) change the nature of that pattern. In Don's case, as the pusher lost energy, the vulnerable and playful child became stronger. Consciousness was now available to both selves, and this made it possible for Don to carry the tension between these two opposites.

The Possibility of Conscious Choice

As we have seen, a great deal of what we do is not done out of free choice but is a response to the demands of the pusher. However, the pusher's drive is not totally negative. Few of us would have gotten through school without its pressure to urge us on. This book would never have been written without its help. A great deal of activity in the world is based on the pusher's power in concert with the critic and the perfectionist.

There comes a time, however, when we wish to exercise more choice in our lives. But to choose, we must first develop an awareness of who is driving our psychological car. The thought patterns of the pusher and critic (whom we shall meet in the next section) are deeply ingrained in societal personality structures, as well as in individuals. We often think these voices "speak the truth." Unless we become aware of their presence and develop an awareness separate from them, they continue to dominate our lives and convince us of their wisdom and benevolence.

Only when our aware ego separates from these voices and objectively considers what they are saying can we perceive their malevolent qualities. They *always* sound as though they want to improve us, as though they have our best interests at heart. It is important, therefore, to listen carefully to what they say and, from the vantage point of an aware ego, ascertain the validity of their comments. Then, and only then, can we make conscious choices.

These choices are invariably more pleasurable, more creative, and more rewarding than those dictated by the critic and pusher. They move us toward self-actualization and therefore feel effortless rather than burdensome.

Life is not meant to be lived on a freeway full time. Neither was it meant to be lived in constant pain over our errors and imperfections. Although we, as psychotherapists on behalf of the health care professions in general, thank the critics, perfectionists, and pushers of the world, we do feel that it is time for a new management team—a team headed by an aware ego.

Critics We have Known and Loved

It is with a real sense of delight that we share in this next section, with deep admiration and unbounded respect, critics we have known and loved. These critics are particularly powerful subpersonalities that exert an untoward influence on our lives. The critic is a remarkable subpersonality who prevents many of us from experiencing life as pleasurable. After all, too much pleasure could be dangerous.

We are sure that you will recognize many of these critics, both in yourselves and in people close (and not so close) to you. In meeting the critic, one basic idea is important to keep in mind: Even critics need loving. It is good to remember how helpful these often difficult subpersonalities can be.

How the Critic Works

How do we begin to describe this highly versatile voice? First, we might note that it has a great talent for teamwork. It collaborates beautifully with the protector/controller by pointing out potential dangers to the protector/controller.

> CRITIC: Tom is doing it again! I keep telling him that if he doesn't ignore his wife when she hurts his feelings and if he doesn't get that temper of his under control, she's going to leave him. She doesn't like it when he blows up at her for no reason. He's being stupid again. So what if she didn't say hello when he came in? He's too sensitive, too needy. And now the poor dear's feelings are hurt (sarcastically), and he's going to have a temper tantrum because she forgot to close the garage door.

Now the protector/controller can take over the job. Tom's hurt feelings are to be ignored and his anger is to be squelched. He is to behave rationally and manfully. (He will probably take the newspaper, ignore everyone, and go into the next room to watch TV.)

Another of the critic's great partners is the pusher. The pusher sets up enormous tasks and unreasonable deadlines and then the critic criticizes when these are not met. Another of the critic's cohorts, the perfectionist, sets up ideal standards of behavior or achievement and the critic criticizes when they are not met.

The following dialogue illustrates how the critic works with the perfectionist. It is an excerpt from a woman who has, with great persistence, become aware of her subpersonalities and how they interact. Her perfectionist, needless to say, expects her to be perfectly aware and act consciously all the time. Carol, because she is human, has her moments of unconsciousness. One of her biggest challenges has been to control her critic's power. Her critic is delighted to criticize, among other things, her inability to limit its power.

> CRITIC: I can't believe her (with total disgust). After all these years, you'd think she'd know how to handle her own critic! She did a wonderful job over Christmas—even *I* have to admit that—but then she let me get her. I started in gradually, reminding her that she'd gained a little weight and had stopped exercising during the holidays, and next thing you know she really let me in. She listened to me when I told her how she's always dealing with the same stupid problems yet never made any headway. Then I told her that she'll never be perfect at work, she's bound to make mistakes, and then I told her that her marriage isn't as perfect as it should be. By the time I was finished with her, she was fully depressed. You'd think she would have learned not to listen to me by now. She even let me wake her up at night and pick on her (mockingly). And then I even criticized her for letting me do that.

The Unusual Abilities of the Critic

We never fail to be amazed at the intelligence of the critic. It must have an I.Q. somewhere between 395-470. If you understand I.Q. scores, you will recognize that this is at the top of the scale. The critic is absolutely brilliant in its ability to make us feel rotten about ourselves.

In addition to the logical intelligence represented by its high I.Q., the critic seems to have a deep sense of intuition.

Somehow, it always knows where our soft spots are and how to dig the knife sharply into them. If we are worried about our physical appearance, if we are worried about being unlovable, if we are worried about being stupid, about being undereducated, disempowered, sexless, selfish, not as good as the next person, or too aggressive—all of these are acceptable targets for the critic. It is holistic in its orientation. It uses its keen clinical intuition to find out what we most fear to be, and then it attacks.

Its powers of perception are remarkable as well. Nothing is too small or too large to escape its notice. From something as small as a spouse failing to appreciate a new haircut (the critic will point out how unattractive it is) to something as large as the threat of worldwide destruction (the critic will criticize our inadequate involvement), the critic is always ready to point out our inadequacies and failures. It monitors our actions thoroughly and will wake us in the early morning hours to review, with distaste, our behavior at a party the night before or an interaction with a loved one, a colleague, or a family member. It will remember every negative detail and, unless we are very alert, it will convince us that we have behaved abominably and done irreparable damage.

Another quality to be admired in the critic is its capacity for total candor. It has no desire to hide its power, and when spoken to directly it seems to revel in the possibility of sharing its philosophy and methodology with any reasonable listener. Critics have been known to brag of their ability to snare an individual no matter which way he turns. In fact, they often get so carried away by sheer delight in their power, they give away valuable information. Let us see how this arrogant honesty helped Alice discover the impossibility of pleasing her critic.

CRITIC: Basically, I just don't think that she measures up. That's all.

FACILITATOR: Can you be more specific? For instance, we

were just talking about her weight. How do you feel about that?

CRITIC: She's too fat. You know that.

FACILITATOR: But when she'd lost weight, remember what you said?

CRITIC: Sure. She was too thin. Bony in the shoulders. She wasn't sexy enough. I think she should look sexier.

FACILITATOR (teasing): And what would you say if she looked sexier?

CRITIC: I'd tell her she looks like a tramp. I agree with her father. A woman shouldn't be too provocative.

FACILITATOR: But you just said she should be sexier.

CRITIC: I know. I don't like it when she's too sweet—too much the girl next door.

FACILITATOR: It seems to me that you've got her coming and going.

CRITIC (triumphantly): That's right. I'm like her father. Nothing ever pleased him either. I just think that everything she does is wrong. Besides that, she's stupid.

FACILITATOR: But she does well in all her courses.

CRITIC: That's because she's a perfectionist and compulsive and she studies too much.

FACILITATOR: What if she relaxed more?

CRITIC (very self-satisfied): Then I'd tell her she's lazy. She can't win with me. She might as well give up.

A top-notch critic can get us from any angle. Only constant vigilance and a keen awareness of that sinking sensation in the pit of our stomach can alert us to its brilliant and well-aimed attacks. If we pay close attention, we will soon realize that however we are, whatever we hope to do, it is not okay with the critic.

The critic knows just where to stick the knife blade. It is always some sensitive spot, and once the blade is in we tend to focus on the critic's complaint rather than on the knife being shoved into us. The critic is an outstanding knife-wielder. To become aware of its capabilities, to be able to look beyond the content of its comments, and to recognize its destructive capacity requires a powerful awareness and an impressive development of consciousness. Before this awareness has evolved, we will continue to be the critic's victims.

The Incomparable Comparer

The comparer is a potent aspect of the critic and has great versatility. It is totally holistic in its approach to comparison. With ease and delight it will remind you that your friend is brighter or has accomplished more—possibly she has written a book. Another friend might be a better mother who spends inordinate time with her children and seems to love them no matter what. A business associate may have a better marriage, and a friend dresses with more imagination. Someone has a penis that is larger, and someone else's figure is the way yours should be. Whatever the comparison, the comparer always uses a particular watchword: However you are, someone else is better. Whatever it is you plan to become has already been surpassed.

The following dialogue with the comparer of an intelligent and successful middle-aged man gives us an idea of how this self works:

> COMPARER: I say, "Why bother? Why bother?" It's too late in life and he's just not going to do as well as his friends.

The comparer, by the way, does not necessarily burden itself with facts.

> COMPARER: As I said, he's not going to do as well as his friends. His work isn't as meaningful as E's, his relationships

> aren't as deep as L's, his sex life isn't adequate. I don't think that people like him as much as they like other people. I look around at everybody else, then I look at him and I say again, "Don't bother."

The comparer is incomparable when it comes to making us feel miserable. Somebody will always be more evolved, richer, sexier, more brilliant, more attractive, younger, older, wiser, more relaxed, more accomplished, more efficient and so on, and so on. Once the comparer starts its refrain, we feel diminished, reduced to second-class status, hopelessly outdistanced by those carefully selected others held up to us as examples.

How the Critic Examines Physical Appearance

The critic often combines with the perfectionist, especially in women, when it comes to appearance. Their appraisal, as in the following example, often has no relationship to reality whatsoever. The subject, Elaine, was a very beautiful woman and a talented actress. (It is to the credit of the critic that it is singularly unimpressed by the way people actually look. The critic criticizes equally, no matter what the objective state of attractiveness may be. It is important to appreciate this egalitarian attitude.)

In the following dialogue, Elaine speaks about her competition for acting roles:

> ELAINE: I just feel unsure of myself whenever I go for an interview. I feel awkward and unattractive.
>
> FACILITATOR: Could we talk to that part of you that makes you feel unattractive? (Elaine shifts into a different seat.)
>
> FACILITATOR: You're the part of Elaine that makes her feel she's unattractive.
>
> CRITIC: I don't have to make her feel that way—she *is* unattractive.

FACILITATOR: Well, I have to tell you, friend, she looks pretty good to me. What do you see that you don't like?

CRITIC: Well, that's a rather open-ended question. I could go on for a long time.

FACILITATOR: Well, just start somewhere. What's the main thing you want changed or don't like?

CRITIC: Well, obviously, her breasts. They're much too small. That's why I want her to have surgery. (It was not obvious to the therapist.)

FACILITATOR: What kind of surgery are you referring to . . . breast enlargement?

CRITIC: I want her breasts enlarged . . . of course. How can she pursue a career as an actress if her breasts are too small? You've seen actresses. You know what they look like.

FACILITATOR: How do you manage to make Elaine feel so terrible about her breasts? I really have to tell you that they look pretty good to me.

CRITIC: I remind her of different women . . . especially different actresses who have very large breasts. I say to her, "How did you feel at the party when you saw Lisa with that low-cut gown? Now *those* were breasts."

FACILITATOR: You sound like a man.

CRITIC: I am. That's why I'm such an expert on the subject of women and what's wrong with them.

FACILITATOR: And apparently, if I understand you, comparing them to other women is a favorite method.

CRITIC: Not just women—men, too. If I can compare Elaine to a man, that can work just as well.

FACILITATOR: Not with breasts.

CRITIC: Oh, you know better than that. The issue isn't breasts. The issue is how to make Elaine feel bad about herself. I love telling her how dumb she is. Otherwise, she wouldn't want to be an actress. And when she does act, I make sure to look at her films and tell her she looks dumb.

The critic is quite remarkable in its ability to change its point of view once a woman has followed its suggestions for surgery. In the following dialogue, a disgusted critic gave an opposing point of view after breast surgery:

> CRITIC: She was really stupid to let them talk her into breast enlargement. Her breasts were perfectly good before and now they're too big and they're heavy and they ache. Do you see how she sometimes rests them on the table? She tries to be discreet about it but I point it out to her every time she does it. I just can't believe how stupid women can be about their looks.

There is no satisfying an out-of-control critic. First it attacks from the right and, as we swing round, it gets us with an uppercut. We listen to its criticisms, try to make things better, and it criticizes us for our new looks or our new behavior. That is why it is so important to go beyond the details of content to experience the energy operating. If someone is sticking a knife into us and, at the same time, talking to us very reasonably about our shortcomings, it might be more advisable to focus on the knife rather than the words.

The Critic Transformed

As we think back over the many critics we have known, we realize that they do provide some valuable services. It is frequently the critic—and the discomfort caused by its complaints—who launches us on our journey of transformation. The critic points out, in no uncertain terms, that there is something wrong and we had better correct it. Furthermore, gold nuggets are frequently buried in the trash. The critic forces us to look at the distasteful sides of ourselves and, if we are not incapacitated by its judgments, we can begin to deal with these aspects through an aware ego. It can be very difficult to sort through the barrage of negativity in the beginning of this process, however.

Last and best, the energy of the critic when transformed (after it has been made conscious), introduced into awareness, and clearly differentiated from the aware ego, can serve as a true ally. It can evaluate our actions objectively and help us improve our performance in any field of endeavor. It can also alert us to areas of unconsciousness, point out disowned selves, and let us know when we are caught in a bonding. As its judgments lose their bite, it can become a very effective, discerning, rational friend.

Its tendency to destroy remains a possibility, however, and a critic is able to become deadly again after a period of benign cooperation. Never turn your back on a sleeping critic! Accept its gifts, love it, but remember: You never know when it will revert to its original untamed state . . . and attack.

The Perfectionist

We have seen how the pusher energy drives people to do things. Together with the perfectionist, it sets standards that can be used creatively, if we are aware of these energies. Or, conversely, it sets requirements that make life an intolerable burden.

When the perfectionist works with the pusher, we are required to do things perfectly. This combination is very powerful (although the perfectionist can exist by itself), and the inner critic is usually part of the equation as well.

Henry was a professional man who wanted to write a book, but he had a writing block. In the course of our conversation with him, it became clear that Henry was driven by a very demanding taskmaster. This internal pharaoh didn't like shoddy work; he only appreciated "class" writing (and "class" anything else, for that matter).

FACILITATOR: I hear a voice, when you talk about life, that seems quite strong in you—someone who demands that things be done in a certain way. Could I talk to that part of you? (Henry moves over.) Good morning.

PERFECTIONIST: Good morning. What can I do for you?

FACILITATOR: I heard your voice while Henry was talking so I thought I would talk to you directly. What is your job in Henry's life?

PERFECTIONIST: Well, if you're going to do a thing, do it right. That's what my father used to say.

FACILITATOR: So, Henry's father was one of your teachers?

PERFECTIONIST: He sure was. He was perfect in everything he did.

FACILITATOR: Well, how about you and Henry? What's your function in him now?

PERFECTIONIST: I keep him clear. His book is going to be a real work of art. I hate shoddy writing. I hate shoddy workmanship. I hate shoddy people.

FACILITATOR: What's a shoddy person?

PERFECTIONIST: Someone who does shoddy work.

FACILITATOR: Do you know many such people?

PERFECTIONIST (somewhat embarrassed—an indication that other parts are somewhat ashamed of what the perfectionist is about to say): Well, he's surrounded by them. His wife is just the opposite. She doesn't care about whether the house is neat or not. I'm always picking up. And his son is the biggest slob you ever saw. I'm always after him. His daughter is like me (proudly).

From our discussion of energy patterns with which we identify and energy patterns that we disown, it is clear that Henry is identified with a strong natural pusher and perfectionist. He has obviously disowned his more relaxed selves, as well as his vulnerability. By the laws of energetics, Henry will always pull people into his orbit who reflect his disowned selves. As long as his awareness level is identified with his perfectionist and his pusher, he will polarize his environment and his already easygoing wife will be driven into a "sloppy daughter" reaction to his perfectionist father.

Remember that no energy pattern is inherently good or bad. At issue is whether Henry's awareness is separated from the perfectionist energy. So far, from our dialogue, it is clear that it is not. Until Henry has an awareness separate from his inner perfectionist father, his relationship to his own son is doomed to perpetual conflict as the father pattern drives his son, "the slob," into deeper and deeper withdrawal and fantasy, or active rebellion. In this way, the son will live out more and more of Henry's unconscious self. Let us go back to the dialogue.

FACILITATOR: So you have a hard time with all these slobs around.

PERFECTIONIST: Well—other parts of Henry are coming in now. They feel I'm too dogmatic. I don't think I am.

FACILITATOR: Are there other areas in Henry's life in which you operate?

PERFECTIONIST: I don't like the way he reads documents at work. He needs to be more careful. He needs to study them more carefully. A mistake can be very costly.

The dialogue proceeded to explore the many areas in which the perfectionist operated. The facilitator at a certain point decided to explore the team that was repeatedly alluded to by the perfectionist.

FACILITATOR: I have the feeling when you speak that you're very afraid—as though if Henry doesn't listen to you, something terrible is going to happen. Could I talk to the part of Henry that feels that fear? (Henry moves over to a different place, sits very quietly, and doesn't speak. He looks totally different physically from the way he looked in the perfectionist voice. A few minutes pass during which time the facilitator simply remains energetically connected to what turns out to be the frightened child. After three or four minutes of silence, the facilitator speaks.)

FACILITATOR: Hello—you seem rather scared.

CHILD: I am. I'm always scared. He always wants to get rid of me. He hates me.

FACILITATOR: You mean our friend over here (perfectionist) hates you.

CHILD: I don't know who hates me. They all hate me. He never lets me be around.

FACILITATOR: How does he get rid of you?

CHILD: He just never lets me out. I hate his work. I hate law. I hate documents. I'm always scared at work. I'm always afraid something terrible is going to happen.

It was clear that Henry had developed an elaborate system of energy patterns to strengthen himself against a very vulnerable and very frightened little boy inside him. The more perfectionistic he became, the more he drove himself, the deeper the *angst* of his inner child became. This *angst* may translate itself into anxiety, depression, physical symptoms and, quite sadly, confused and disturbed family relations.

For the inner child, it was the first time he had even been allowed to be present in Henry's life. Henry's awareness now had the opportunity to separate from the perfectionist and the pusher and to witness the feelings that had been negated for such a long time.

The following dialogue shows us the perfectionist of a woman who would be considered eminently successful by all who knew her:

FACILITATOR: Would you be willing to tell us your expectations of Barbara?

PERFECTIONIST: I'd be delighted! (With extreme self-righteousness.) My basic philosophy is quite simple: I expect her to be perfect. There are to be no mistakes. None whatever. I don't compare her to anyone else; my standards are absolute. She must never say or do anything that could be reasonably questioned by anyone else.

FACILITATOR: That could be a bit limiting, couldn't it?

PERFECTIONIST: I'm *quite* clear. I'd rather have her say and do nothing than let someone else find a flaw in her. My aim is to be sure that she's perfect.

FACILITATOR: In what areas?

PERFECTIONIST: In all areas. When she speaks, it should be clear, well thought out, rational, in complete sentences, and concise, but it should not be pedantic. She should be spontaneous, entertaining, and perceptive. When she writes, there should be no errors anywhere in grammar or spelling. Each paragraph should flow beautifully into the next. There should be a perfect marriage of meaningful content and elegant style. And, again, nothing that anyone could possibly criticize. I do want her to be sure that nobody can find fault with anything she says or writes.

FACILITATOR: That sounds a bit difficult to achieve. What about other areas of her life?

PERFECTIONIST: Whatever bookkeeping she does must be faultless. I can't tolerate a checkbook that doesn't balance with a bank statement. She should always do everything on time, have reports and repairs done immediately, return phone calls within hours, remember people's birthdays, be thoughtful.

FACILITATOR: I'm getting exhausted. You're not kidding, are you?

PERFECTIONIST: I most certainly am not! The world tolerates entirely too much imperfection these days. I'm here to uphold standards. Now, I also expect her to maintain herself in peak physical condition. She should be in perfect health—poor health suggests an imbalance somewhere and I can't tolerate imbalances—and she should always look good. She should be rested, centered, and conscious at all times. Her relationships should be conscious, clear, and intimate and she should always

> be on the best possible terms with everyone. I don't like tension or unpleasantness any more than I like mistakes!

This perfectionist went on and on, gaining momentum and self-satisfaction as its demands multiplied. As our aware ego listens to such demands, as it becomes conscious, we are able to make informed choices for ourselves. We can see the futility of trying to please a perfectionist like this whose demands are totally unrealistic and can never be fully met no matter what we do.

Needless to say, there are areas in which perfection is necessary and mistakes are catastrophic. We *do* want perfectionists supervising the designing and building of our planes, bridges, buildings, and nuclear plants. But the same perfectionistic demands brought to bear on all aspects of daily living can be totally debilitating.

The Power Brokers

Power is a fact of psychic life that many people today would like to believe can be eradicated or transmuted. But power *is* a reality, and, as with all energy patterns, the real issues are whether or not it is used to control people and whether it is used with awareness.

The power brokers are a group of energy patterns that may include power, ambition, pusher, money, selfishness, and a variety of other voices. If a facilitator chooses to talk to the protector/controller, the subject's power group may respond instead. The protector/controller's interests often coincide with the interests of the power group in charge of operations. The following transcript is an example of how this power group operates.

Sam was a thirty-eight-year-old man who was very successful in business and not very interested in anything related to the evolution of consciousness. One day his wife decided to leave him. He was very upset by this and didn't understand it, but he felt forced to take a closer look at himself—something his wife had been asking him to do for years.

In the course of his training he did the following piece of dialogue work with his facilitator:

FACILITATOR: Well, Sam, it would appear that power is a major issue for you in your life.

SAM: Well yes—I've been very successful. You don't do that by being passive and retiring.

FACILITATOR: Could I talk to the voice of power?

SAM: I'm not sure there is anyone else.

FACILITATOR: Well, why don't you move over and let's see? (Sam moves over.) Good afternoon. The person I wanted in Sam was his power voice. Is that who you are?

POWER: So, who else? Of course it's me. He hasn't become a multi-millionaire by twiddling his thumbs.

FACILITATOR: Making him rich is one of your jobs?

POWER: It certainly *is* one of my jobs. And a good one it is. How much money do you have?

FACILITATOR: Well, I'm comfortable. But why is that important to you?

POWER: Money is a measure to me of whether someone has made it or not.

FACILITATOR: What are the criteria you use for how much money is enough for success?

POWER: I always told Sam he had to be a millionaire by the age of thirty. He made it.

FACILITATOR: Did that satisfy you?

POWER: Not really. I looked around at all the other investors and realized he was a little fish in a big sea. So I upped the ante, to ten million. I told him if his net worth was ten million dollars, it would be a different ball game. He would have the power then.

FACILITATOR: Well, how has he done?

POWER: He's worth more than that now, but a lot of it is in real estate. He's actually cash poor.

FACILITATOR: What does it mean to be cash poor?

POWER: His income isn't more than half a million a year. You may think that's a lot, but he has friends who have incomes of over a million a year.

FACILITATOR: Well, tell me—what would ultimately satisfy you?

POWER: A net worth of a hundred million and an income that could simply keep building accordingly.

The compulsive accumulation of wealth is, to a great extent, an attempt to allay the anxieties and fears of the vulnerable child. This and the need to control others are always inextricably interwoven with the fears and vulnerability of the child. Compulsive wealth-building is one aspect of the power broker in action.

It is obvious that the power, pusher, and ambition voices are all inextricably interwoven. We know from our theoretical structure that Sam's vulnerability must have been totally unconscious. He had to keep building wealth to maintain the dominion of power and repress his vulnerability. He became more and more isolated as he distanced himself increasingly from his vulnerable core. His wife knew it and, because of her own process, was no longer seduced by the pure glamour of money. She left him because he was incapable of sustaining a healthy relationship.

At a later point in Sam's process the facilitator attempted to talk to his vulnerable child.

FACILITATOR: We've talked about the issue of vulnerability, Sam. I'd like to meet your child, if I could. Are you up to that?

SAM: It doesn't thrill me, but I'll try. It's what my wife keeps talking about. (Sam moves over to the child space.)

FACILITATOR: Hello—are you there? (There is no real feeling yet of the child being present. The facilitator could choose to be silent and try to induce the child energetically, or he could start talking even though the child energy isn't fully present. He chooses to start talking.) Well, I'm glad to meet you finally. How are you doing?

CHILD: I don't know. I don't know who I am.

FACILITATOR: Well, you're the part of Sam that would carry his fears—the part whose feelings get hurt easily—the part who feels overwhelmed very easily.

CHILD: He never lets me out. I don't think he even listens to me.

FACILITATOR: Does he even know about you?

CHILD: I don't think so. He's too busy. He doesn't know about me at all.

FACILITATOR: Did he ever know about you?

CHILD: It was too long ago.

FACILITATOR: Would you like to come out?

CHILD: I don't know. I'm no good. I can't do anything.

FACILITATOR: Actually, those are other voices in Sam that say you're no good. You're so used to hearing them you think it's you who feels that way. Sam has a lot of parts in him who don't like you.

CHILD: Why not? Why am I so bad? I know I'm scared all the time. I always feel scared.

The dialogue proceeded a while longer and then shifted to other work. The child was able to speak and identify itself in a very limited fashion, but its real energy was not present. The controller/power axis was still much too powerful. A facilitator cannot force a disowned self to be present if the weight on the other side is too great. Such a situation calls for patience; the process must be allowed to work its way through.

The Pleaser

We have included the pleaser in the heavyweight section, because even though its energy is decidedly different from the others discussed here and it may look like weakness to some, it wields immense power and deserves to be considered a heavyweight along with all the others. There is nothing wrong with pleasing. The only question is, as with all energy patterns, who is doing the pleasing? Is there a real choice made by an aware ego? Or is the pleasing an automatic, unconscious response to the world?

Nancy was a committed wife, mother, and daughter. She always did the right thing to make people happy—she drove her children wherever they wanted to go, she was available to her parents, and she doted on her husband. She always smiled and was generally very gracious.

Over time, she began to have difficulty sleeping at night. She was aware that she was having bad dreams, but she could not recall what they were; she only remembered that things were after her. Eventually, bedtime became nightmarish and she began to use sleeping pills to get a good night's sleep. She was in a state of physical and psychological exhaustion by the time she sought help. After the preliminaries of the process, the facilitator asked Nancy about her role in the household.

> FACILITATOR: It sounds like making people happy is a very important part of your life.
>
> NANCY: It always has been. My father was a "growler" and I was the one who could keep him happy. So I did. But aside from that, I really enjoy having happy people around me.

FACILITATOR: Why don't you move your chair over? I'd like to talk to the part of you that needs to keep everyone happy. (Nancy moves over.) Tell me, how do you function in Nancy? How do you keep all these people happy?

PLEASER: Well, I've learned to recognize when people want things. My job is to see that no one gets grouchy. I'm very sensitive to moods and I can tell when they're coming on. So I do whatever I have to do to stop the moods.

FACILITATOR: Can you give me an example that actually happened recently—one where you were actually dealing with such a situation?

PLEASER: Well, Nancy's husband was going to work this morning and he asked Nancy to drop off his clothes at the cleaners and then to pick up some supplies at the stationery store after her appointment with you. So, I told him that of course I'll take care of these things. I know he's nervous about my coming here this morning.

FACILITATOR: Did he say something to Nancy to indicate that he was scared?

PLEASER: People around me don't have to talk. I'm a kind of psychic pleaser. I know. This way he went off to work happy and I don't have to contend with any difficulty.

Nancy's pleaser clearly worked automatically. Nancy's behavior certainly involved no choice—she always had to please. After considerable exploration of this pleaser energy, the facilitator decided to investigate an opposite energy pattern. There are several ways to approach this in dialogue work. The facilitator might say: "I'm curious as to what part of Nancy is the other side of you. If you weren't around, what would happen? Who would be present?" The pleaser responds by saying there would be anarchy.

The facilitator knew that Nancy must have enormous rage. She also knew, from the nightmarish quality of Nancy's sleep, that Nancy must disown her whole demonic nature. The facilitator chose to pursue Nancy's selfishness, a relatively nonthreatening energy that contrasted sharply with the pleaser. Although the facilitator could have had Nancy move over to the "other side" and see what appeared, instead she followed the pleaser's lead.

FACILITATOR (still talking to the pleaser): Anarchy means what?

PLEASER: Without me she would do exactly what she wants.

FACILITATOR: Could I talk to the part that would like to do exactly what she wants?

PLEASER (not happy): If you insist. I warn you though—it's anarchy. (Nancy shifts to a new chair.)

We will label the voice Selfish Nancy. Please keep in mind that we do not have to give it a name at all. Nancy might give a name to this part, or we might simply work without a name.

FACILITATOR: Good morning.

SELFISH NANCY: If you're going to talk to me you can forget the niceties.

FACILITATOR: Well, who are you? What do you do?

SELFISH: *I don't do anything*. That's the trouble; I don't do anything.

FACILITATOR: What would happen if you did do something? What would happen if you were in charge of Nancy's life?

SELFISH: One thing I can tell you—I wouldn't please anyone. Not ever again. Her husband could take in his own laundry and buy his own office supplies. He treats Nancy like a slave girl and she smiles and smiles and does and does. And those children! She's creating monsters. She does whatever they want. They're nice kids and she's turning them into monsters.

FACILITATOR: Could you give me an example that's more specific? What are some of the things you'd actually do if you were in charge?

SELFISH: I would go to the gym every morning. It would be the end of "breakfast by Nancy." I would go back to school *now*. I wouldn't wait until the children are grown. Nancy has a thing about waiting until the children are grown. Now she's supposed to take care of everyone. When she's forty-five she's allowed to go out on her own. I'd have her meet new and interesting people. I'd have her dress differently. It would be a totally different scene.

The facilitator had uncovered a core disowned energy pattern in Nancy. Many facilitators are seduced by the anger that they sense is underneath pleaser patterns, and, in fact, it may certainly be necessary to tap into the anger voice. From our perspective, however, too much time is spent trying to elicit anger when, if we can get beyond the anger, we can deal with the problems that are eliciting it.

For example, a man sits down on a chair and in doing so, sits on a tack. He is in much pain, so he goes to someone who has him emote and, though this feels better, the tack is still there, firmly embedded in him. Then he gets involved in meditation training. This helps, too, and he learns to rise above his pain, but he still has the tack in his seat. He tries biofeedback, reflexology, and hypnosis, but when all is said and done, the tack remains.

What is the tack in our lives that creates so much anger in us? It is the ability, or inability, to say yes and no. If we live life on our terms, saying yes and no appropriately, then we tend to have less occasion to be angry.

Nancy had a deep rage, and the negation of that rage was exhausting her. Her rage was the result of living a life of pleasing, a life where her needs came last. Moving into the reciprocal relationship of the pleaser/selfishness energy pattern gave Nancy an awareness of two basic opposites in her—one with which she had been identified, one she had disowned. It was the start of a process of reclaiming her autonomy.

Every disowned self demands a certain amount of energy to keep it unconscious. Too many disowned selves, or too powerful a disowned self, will drain the psycho-physiological battery and eventually the system will go into an exhaustion mode. This can ultimately lead to a serious breakdown on either a physical or psychological level. Thus, getting to know about our disowned selves is very important.

In this chapter, we have looked at a group of common primary selves. Now let us explore some of the disowned selves that these primary selves defend against. Chapter Six will examine our disowned instinctual energies, and Chapter Seven will discuss the area of disowned vulnerability.

6

Disowned Instinctual Energies

We have seen that when instinctual energies are disowned over time, they tend to build in intensity and eventually turn against us and/or channel through us in destructive ways. As these energies become destructive, we give them a different name: We now call them *demonic*. Natural instincts may range from simple assertiveness to fairly primitive energy patterns. By definition, they do not become demonic until they are repressed or disowned.

Hans was a physician who was totally identified with service, compassion, honesty, and kindness. He had denied his natural aggression, selfishness, and drive for personal power. Hans dreamt that a Mafia figure was telling him that he had not been paying his dues. The Mafia figure, despite Hans's protests, then proceeded to beat him up very badly. For Hans, the Mafia was a symbol of the disowned selves that had now become demonic and, unfortunately, had caused serious medical problems. Learning how to work with these energies is fundamental to Voice Dialogue training.

In learning to deal with demonic energies, one basic principle should be followed: The way to work with disowned instinctual energies that have become demonic is to *wait before working with them*. It is essential to first work for a considerable period of time with the primary selves who fear and are opposed to demonic energies. They have been protecting the individual since early childhood from these energies because they perceived them as dangerous. Demonic energies continue to be dangerous until such time as an aware ego is able to handle them as well as the more controlled, rational selves. It is also crucial to avoid being seduced by a subject who says: "I want to work with my demonic." These are not energies to be tampered with.

It is a paradox, we realize, to say that the key to exploring demonic energies is to not explore them, but this approach keeps the work safe and grounded. Having prepared by working with the primary selves, at the right moment the facilitator and subject can begin to explore some of these disowned instinctual energies. The role of the vulnerable child must not be overlooked, either. This self often fears the expression of demonic energies because it either fears abandonment or envisions some catastrophic retaliation.

Aside from the primary selves and the vulnerable child, many other parts of the personality have been conditioned by society to negate demonic energies, including the rational voice, the pleaser, and the spiritual voice. With such a well-developed barricade of selves to face, it is no wonder that demonic energies constitute one of the most profoundly negated psychic systems we will encounter in the evolution of consciousness.

The more energy we invest in holding back these energies, the more drained we become, physically and psychically. The African Bushmen have a saying that one should never go to sleep on the veldt because it means there is a large animal nearby. When we first heard Laurens van der Post make this statement, we were struck by its psychological implications. Exhaustion and fatigue, more often than not, are a function of strong instincts (animals) that are being disowned.

We worked with a woman who found the Bushmen's statement to be literally true. She discovered she had disowned her anger so totally that when she was deeply irritated by her husband, she experienced not anger but an overwhelming desire to go to sleep. When she learned her drowsiness was a substitute for natural aggression, she began to search for the anger concealed by her overwhelming fatigue. As soon as she became aware of her anger voice and learned what it wanted, the drowsiness disappeared.

If the lion in us wishes to roar but the goat bleats instead, we must pay for this substitution in one way or another. Payment will vary: For some, it will be experienced as depression, a loss of energy and enthusiasm, or a growing unconsciousness. For others, it can be uncontrollable, seemingly irrational behavior, during which life, fortune, profession, or marriage may be risked. In its most extreme form, the price may be a physical breakdown that can lead to illness or even death.

On a broader, more planetary level, disowning demonic energies contributes to the pain and darkness in the world. But the darkness of our world cannot be lit by love unless that love is an expression of an aware ego that can also encompass these demonic energies.

If an animal is kept locked in a cage for many years, it will become wild. If the door is opened inadvertently, the animal comes out raging. From this, its keeper accurately concludes that the animal is inherently dangerous. But this is not necessarily so. The danger is, at least in part, a result of the long imprisonment.

So it is with our instinctual life—those selves who fear instinct help lock our instinctual energies in a cage where they eventually become demonic. Periodically these energies erupt in vicious ways. The "keeper of instincts" within us tells us that this viciousness is proof that the animals inside us are bad. If we listen to the keeper, we will force our animal/instinctual nature back into the cage.

It requires great courage to allow the voice of the demonic to speak, for so much of what it has to say is unacceptable to our traditional values. We are challenged to allow this power energy to speak while we honor that part of ourselves that is fearful. The protector/controller's fear of the demonic is legitimate, for it possesses an enormous potential for destruction. The longer and more powerfully the demonic is negated, the greater its capacity to destroy.

Among the many ways available to work with this kind of energy, Voice Dialogue is effective and safe if the facilitator is adequately prepared to deal with these energies. Let us look at some examples of how the dialogue process is used with demonic energy patterns.

Beginning the Dialogue with the Demonic

Entering into a Voice Dialogue session involving demonic energies requires real choice on the part of the facilitator. We might ask one person to talk to the demonic, and this request would result in a good experience. Another subject might be totally put off by such a request, which would send the protector/controller into a spasm of contraction. The following are possible leads for entering into Voice Dialogue with demonic energies.

> May I talk to the part of Sue who would like to be able to do what she wants whenever she wants?
> Might I talk to the selfish Jim?
> May I speak with the not-nice Ruth?
> May I speak with the part of Ralph that would like to rule the world?
> May I talk to the part of Lorna that would like to be a hooker?
> May I talk to the angry voice?
> Might I talk to the part of you that would like to be all-powerful?
> May I talk to dirty Harry?
> Might I talk to the part of you that feels like killing insensitive people?

May I talk to the demonic in you?
May I talk with the part of you that sometimes gets so frustrated that it feels as though it could kill?
May I talk to the Hell's Angel?

All of these are lead-ins to disowned energy patterns that are usually related to repressed instinctual energies. They are difficult voices for the vast majority of people. Facilitators must be flexible and alert enough to ask for the self that a particular subject is comfortable to bring out. The way the voice is invited to speak must be strong enough to evoke the disowned energies but not so strong that it threatens the subject's protector/controller.

Another approach that works well is to ask for the voice that has fantasies or daydreams. This often elicits very powerful and interesting information relating to repressed instinctual energies. It is also one of the easiest ways to reach fantasy material that is often unaccessible.

Power

Georgine, a feminist, loved to wrestle with men verbally. She waited for a man to make a statement that revealed his chauvinistic tendencies, and then, like a vicious dog, she pounced. She bit into his leg and would not let go. Her facilitator noticed this pattern and decided to speak to Georgine's disowned power, the power that her feminist projected onto the male chauvinists it encountered.

FACILITATOR: Georgine—you feel like a bulldog when you go after these men. I don't imagine that your relationships last very long.

GEORGINE: I've had so many men I can't count them anymore. I used to be their victim, but no more. I know how they treat women. Now I go for the jugular. It's the law of the jungle—kill or be killed. If they can't handle it—tough.

FACILITATOR: Could I talk to the bulldog? (Georgine moves over.) Well, you certainly have powerful jaws.

BULLDOG: You recognized me—I'm surprised.

FACILITATOR: Well, she keeps you disguised with her feminist teachings, but a bulldog is a bulldog.

BULLDOG: I love biting in deeply and not letting them go. I love watching them squirm. I'm so grateful for Georgine's mind. She's a genius, you know. And I use it. I use her mind to kill her adversaries. The more assured they are, the more I love it.

FACILITATOR: Do you work alone or with someone else?

BULLDOG: I work with her sensuality. We dress smashingly—soft clothes—light perfume—soft blouses—no bra. We drive them crazy. Sensuality spins a web and then I bite, and hard!

Georgine's bulldog and her sensuality developed an alliance, drawing their power from Georgine's need to protect her vulnerable child. In reality, of course, this child was totally isolated and fearful. The protection was no longer effective, although it did serve its initial protective function. Actually, Georgine *was* the victim of patriarchal consciousness. She *is* still the real victim, albeit it is now her own inner patriarch who keeps her isolated.

Georgine's demonic energies channeled through this bulldog and the sensual part of herself. She attacked men with the combined energy of these two selves, and with each attack she became more and more isolated. Her dreams were filled with images of orphanages and crippled children and eventually assumed nightmarish proportions. Her demonic energy pattern was subtle: In her job and interpersonal relations, Georgine was relatively disempowered. She was not able to bring a natural assertiveness and expansion into her entire life, but confined her aggressive energies to this one channel.

Sensuality

For years, Sandra was plagued by a repetitive nightmare of being chased by wild animals, particularly feline animals.

She began therapy and in an early dialogue session the facilitator asked to talk with her cat nature.

> CAT VOICE: She doesn't know me or like me.
>
> FACILITATOR: Why not?
>
> CAT VOICE: She's afraid of what would happen if I were around.
>
> FACILITATOR: Well, let's imagine that you were around all the time. What would you do? What would happen?
>
> CAT VOICE: I'd preen a lot. I'd take hot baths all the time—hot sudsy baths with smelly things in them. I'd eat when I wanted, not when others wanted. I'd never, never cook for anyone, unless I wanted to cook. Then I'd make sure the man was with me while I was cooking, and I'd make sure he was making love to me all the time. That's another thing. I'd make love all the time. I'd never stop. I'd use all kinds of exotic oils and I'd massage myself all over.

Sandra had grown up conditioned to identify with being a proper lady. In her marriage, she was identified with being a good mother and a pleasing daughter. Her sensual Aphrodite nature had long been eradicated from her awareness. She was not allowed to be selfish, sensual, or self-indulgent. Fortunately for Sandra, her unconscious maintained its pressure. Over and over again, her feline nature appeared in her nightmares, chasing her like the aggressive demon it had become. A few nights after this dialogue session, she had the following dream:

> I'm again walking down the street; it feels very familiar. I'm aware again of the fear reaction and the sense of being followed. I know the cat is there. I start to run. Then I stop. I am tired of running. I turn around to face my pursuer. It is a lion. It comes racing up to me and then stops and licks my face. Why have I always been so afraid . . . ?

Because Sandra had been identified with a good girl/pleaser psychology all her life, it is no wonder that her natural instincts were negated. Having been rejected, they are now enraged; because she refused to look at them, they grew in power and authority. This made it even harder and more frightening for her to face them and listen to their demands.

What is remarkable about this whole process is that when we have the courage to look at our disowned parts, they change. The raging lion licks our face. He does not need to take over our personality; he only needs to be honored, to be heard, to be allowed to speak.

Inner Critic

Disowned demonic energies often express themselves through the inner critic. It is amazing to watch the transformation that occurs when a facilitator asks to speak with the critic in a passive individual who essentially lives life as a victim. As the critic starts to speak, the bedraggled subject sits up straight, looks at the facilitator with a direct and unwavering stare, and begins to speak in a strong, self-assured voice. Suddenly we see real power. Unfortunately, this power and all the available aggression and related instinctual energies have turned demonic and are directed against the subject. It is as though the natural channel for these instinctual energies has become blocked through the disowning process, and the demonic system in its growing power turns against the subject. This may happen through an inner critic or a pusher whose energies are clearly killing the person. These energies may also invade the physical body itself and cause physical illness.

This redirection of instinctual energies was evident in Nan's case. She had had cancer surgery—a radical mastectomy. Shortly after the surgery she had the following dream:

> I am in a room high on a hillside. Around the room are lush green meadows and trees but I cannot get out of my prison. In the prison with me is a demon dancing around a fire.

Earlier in her life Nan drank a good deal, and, when she drank, her more expressive Dionysian energies were loosed. This is not at all unusual in people with drinking problems. If our more expressive nature is blocked, then alcohol becomes one of the primary ways to unblock this energy or to alleviate the stress that builds when this energy is disowned.

Unfortunately, when Nan gave up drinking she became sober in every way. Her extroversion was disowned, along with a number of other expressive and sensual energy patterns. Her instincts turned against her and one avenue to express them was her inner critic—a self that developed in power in the same way a runaway tumor gains in destructiveness.

In her dream, Nan was locked up with a demon. This is the tragedy of the disowning process—we literally become victims of the energy we have denied. We become a prisoner along with the very energies we are trying to imprison. If we think of demons as the mythic expression in Western culture of our disowned instinctual heritage, then making them our enemies only empowers them to a much greater degree. If we see in the demonic a figure that must be honored along with all the other energy patterns, then demonic energies can be transformed and can actually serve us in our lives. When they are recognized and honored and given the opportunity to speak, they are transformed back into our natural instinctual heritage.

Because of how deeply Nan had repressed these impulses, her inner selves turned against her ragefully. When her inner critic became demonic, she was paralyzed in her ability to express herself in life. From our study of many cancer patients, there is little question in our minds that the denial of our natural instinctual heritage can be a major etiological factor among the many causes of cancer.

This tendency for disowned energies to turn against us is an important consideration in the dialogue process. Whenever we deal with a voice that exhibits this energy quality, we know we have the demonic at hand. However, we also have the possibility of reclaiming and rechanneling these energies.

Loretta had a very strong inner critic, although she, herself, appeared rather passive and disempowered. The following is an excerpt from a dialogue with her critic:

> FACILITATOR: Why do you hate her so? It sounds like you want to kill her.
>
> CRITIC: I do—I would—I hate her. The trouble is, if she dies I can't torture her anymore.
>
> FACILITATOR: But why do you do it? Is it just for fun, or are you like a cassette tape that simply repeats itself automatically?
>
> CRITIC: She's weak. I despise weakness. I despise her. If she would ever stand up for herself it would be a miracle.

The rage, the passion, the vindictiveness of Loretta's inner critic alerts us to the underlying energy. Disowned demonic energy becomes like a cancer in the individual psyche and in the collective psyche as well. It will work to destroy the individual organism and the collective until we learn to deal with it.

The Demonic Voice

John was considering a serious career change after practicing as an attorney for twelve years. Following the rather nasty breakup of his marriage, he became involved in a spiritual process that led him to feel he should give up his law practice. His spiritual self, with the support of a spiritual teacher John had become involved with, told him he needed more time for his spiritual development. His meditations inspired a number of profound experiences, but he felt an inner doubt about so radical a change. A number of his friends felt he had become too one-sided, so he sought help to find more of a balance in his life.

After an initial period of discussion, John's therapist asked to talk to John's spiritual voice. This voice spoke at great length about John's spiritual process, how much he had changed, and his need for time to devote to more introverted pursuits. The voice was quite positive and supportive and pointed out a clear direction for John's life. The therapist then asked John if another voice was available to speak with, one that would be the opposite of the spiritual self. What emerged was the voice of power, an energy John referred to as his demonic side.

THERAPIST (to demonic voice): How do you feel about John's decision to give up his law practice?

DEMONIC: I resent it and reject it. That son of a bitch has rejected me all his life. Then he gets into this spiritual trip and I go down another 2,000 feet into the earth.

THERAPIST: Why are you so angry at the spiritual side? It has some very good ideas and John has been helped considerably by it.

DEMONIC: I'm angry because I'm left out. Whatever I'm not part of is crap. His marriage was bullshit because I wasn't a part of it. I'm glad his wife nailed him. He deserved it. He was always the angel and she was the bitch. That's because I was buried. I'm telling you something—his blood is made of saccharin.

THERAPIST: Have you always been this angry with John?

DEMONIC: Look, wise up. I'm angry because he ignores me. He's Mr. Nice Guy. So long as he tries to act like Jesus Christ, I will do everything I can do to defeat him. All I want is to be acknowledged.

THERAPIST: What would it mean for John to acknowledge you? I mean this in a very practical way. What does acknowledgment mean?

DEMONIC: Right now he thinks I don't exist—that I'm not real. Before he got into this spiritual stuff he just rejected me. Now he's learned that I'm supposed to be transmuted. How would you feel if every time you expressed yourself someone tried to transmute you into something better or higher? It's insulting.

THERAPIST: Well, I'm still not sure what it would mean on a very practical level.

DEMONIC: I don't like his passivity with his wife. She controls everything in regard to the children. He thinks that by being nice, everything will get better. Well, it's not getting better. It's getting worse. And before he signs the final property settlement I suggest he listen to me. Mr. Nice Guy is giving her ten times too much. I also don't like some of the people in his group. I'd like him to listen to me, to take me seriously, to honor what I have to say.

John's demonic voice was like a caged animal—filled with the power and energy of being rejected for a lifetime. His marriage ended in disaster, in part because he forced his wife to carry the demonic side of himself. Because John had been unable to show his anger, negativity, or selfishness, it became necessary for her to express these points of view. Conversely, as she became more identified with these patterns, he was thrown ever more deeply into an identification with his peaceful and loving selves. It soon became apparent to everyone that his wife was the demon and he was the good guy. How often our mates and partners live out our disowned selves in this same manner.

John had slipped very easily into the spiritual mode. It was a natural way of expressing his very loving and positive nature. Unfortunately, his awareness was identified with these spiritual energies. Furthermore, the spiritual voices were identified with his previous "nice guy" mode, which precluded all expressions of power, anger, negativity, and selfishness. No wonder this voice was enraged!

It takes great courage to face our disowned demonic patterns. The energies of these selves have lived in isolation for years, like lepers shunned by regular society. When we see people who embody these qualities, we avoid them if possible. They are reprehensible to us. How easy, and yet how difficult, it is to take the next step to recognize that those people whom we cannot stand are clear reflections of our negated parts. What golden opportunities are presented to us with great regularity, if we are ready to hear and see them and begin to find appropriate ways to include them in our lives.

7

The Inner Child

The Vulnerable Selves

The vulnerable selves that represent various aspects of the inner child are the other major group of selves that are usually disowned. Working with these is one of the most significant and rewarding aspects of Voice Dialogue, and it requires a deep sensitivity to the subject. Three aspects of the child are of particular importance: the vulnerable child, the playful child, and the magical child.

The vulnerable child embodies the subject's sensitivity and fear. Its feelings are easily hurt and it generally lives in fear of abandonment. It is almost always frightened of a multitude of things that the protector/controller and the heavyweights know nothing about. Remember that the protector/controller evolves to protect this vulnerable child and, in doing so, buries it so that it will not be hurt.

The playful child is just what the name implies—playful. It knows how to play as a child knows how to play. It is generally easier to reach than the vulnerable child, because the protector/controller is much more likely to permit play than tears and pain.

The magical child is really a brother or sister to the playful child. It is the child of imagination and fantasy. It is the child of our right brain, our intuition and creative imagination. It is, in part, the source of visions. It, too, is lost very early in our lives as the heavyweights take over. It often has to be coaxed out, and this requires great sensitivity on the part of the facilitator. The magical child needs to know the facilitator's own magical child energy is present before it will show itself because it is usually quite shy.

The inner child never grows up. Over and over again in dialogue work facilitators encounter the child's great surprise at learning it is not required to grow up, act adult, or even use words at all. Some of the most profound Voice Dialogue sessions with the inner child are held without words. This is less true of the playful and magical children than it is of the vulnerable child.

The children of our inner world know how to "be," while the rest of our personality knows how to "do" and how to "act." In working with these patterns the facilitator is given the opportunity to learn how to "be" with them; otherwise, they cannot emerge. When dealing with the inner child, the dictum is: "There's nowhere to go and there's nothing to do."

The loss of the inner child is one of the most profound tragedies of the "growing-up" process. With its loss we lose so much of the magic and mystery of living, the delight and intimacy of relationship. So much of the destructiveness we express to each other is a function of our lack of connection to our sensitivities, our fears, our own magic. How different the world would be if our political figures could say: "I feel very bad. You really hurt my feelings when you said that." Or: "I want to apologize to my colleague for my remarks yesterday. My feelings were hurt and I was angry and I am sorry."

If the inner child is operating in our lives autonomously and without protection, we can be fairly sure that we will end up as some kind of victim. The child, however wonderful, cannot drive our car any more successfully than any other single energy pattern. It, too, needs balancing. But as long as the protector/controller is in charge of the personality, the child will remain buried and therefore inaccessible.

As we separate from the protector/controller and become more aware of the inner child, our aware ego gradually becomes the parent to our child. We can then take responsibility to use the energy of the inner child in our lives and provide it with appropriate protection when needed.

When the aware ego becomes more effective, the protector/controller quite willingly surrenders control. As long as we are protected from being hurt too badly, as long as the protector/controller feels our vulnerability is being protected, it can begin to relax, knowing that the fundamental integrity of the system is in good hands. Let us look now at how the inner child manifests in the Voice Dialogue process.

Vulnerability—a Primary Disowned Self

Perhaps the most universally disowned self in our civilized world is the vulnerable child. Yet this child may be our most precious subpersonality, the one closest to our essence, the one that enables us to become truly intimate, to fully experience others, and to love. Unfortunately, it usually disappears by the age of five. This child cannot exist in our civilized societies without the protection of a very strong protector/controller. The only way a protector/controller can handle the vulnerable child is to disown it. It is usually so completely disowned that the protector/controller no longer even worries about it.

What is this child like? The most striking quality is its ability to be deeply intimate with another person. The facilitator can feel a physical warmth and a fullness radiating from this child. It is as though the space between the two people is alive and vibrating. When the vulnerable child withdraws (as it does at the slightest provocation), this warmth and fullness disappear, leaving behind a slight chill. This experience is somewhat similar to the special feelings that might occur with a small child or with a dog in a moment of deep affection and mutual trust. This ability to be fully "with" another human being is most precious.

However, being fully with another brings its share of discomfort as well as pleasure. The vulnerable child is tuned in energetically—it is aware of *everything* that is happening. Words will not fool it for a moment. As you speak, the child will know if there is any change whatsoever in your energetic connection to it. An outside thought may have intruded—you may be wondering what time it is, you may suddenly decide you're hungry—and the child will know you have withdrawn. It is exquisitely sensitive and reacts immediately to any abandonment it perceives. It may not know why the withdrawal has happened, but it will know that one has occurred.

Getting in touch with this subpersonality can open us to the most embarrassing feelings of rejection, such as experiencing a sense of abandonment when a spouse leaves the bed in the morning to go to the bathroom. However, when made conscious, this subpersonality can often tell us who is to be trusted and who is not. It usually recognizes the people who have disowned their vulnerable children and who can, therefore, hurt others, either accidentally or deliberately.

The first dialogue with a vulnerable child may simply involve sitting quietly and encouraging it to come forth. It is often preverbal and may sit quietly or cry. In its initial emergence, it might curl up in a foetal position, cover its head, and weep with great wrenching sobs. Another might be very tentative, checking out the facilitator's ability to sense its presence or absence. Above all, no vulnerable child will appear unless the facilitator can be trusted not to hurt it. It has invariably been hurt in the past and is fearful of being hurt again. This was dramatically illustrated by the vulnerable child of a Jewish woman who had managed to stay alive in Europe through World War II.

CHILD: It hurts so to think of everything that she's been through. I had to go away when she was very, very young (crying). It's too painful to exist. It just feels like a skin full of tears.

FACILITATOR (with concern): Do you want to go away now?

CHILD: No, it feels good to have you here with me. I always go into hiding, but it hurts even worse when I'm alone. I need someone to be with me and let me be sad.

The pain of the vulnerable child is a deep pain that requires respect and empathy. The child will know if you are feeling aloof or rational and it will not emerge. It sometimes demands that a facilitator actually search for it. With Natalie, a therapist, the vulnerable child emerged in a most surprising fashion. Natalie began the session by expressing her discomfort at hugging the facilitator. Actually, this was Natalie's rational voice, as it turned out later, but it certainly sounded like an aware ego at first.

RATIONAL NATALIE: I've been thinking a great deal about this business of hugging you at the end of our sessions and it's not comfortable for me. It seems to me that it's a way of discharging anxiety and it works against the therapy. Also, I don't feel I have free choice in the situation.

FACILITATOR (equally rational to protect her own vulnerable child): Well, why don't we forget about hugging and see how that works? I can certainly see your point about the discharge of anxiety and tension and it's not comfortable for me if it feels compulsive.

At this point, the facilitator noticed a change, a sense of sadness in Natalie.

FACILITATOR: Wait a minute. Let me talk to the part of you that wants me to hug her.

VULNERABLE CHILD (bursts into tears): I was afraid you wouldn't know I was here. She's so sensible—I was afraid she'd hurt your feelings and you wouldn't think of looking for me. I *want* you to hug me. I like it. I *want* you to pay attention to me. (A fresh outburst of tears.)

FACILITATOR: I'd love to pay attention to you. Tell me about yourself.

CHILD: I'm very little, about four years old, and I'm cute. But I'm scared. And I'm hiding. I'm hiding in the closet. And I hope that someone will come looking for me but (more sobbing) nobody comes, nobody ever comes. I really want somebody to come and look for *me* and pay attention to *me*. She's acted grown up and sensible ever since she was little and nobody has ever even thought to look for me. Nobody ever misses me. I need people to notice I'm gone, and to care.

This dialogue is a most touching portrait of the vulnerable child. It wants to be missed, sought after, and valued although the protector/controller and other rational subpersonalities do not want it to exist at all.

Men have even greater difficulty than women in agreeing to contact their vulnerable children because it is socially unacceptable for men to be vulnerable. Their children, too, are often in hiding. They have been found hidden in closets, under the kitchen sink, in a cave, up in a tree house, in the woods, in a barn, or in an attic. Sometimes the facilitator can make an initial contact by asking for the part that runs away from people or stays hidden.

FACILITATOR: I know that Mike is very efficient and successful but I'd like to talk to the part of him that's a little more sensitive and needs to keep away from people; maybe it even needs to hide.

CHILD: I certainly do need to hide. When he was little, I used to go out into the woods when somebody hurt my feelings. I'd wait and wait for somebody to come looking for me. I was really scared that if they found Mike, they'd hurt my feelings again, but I really wanted them to notice he was gone and to come looking. And do you know what? They never did. And then I'd really feel bad.

Once Mike knows how his feelings have been hurt, he can speak to his wife about this issue. If he doesn't know, he withdraws into a cold parental subpersonality, and his wife's vulnerable child is hurt by his withdrawal so she becomes even more rejecting to protect herself.

The vulnerable child helps us to remove ourselves from painful situations if they cannot be changed. The vulnerable child will also pull us out of an unrewarding relationship or a thankless job, once we listen to it. For instance, Frank was in a relationship with a younger woman who was fond of him but clearly let him know that she didn't love him enough to see their relationship move toward marriage as he hoped it would. Frank had disowned his vulnerable child so completely that at first we could only talk to it through the protector/controller. However, the protector/controller finally agreed to let us consult directly with the child.

FACILITATOR: Would you please tell us how you feel about Frank's relationship with Claire?

CHILD: I don't like it at all. I get hurt all the time. He keeps thinking that she's going to learn to love him but I know she's not. She's just sticking around for what she can get. He's nice and he does things for her so she stays around. I know that she doesn't love him and it makes me feel bad. But he doesn't care how I feel.

FACILITATOR: If you were running Frank's life, what would you do?

CHILD: I'd get away from her. It makes me feel too lonely when he's with her. It's much worse than being alone.

As we have said before, the vulnerable child often sees emotional matters clearly and can give good advice. Frank had to decide what to do with this information. He also consulted other subpersonalities but in the end he followed his vulnerable child's advice—he confronted the situation and, with tact and diplomacy, ended the relationship.

In contrast with its ability to end an unrewarding relationship, the integration of the vulnerable child into a relationship encourages unparalleled intimacy and depth, as we will see in Suzanne's experience.

Suzanne had been raised by a very cold and rejecting mother. Her vulnerable child was disowned quite early in life and replaced with charm, sophistication, and a whimsical, delightful wit. Suzanne was irresistible to men but very lonely. She was shocked to realize she had vulnerable feelings and her child felt worthless.

CHILD: But what good can I do her? I just get hurt and frightened.

FACILITATOR: I know it feels awfully good to be with you and you have lots to tell both Suzanne and myself. You're delicious.

CHILD: I don't know about that (but she smiles because the energetic contact is good).

FACILITATOR: Tell me, why did you have to hide?

CHILD: Her mother (she starts to cry)—her mother is very mean and she made her cry all the time. She always told Suzanne that she was ugly and stupid and that she didn't want Suzanne in the first place. Do you know that she still tells Suzanne that she never wanted her? (She cries for a while as the impact of this revelation is absorbed.)

FACILITATOR: Well, I can certainly see why you wanted to hide. Tell me more about yourself.

CHILD: I'm really sensitive and lots of things hurt my feelings. Suzanne keeps getting into these relationships where another part of her laughs and I feel bad. Like with Eric. He has lots of girlfriends and he likes them all to think he's terrific but he never really loves them. He just collects them. It hurts my feelings every time she's with him but she just gets sophisticated and laughs.

FACILITATOR: That sounds as though it must be difficult for you. Tell me, how do you like being here now?

CHILD (shyly): I really like it. I trust you and it feels good.

Suzanne embraced her vulnerable child quickly. She enjoyed the special opening of her heart energy that it brought and she wanted to seek it elsewhere. She had a great deal of strength, above-average looks, and the intelligence and social skills to protect her vulnerable child. She used everything she had quite consciously. She calmly and objectively confronted Eric with her child's observations (over an expensive dinner) and ended her romantic involvement with him, but not her friendship.

Her next relationship, begun shortly after her introduction to this vulnerable child, was like none she had ever before experienced. She found herself communicating her feelings and reactions immediately and actually discussed her past and her mother with her new partner. She verbalized each "little" hurt and fear as it arose, and the man did likewise. For each, it was a depth of sharing never before experienced. It took real courage, but Suzanne was a determined woman who learned quickly and her bravery inspired equal intimacy in her partner. As each risk was rewarded with deeper mutual understanding and love, they became less fearful and more daring in this mutual exploration of their complex humanity. Although this was not always easy or pleasant, it was deeply satisfying to each of them. With the information provided by their vulnerable children, they were able to deal practically with pain in the relationship and protect the delicious energetic interchange—that warm pulsating energy that vibrates between people when they are truly open and trusting.

A warning—this is not to say that all is forever perfect. Circumstances beyond the control of the aware ego sometimes cause the vulnerable child to withdraw from a relationship. But once this warmth has been experienced it is something to strive for and return to, and most of us are willing to experience much discomfort in order to do so.

We would like to give you one final example of an excerpt from a Voice Dialogue session with the vulnerable child. In this instance, the facilitator asked questions that would allow the subject's awareness level to witness the requirements of the vulnerable child.

FACILITATOR: We've been talking so far about how lonely things are for you and how much you feel left out in Peter's life. Is there anything that Peter could do that might be helpful to you?

CHILD: I don't know what he could do. He always runs away from me.

FACILITATOR: Well, I know that—but Peter is listening to our conversation and he might learn a thing or two about you. I can't guarantee it, but Peter could learn how to be a proper parent to you. I know that he's never done it before, but it could happen.

CHILD: I'd like that. I'd feel better if he took care of me. It's especially when I get scared that I need him, and I get scared a lot. I wish he would just learn to be with me and not run away all the time. If he would just talk to me I'd feel so much better.

FACILITATOR: So one of the things he could do for you is just learn to be with you.

CHILD: And maybe he could save more money. I get scared when there's no money. He likes to do things with money that are scary to me. I hate the stock market. I hate the feeling that he could lose it all. He likes to gamble.

FACILITATOR: So now we have another thing that would make you feel better. You need the feeling of financial security. Is there anything else?

CHILD: He could let me out more. Nobody knows about me. Everyone thinks Peter is strong and tough. That's what every-

> one sees. No one ever sees me. That makes me feel lonely. Even Margaret (his wife) doesn't know about me. He never tells her about my feelings.

As a child grows up, it is common for parents to reject its vulnerability because life demands strength. Additionally, parents usually have no conscious relationship to their own vulnerability. So it is that we, as adults, reject our inner child, further perpetuating this ancestral disowning process. Through dialogue work, we can hear the child's voice and gradually take over the responsibility of child-rearing from the protector/controller.

We have seen individuals do very interesting things as they begin tuning in to the needs of their inner child. Cynthia built a large doll house and furnished it, and then made it clear to her children that it was *her* doll house. John constructed an imaginary home for the child where he would visit him regularly. Ann took her special pillow to sleep on when she went on business trips. Sam started reading spy novels rather than purely redemptive literature. Lianne got a job to help her child feel more secure about money. A multitude of different activities can support the needs of the child.

Once the reality of the child has been established, journal writing becomes an excellent tool for working with it. Prior to making this connection, the question will be: Who is doing the writing? If an aware ego has not separated from the protector/controller, then the protector/controller itself may be doing the writing.

Dialoguing with the inner child is very satisfying and very revealing. One excellent approach to this kind of writing is to use the nondominant hand for the child and the dominant hand for the primary self. This same principle can apply to any primary/disowned self system while doing dialogue work in a journal format.* For an aware ego to

* Capacchione, Lucia, M.A. *The Power of Your Other Hand*. Van Nuys, CA: Newcastle Co., Inc. 1988.

properly take care of the child, it must have the power energy available to it. Without the protection of the heavyweights, the child will not be safe, and generally it knows this. What we aim at here is an aware ego related to the energies of the heavyweights on the one side, and the vulnerability, playfulness, and magic on the other. This is true empowerment. Learning to be powerful and knowing how to consciously use our heavyweights is generally an important step in attaining this empowerment.

The Paradox of Omnipotence

When we disown our vulnerability, we identify instead with our omnipotence. It feels so good to identify with an omnipotent subpersonality, one who knows its superiority to the rest of humanity. This omnipotent voice may feel superior due to a high I.Q. or great spirituality as a result of achievements in life (the more varied the better), good looks and youthful appearance, good taste, social standing, charisma, intuition, depth of wisdom, exquisite sensitivity, efficiency, and so on.

Any quality admired by any segment of our society can be used to create and build upon a subpersonality who feels it has mastered its environment. Of course, the subpersonality must be used in the proper setting. It probably won't do much good to try to impress a group of psychics with the announcement that you graduated first in your class at Harvard Law School. Conversely, the ability to see auras and read energy fields is not likely to carry much weight with the admissions committee at most medical schools.

Each of us has our particular omnipotent, or "top dog," personality that we love dearly. This subpersonality is fun to share with "like-minded" people, to gather all the special voices together in a little group and enjoy feeling superior to the ordinary people out there. This occurs throughout social groupings such as fraternities, sororities, and country clubs. We can see it in the prestige associated with Ivy League colleges. It also happens in spiritual communities, many of which feel they have exclusive knowledge of the secrets of the universe. This superior attitude is also found in groups that see themselves as the lowest, the most dangerous, the most dissipated, or the worst. Any superlative will do.

When this omnipotent voice takes over, we feel terrific, as did Laura in the following dialogue:

> LAURA: I was feeling so great, I couldn't believe it. I suddenly realized how clearly my mind worked, how many rich experiences I had, and how much more advanced I was than all the other people around me. I felt like I could do anything, and so I started to make contracts to sell my product.
>
> FACILITATOR: Let's talk to the voice that was operating on that day. (Laura moves over.) Hello there.
>
> OMNIPOTENT VOICE: Hi (looking very self-confident). I really did beautifully that day. You know, Laura *is* quite special. First of all she's unusually smart—I'd tell you her exact I.Q. but she doesn't want me to brag. Actually, I *love* bragging. Also, she has a great ability to see through to the essence of a problem and do away with all the trimmings that other people waste time thinking about. She abstracts well, verbalizes well, and knows how to approach people so that she gets what she wants without seeming pushy. I think she's terrific and I tell her so. It's important to me that other people realize that as well. When they do—when they compliment her—then I'm *really* happy.

Now we come to the paradox of our omnipotent voice: If we let it take over, if we identify with it because it feels so good, the opposite energy will not be far behind. As high as the omnipotent voice flies, that's how low the frightened voice will fall. An aware ego will enable us to assess our assets and use them wisely. It will allow us to enjoy a feeling of mastery or accomplishment, but we must be wary, for a line must not be crossed. A certain feeling of self-satisfaction is a signal that we have gone beyond an appropriate level of self-appreciation, that our awareness level has disappeared and we have begun to identify with the omnipotent voice.

It does not take long before the opposite energy takes over. If the omnipotent voice has confidently made promises about a product, an investment, or a workshop, then the frightened child wonders if we will be able to back up those promises. For instance, let us see what happened to Laura after she made her phone calls.

> LAURA: When I finished setting up all the appointments, I suddenly became frightened about what I had done. I started to worry about all kinds of details.
>
> FACILITATOR: It sounds as though your omnipotent voice made the appointments, and then your frightened child took over. Let's see what she has to say.
>
> FRIGHTENED CHILD: I'm scared. Just plain scared. I don't feel ready to meet those people. What if they don't like her? What if they ask questions about her products?
>
> FACILITATOR: Her omnipotent voice feels pretty good about Laura, but you don't sound so sure about her.
>
> FRIGHTENED CHILD: I'm not. I worry. I worry all the time. First of all, I don't think she's done her homework. She should know more about what it is that she's trying to sell. People are pretty sophisticated these days. If she's trying to sell tax shelters, there's a lot to learn. You know, about tax law and investment credits and about the oil drilling itself. People ask questions and I'm scared because she doesn't have the answers.
>
> FACILITATOR: You also said something about being scared that they won't like her.
>
> FRIGHTENED CHILD: I certainly am. What if they don't like her? What if they don't think she's smart? Worst of all, what if they can see right through her brave front and see me? I'm most scared that they'll find out about me and how scared I am. I'm only about nine or so, and I need to be sure about things,

but I'm not sure about anything anymore. Other people look so sure of themselves. I want her to be like them. I don't like me. I feel awful. Just awful! I wish she could make me feel better. Or make me go away.

FACILITATOR: So you're afraid they'll find out about you?

FRIGHTENED CHILD: Sure. Then how are they going to trust her and buy anything from her? It's hopeless . . . just hopeless. The more I think about it, the more scared I get. The more she impresses everybody else with her cleverness, the more scared I get.

FACILITATOR: What if she doesn't promise too much?

FRIGHTENED CHILD: You know, that sounds a teeny bit better. After all, if she promises less, I'd have less to worry about. There'd be fewer things she'd have to know. If she'd only be able to tell people that she didn't know something—that she had to look up the answer . . . .

OMNIPOTENT VOICE (interrupts here): I don't like that. You're not giving me enough credit. I bring the customers in. They need to have faith in her, to know that she knows what she's doing, that she can answer all questions.

FACILITATOR: Can she?

OMNIPOTENT VOICE: Listen—she can figure anything out. She can learn all the answers. I told you—she's terrific. She's more clever than those people she'll be talking to. She should be able to answer all the questions. Just watch her. She can do it.

FACILITATOR: I appreciate your feelings and I do agree that Laura is smart and special, but I'd like to go back to the part of Laura that is scared.

OMNIPOTENT VOICE: I don't like that one. I don't really believe that she needs to exist. From my point of view Laura doesn't need her.

FACILITATOR: But she has her and we need to find out more about her needs, so that Laura can function more efficiently.

> FRIGHTENED CHILD: Do you see why I'm scared? She wants Laura to be perfect and to impress everybody. Then I get scared that they'll find out she's not perfect and they'll make fun of her. I don't want anyone talking badly about her.

We see here the war that rages between the omnipotent voice and the frightened child. The more Laura identifies with her omnipotent voice and needs to impress everyone with her superiority, the more frightened the child becomes, and the more miserable Laura feels.

As Laura stops identifying with her omnipotent voice—as she stops allowing it to seduce her with sweet words—she begins to pay attention to her frightened child and take care of some of its concerns. Her aware ego becomes the parent to her frightened child. She does her homework. She learns the basic facts she needs so that the frightened part of her no longer has to worry about her lack of preparation. She has integrated her vulnerability and fear into her life and work.

Most important of all, she has stopped relying on her omnipotent voice to provide her with a sense of strength. She realizes that, although she feels absolutely terrific when her omnipotent voice supports and validates her, this strength is illusory. Her real strength emerges from her awareness and her aware ego after she integrates her vulnerability. Her ability to sell her product is now based on a commitment to, and a belief in, her work, rather than a need to impress others and get something from them. Others can feel this change and will respond with increased support and realistic encouragement. Laura has finally freed herself from the extremes of self-importance and self-doubt.

Power by itself is illusory. It depends on our superiority and the disempowerment or inferiority of others. This is beautifully illustrated by the following dream:

> A very well-dressed man from a middle-Eastern country is driving a huge Rolls Royce. His totally disempowered wife sits in the back seat and he makes disparaging comments to her from time to time. He thinks he knows everything. She thinks

> she knows nothing. Actually, his experience is limited because he comes from a very small country and it is quite different from America, where he is now driving his car. He sees a small dirt driveway off to the right and because this looks like roads look back home, he veers off and drives down it quickly. He comes to a dead end almost immediately. His wife, incidentally, could see that this was the wrong turn.

Here is a perfect picture of an omnipotent or power subpersonality. The man's superiority depends on superficial conditions—his beautiful clothes and his Rolls Royce. His superiority is also built on the acknowledged inferiority of his wife, who sits in the back seat while he drives the car and thinks he knows everything. He is unconscious—he does not know that he does not know. He does not even have a clue; therefore, he drives right into a dead end.

This is how our power subpersonalities work. They are dependent on the disowning of our vulnerability. Although they may have acquired the trappings of success, there is no consciousness, no empowerment from within. They can be toppled by someone more powerful or even ousted by the critic.

The omnipotent parts of us provide the *most* delicious feeding-grounds for our critics. Even if nobody else can tell when we have become identified with an omnipotent voice, the critic can. And the critic will be more than happy to let us know about our inadequacies. Let us see how this works. Arnie's power voice had been outlining a financial plan that would make him quite wealthy in just a short time.

> POWER VOICE: It's quite simple. With his background and his contacts in the business, he should have it all tied up in about eight weeks. It will only take a few calls and a little razzle-dazzle.

This power voice is quite convincing. It could sell anyone anything . . . anyone, that is, except Arnie's critic, who had the following response to these plans:

CRITIC: He'll never do it. He's really good about making an impression and starting something, but he can't follow through. He has no self-discipline, and besides that, he's a coward. You know those calls he's talking about?

FACILITATOR: Sure, what about them?

CRITIC: He's never going to make them. He'll procrastinate until it's too late and the whole thing falls through. He's chicken.

The critic was right. The plans had been made by the power voice, but there was no real empowerment to back them up and they faded into oblivion, as so many others had before.

We see again in these examples the basic difference between being powerful and being empowered. Being and acting powerful means that we are identified with the power energy patterns. Empowerment means that our aware ego honors, and to some extent embraces, both power and, ironically enough, vulnerability. Empowerment is certainly one of the inevitable outcomes of the Voice Dialogue process.

The Playful and Magical Children

The vulnerable child is important in matters of relationship and empowerment, but the two other aspects of the inner child—the playful child and the magical child—bring joy and magic to our lives. We can see how this operated in Jon. He had been introduced to dialogue work but this was the first time his playful child had been expressed. Jon was Dutch; he was serious and hardworking and respected the father's authority.

FACILITATOR: From what Jon has said, I've wondered whether you would be available or not.

PLAYFUL CHILD: Oh, I'm here, but just barely. He would rather suffer than have fun. (Wistfully.) I could really show him how to have a good time if he'd let me. Take this workshop for example. Everyone is so serious. Jon is so serious. (He makes a mock-serious face.)

FACILITATOR: What would you do if you were in charge of the operation? (This is a common question used when eliciting information about a particular subpersonality.)

CHILD: I would have fun. I would make faces at people. I would play tricks on people.

FACILITATOR: What would you do if you were in charge of the operation? (This is a common question used when eliciting information about a particular subpersonality.)

The facilitator gradually led Jon's playful child into an increasing amplification of its own energy, always keeping in mind the protector/controller who might have objected to what was happening. In such a position it is possible to engage in a variety of Gestalt techniques, creating experiments for the child, but always being ready to reduce the risk level as the occasion requires. The facilitation of the playful child requires both tact and whimsy.

Sean was a serious man, long involved in the spiritual movement. He had done dialogue work before, but the facilitator on this occasion asked him whether he would like to learn something about his magical child. He was a fundamentally rational man but had learned enough about energy patterns to be intrigued by the idea. Once Sean's magical child was fully present, the facilitator asked the following question:

FACILITATOR: It seems that Sean doesn't use you very much in his life.

MAGICAL CHILD: He's afraid of me. I don't make sense.

FACILITATOR: What do you mean—don't make sense?

MAGICAL CHILD: I make up things. He (Sean) always has to make sense. I would make up stories and say things that didn't make sense.

FACILITATOR: Can you give me some examples?

MAGICAL CHILD: Sure—the moon is blue and cheese is blue and you're blue, too.

FACILITATOR: Well, you're a poet—and you don't know it.

MAGICAL CHILD (beginning to get warmed up): Onions and garlic are dear to my Harlick/Nunchies and crunchies have bunches of lunches.

FACILITATOR: That's really amazing. Let's play a game—I'll say a word and you make up a poem. Do you sing?

MAGICAL CHILD (contraction occurs): I would, but he won't let me.

FACILITATOR: Well that's okay. Remember all this is pretty new to him (pointing to the chair of the protector/controller) so we have to give him the right to stop whatever is going on when things feel too uncomfortable.

It is abundantly clear that in drawing out the magical child, the facilitator's connection to his or her own magical child is quite significant. Conversely, as we facilitate, certain energies in ourselves are activated, so we can then do the necessary work to connect to them. Thus, in facilitating the magical child in someone else, we can strengthen our own.

In general, the playful child is easier to access than the vulnerable child. Many people who are spiritually identified have access to the playful child but not to the vulnerable child, so they tend to confuse the two. Marie was such a person. During a session the facilitator asked her the following:

FACILITATOR: Marie, could I talk to your child—the one who carries the sensitivity and hurt?

PLAYFUL CHILD: Oh, I'm an important part of her. We have lots of fun and she takes me very seriously. I sing a lot and I love to dance.

Playful children generally love to talk. Vulnerable children do not. The facilitator sensed this and commented as follows:

FACILITATOR: It isn't really you that I want to talk to. It's your sister, the quiet one. Could you move over again? (Marie moves over and immediately starts talking.) Let's just sit quietly for a few minutes. (Facilitator makes contact with her own vulnerable child and simply sits quietly with Marie in the new place. After a few minutes tears start to come, slowly at first, and then with more intensity. After about ten minutes the facilitator responds.) I had a feeling you were in there somewhere. How does she get rid of you so easily?

VULNERABLE CHILD: It's easy—she loves everyone and she takes care of everyone. She has time for everyone except me. When she begins to feel small and vulnerable, she gets chatty and acts cute and playful. She doesn't really know about me (looking very woebegone).

In this dialogue, the facilitator's awareness helped her perceive that Marie's playful child was not the real issue. Marie was convinced she had a real connection to her inner child. In fact, she did, but only to one aspect of it.

We hope we have demonstrated the beauty and complexity of the inner child. Facilitators of Voice Dialogue work, lacking a connection to these patterns within themselves, would not be able to enter into some of the deepest and most profound feelings that exist in the subjects being facilitated. Without the inner child, we lose a great deal in our personal lives because we are continually forced into an identification with the heavyweight subpersonalities inside of us. It is their job to attack, erect defenses, and avoid showing feelings, pain, or need. They keep us from our deepest selves.

The discovery of the inner child is really the discovery of a portal to the soul. A spirituality that is not grounded in understanding, experience, and an appreciation of the inner child can move people away from their simple humanity too easily. The inner child keeps us human. It never grows up, it only becomes more sensitive and trusting as we learn how to give it the time, care, and parenting it so richly deserves.

8

The Parental Selves

Properly speaking, the parental subpersonalities belong among the heavyweights, for heavyweights they are. They occupy a unique and central position in our interpersonal relationships. Therefore, in this chapter we will introduce you to some parental subpersonalities currently common in our society. We are well aware that parental subpersonalities differ from society to society and from one epoch to the next.

We will start with the good mother. Although she probably does not know it, her roots are found in the philosophy of child-rearing popularized by Rousseau. In this system, the mother must be ever-present, loving, giving, and supportive at all times so that the child will grow up brave, trusting, and self-confident. A woman must similarly provide this abundance of nurturing to all those around her or society will crumble. The early Freudian view of femininity and the importance of self-sacrifice in child-rearing give further support to this particular subpersonality. In her book, *Mother Love: Myth and Reality*, Elizabeth Badinter traces the development of this particular good mother role.

The Good Mother

The good mother is a most seductive subpersonality. It makes women feel good and indispensable (a lovely attraction for the vulnerable child within), and it is pleasing and comforting to those around it.

Why, we might ask, is there anything wrong with this? There is nothing wrong, as we have said before, when an element of choice is also present, when an aware ego chooses whether or not to do something for someone else. The good mother, as with any other subpersonality, is fine as long as she is not in complete control. The good mother/obedient daughter combination predisposes us to physical illness because the natural instincts are ignored when these patterns are in control.

When the good mother is in operation, the woman has no choice but to give and give until she is depleted. She finds herself boxed in by dependent children, a demanding husband, and needy friends. She finds herself rescuing others, cheering them up, and supporting them unstintingly. Their needs are always greater than hers—in her estimation. Marilyn, whom we discussed in Chapter One, was a perfect illustration of this.

A good mother will give to everyone—even the therapist who is being paid to pay attention to her. This was touchingly illustrated by Pat, who came in for her session, sat down, looked at the therapist, and said, "How are you doing? You look a little tired today. Is there anything the matter?" This is a hard one to resist! It's so tempting to say, "Yes, I am a little tired," and launch into a long conversation. But this temptation was resisted, with great effort, we might add.

> THERAPIST: Now that certainly sounds like your good mother voice to me. Much as I'd love to have her take care of me, you're the one paying for the session so how about changing chairs and we'll talk to Mom. (Pat moves over to another chair and begins.)

GOOD MOTHER: Things haven't been going too badly for Pat, and I noticed you looked a little tired. I feel the need to see how you're doing. It's very uncomfortable for me to think that something might be troubling you, and Pat would just be talking on about her own little problems. (All of Pat's problems are little ones according to this subpersonality.)

THERAPIST: But that's why Pat is here—to talk about herself, not to take care of me.

GOOD MOTHER: I know (shrugging), but it makes me uncomfortable if anyone around her is uncomfortable. I always come in and make them feel better. That's what I did in group. I was really good. I knew just what everybody needed and I helped them a lot. I even helped the therapist sometimes. People really like having me around.

THERAPIST: I'll bet they do. But what happens to Pat?

GOOD MOTHER (contentedly): Pat's strong. She can take care of herself and of everybody around her, too. She likes having me around. As I said, people like me and want to be near me.

Just as the pusher can be balanced by the energies of the do-nothing, so can the good mother's energies be balanced by the selfish subpersonality. Pat's selfish voice saw the situation quite differently.

SELFISH: I wish she'd stop giving, giving, giving all the time. It makes me sick to my stomach! She's always available, always understanding. She'll take her son wherever he wants to go, and, as far as I'm concerned, he's old enough to take himself. Then she spends hours and hours on the phone listening to her unhappy friends complain. Does she *ever* ask for anything? No! Does she ever complain? Never! Does she ever just cut a conversation short and say "I'm busy?" Never! As far as I'm concerned, she's a damned fool. And as for group, she could have taken a little attention for herself once in a while and asked for something. Instead, she made herself a damn assistant leader, for no pay, and didn't get any support at all.

As Pat's awareness separated from her good mother—and this was greatly speeded up by her selfish voice—Pat was able to make conscious decisions. She didn't become selfish, she simply became discriminating in her choices. The change was particularly apparent several weeks later when she came in and announced to the therapist, "You look a little tired and my good mother wants to take care of you, but I have so much to talk about today that I want to start right in with myself."

When a woman is identified with an overly nurturing good mother, other family members automatically identify with childlike subpersonalities, which will vary from family to family. For instance, Mildred was similar to Pat in the way she identified with her good mother. She was loving, giving, and always available. As a result, her daughter, Ann, grew up to be rebellious and selfish, very much the opposite of her mother. The quality of their relationship was evident in their phone calls. When Mildred lovingly telephoned Ann, Ann kept the conversation very short. "Okay, Mom, I have to go," she would say and then hang up the phone. Her mother was crushed by this behavior over and over again.

Ann, rather than Mildred, finally came in for therapy. She was upset because she realized there was something wrong in the way she related to her mother. When Ann visited her mother's home she often took personal items belonging to her mother, without asking or obtaining her mother's consent. Often she didn't really want these things. Mildred, although she might have experienced an initial burst of anger, immediately went into her good mother mode and became quite loving, concerned, and caring again. When questioned about her feelings, she might well have responded: "What does it really matter? I love her so much . . . . It isn't worth the trouble. She'll learn someday."

Let us now consider what this experience is like from Ann's standpoint. The good mother dominated the relationship; Ann never experienced any sense of limitation. Her father left all child-rearing matters to her mother. The overly nurturing good mother could not set limits. Thus, Ann was constantly being thrown into the roles of guilty daughter, grabby daughter, and rebellious daughter. She was never able to be herself with her mother, and she never got a realistic reaction from her mother, who also could not be herself with Ann. Ann alternated between rejecting and fervently loving her mother.

In her work with her therapist, Ann had the following dialogue:

> THERAPIST: Why did you take the perfume from your mother if you didn't want it?
>
> ANN: I didn't . . . it's like something takes over in me . . . . I know it sounds silly, but that's what it's like . . . like it isn't me.
>
> THERAPIST: Could I talk to the part of you that takes over and wants the perfume? (Ann moves over.) So, who are you?
>
> TAKING VOICE: I'm a thief. I really can't help it. I feel like I have to steal from my mother. I know that she'll never say anything . . . anything. I wish she would. I wish she'd stop me once. I really can't stand the way I am, but I can't help it, either. Then I feel guilty and I hate that. I really hate her when I feel like that.
>
> THERAPIST: What happens when you feel guilty? What's the next step?
>
> TAKING VOICE: Then I just want to get away from her (Ann's mother) and I hate myself more. And her mother gets more loving. I really love her, but I can't stand her. I wish one time she'd slap me hard. She never stops me and I can't stop myself.

Ann had become identified with a mode of being that is specifically archetypal. As the daughter of a woman who is identified with the good mother, she became identified with the archetypal role of daughter—first conforming and then rebelling. Ann had been a conforming daughter until adolescence, at which time the rebellious daughter took over and the hostilities commenced. It is to be noted that not *all* daughters of women identified with the good mother will react as strongly as Ann did.

Ann and her mother were caught in an archetypal drama that is highly predictable and mathematically precise. The challenge for each of them was to develop an awareness that could help them separate from these stereotyped ways of feeling, thinking, and responding.

We would like to provide another example of how the situation looks from the standpoint of the daughter of a woman who is identified with the good mother. In this dialogue, the facilitator talked with the part of Shawn (the daughter) who could never keep any secrets from her mother.

> COMPULSIVE TALKER: Sometimes I'll come home from a date and my mother is waiting up for me. She doesn't say anything to make me talk, but I find myself spilling my guts every time we're together. My friends don't tell their mothers everything. I feel like I have no privacy.
>
> FACILITATOR: . . . and you have no choice?
>
> TALKER: None. I'm afraid not to talk. I think I have a lot of anger in me.
>
> FACILITATOR: You mean there's another part of Shawn that is angry?
>
> TALKER: Yeah. She's afraid for it to come out.

Shawn felt she loved her mother, but she also felt trapped. The loving, nurturing, protective side of her mother was very strong and had crystallized a part of Shawn that had become bonded to this mother. This was the compulsive talker—a voice that had become so powerful that it had entirely taken over Shawn's relationship with her mother. Thus, Shawn shared intimacies and the relationship looked close, but beneath this apparent closeness were anger and resentment.

The term "bonding" refers to the fact that the two archetypal patterns, good mother and compulsive talker, have joined together without the benefit of awareness. Shawn had become aware of this bonding, as well as another set of feelings: She began to be aware of the resentment that lay beneath the closeness. This does not mean she did not love her mother or that she would never talk to her again. The process was only aimed at helping her to become aware of the conflicting feelings so she would have a *real* choice in what she did or did not say to her mother.

The Good Father

The good father is just as seductive as the good mother. Who could resist a combination of "Father Knows Best," "Marcus Welby," John Walton, and King Arthur? Our culture has developed an impossible ideal for its fathers as well as its mothers. A good father is steadfast, responsible, loving, understanding, helpful, and gently humorous. He always knows the right thing to do and he does it without fanfare. He can fix anything from a flat tire to a broken heart. And he never gets tired or needs help. What a burden!

Good fathers surround themselves with helpless children. The good father who does his daughter's homework might still be writing her term papers for her in college. The good father who takes care of everything for his wife will get midnight phone calls well after his divorce when the dishwasher overflows or the pool heater breaks. Just as the good mother bonds with the needy, the good father bonds with the helpless. As the good mother is loved by all around her, so is the good father.

A good father is a handy thing for a woman to have around; ask anyone who has married one. They shoulder all the responsibility—financial and emotional—and they usually do much of the maintenance work around the house. In fact, they do so much that many times their wives become infantilized and have trouble taking care of themselves. The helpless daughter bonds with the good father, and all other subpersonalities atrophy.

The good father finds himself trapped by his compulsive need to be responsible for everyone and everything around him. He finds himself surrounded by people who leave decisions up to him or do not bother taking care of details because they know he will. He is indispensable, but at what a cost!

Just as a good mother will trouble herself about the psychological needs of her therapist, a good father will unobtrusively put a new bottle of water in the therapist's waiting room. What a delight!

Bob's good father was firmly bonded to his ex-wife's helpless daughter. Bob was trying to make vacation plans, but his good father kept getting in the way as the vacation was discussed.

> FACILITATOR (to Bob): Wait a minute, I'm confused. I thought that you were going to stay at the ski resort until Sunday and now you're planning to come back on Friday. Let's talk to your good father again. (Bob moves over.)
>
> GOOD FATHER: I think he should come back on Friday. Angela (his ex-wife) has had a bad cold and she might need him to help with the children over the weekend. If she feels better, she wants to go to Palm Springs and he'll need to take care of the dog.
>
> FACILITATOR: Can't she get a baby-sitter or send the dog to a kennel?
>
> GOOD FATHER (horrified at these suggestions): No, I couldn't let her do that. I'd feel too guilty. Bob couldn't have a good time.
>
> FACILITATOR: You certainly make it tough for Bob to take a vacation. He was really looking forward to this one. He hasn't taken one in a year.
>
> GOOD FATHER (virtuously smiling in a superior way): He'll have plenty of other chances. Right now he's needed here.

Actually, the good father's version of being needed doesn't necessarily correspond to the situation. In this case, the good father had the last word—Bob came home early from his vacation, and Angela felt better and went to Palm Springs with the children. The children refused to leave the dog at home and Bob's sacrifice went totally unnoticed. Needless to say, the good father disappeared and the negative father took over.

The Negative Father

As the good father convinces us to do more than we would do if we were making conscious choices, the negative father is building up an equal and opposite energy. After Bob's sacrifice of several prime days of skiing went unnoticed, his negative father emerged in full force. The negative father, in this instance, was judgmental and punitive.

> NEGATIVE FATHER: I don't like the way Angela is handling the kids. She's mean to the older one and she's spoiling the younger one. I keep telling the older one not to listen to her. That's the best way I know of handling the situation. "Just ignore your mother," I say. Then we wink at each other. (When Bob was not under the influence of his negative father, he was quite comfortable with Angela's child-rearing.)
>
> FACILITATOR: I'll talk to Bob about that a little later. In the meantime, I see that you're really angry at Angela. What else has upset you?
>
> NEGATIVE FATHER: The way she spends money. She seems to think I have an unlimited supply. (Here, too, we have an alternation of the good father and the negative father without an intervening aware ego. The good father automatically paid *all* the bills, and the negative father got angry.) She uses up all the money Bob gives her within a week. And then she charges things on her credit cards and sends him the bills. He pays them all and I'm furious. Now she wants money to fix the roof of the house. She says that there's mildew on the walls in a few places and it really smells. *I* decided not to let him pay for that

one. I don't think she should be in that house anyway. It's too expensive. Thank God, he lets me draw the line somewhere.

Until Bob learns to take the decision-making power away from his good father, he will be doomed to seesaw between giving too much and withholding and punishing. This is often a difficult step forward in consciousness because others have a tendency to support the good father. As one of our children, Claudia, asked pointedly, "Isn't there some way of locking in Hal's good father and keeping it there forever?" No, Claudia, there isn't. If you get the good father (and Hal's is one of the most delicious), the negative father is never far behind.

The Negative Mother

The negative mother has been portrayed in all her glory as the witch of fairy tales. She destroys or she devours. The good mother makes all kinds of sacrifices and, as with the negative father, the negative mother is rarely far behind. The good mother understands all and accepts all until her opposite appears.

Karen came to therapy because she was feeling depressed and irritated. She had been a nurturing mother and supportive wife for years, and now everything about her husband and children irritated her. Her sex drive had disappeared totally and she felt despondent about her life. She was surprised to discover the variety of subpersonalities that flourished in this apparently arid desert of her life. But none released more energy than her negative mother.

THERAPIST: How about talking to the part of you that is always irritated?

KAREN: I don't see what good that would do—that's what my

problem is. I'm trying to get over this irritation and back to my old good-natured self.

THERAPIST: It sounds like somebody in there is afraid of your irritation. Don't worry, we don't want you to become an impossible bitch. All we want to do is to give your irritated voice a chance to speak so that you can figure out if there's anything she can do to help you.

KAREN: Okay. All the other voices have been helpful. But you're right. I *am* afraid of this one. (She changes her chair, assumes an irritable and angry expression, and her negative mother begins to speak.)

NEGATIVE MOTHER: Everything any of them does irritates me. Everything. The way they talk, the way they look. I just feel like making them change or pushing them away. I'd really hurt them if I could. Sometimes I feel that I could even murder someone. I get so angry (pause). I just wish they'd all disappear and leave Karen alone. I can't stand any of them to touch her. If her husband kisses her, I want to shove him away. When her children hug her, I want to hit them. They all drive me crazy!

THERAPIST: It's no wonder you frighten Karen. Tell me, what are some of the things that drive you crazy?

NEGATIVE MOTHER: They're always grabbing and she's always giving.

THERAPIST: What do you mean by that?

NEGATIVE MOTHER: When her son's car stalls because he's run out of gas, she's off to rescue him. Immediately. I think she should let him sweat it out a bit. Let him be late for his date and let his date be angry. But no, Super Mom here drops everything she's doing and is off for an hour to do works of mercy. It makes me sick (with disgust)!

THERAPIST: You don't like it when she takes care of everybody?

NEGATIVE MOTHER: You've got it! Big Mama here takes care of everyone. Madame Martyr, I call her. I couldn't care less if she never did anything for any of them again. And she needs to support that husband, too. He gets nervous and she loses sleep. Super Mom can't let him keep his insomnia to himself. She has to get up and worry with him. And she's so understanding. I'm not. I just get angry. But she doesn't let me react. She smiles prettily and stays helpful.

THERAPIST: How do you come out?

NEGATIVE MOTHER: When she's not looking. I'm the one who makes those nasty comments about her husband when they're out socially. She doesn't know why she does it, but it's me. Somehow Super Mom doesn't have the same power in a social setting. And (smiling) if she has a couple of drinks, I can get pretty sharp. I know just how to get to him.

THERAPIST: Oh, so it was you. She was wondering who did that. How do you come out with the children?

NEGATIVE MOTHER: I let them know how hopeless I think they are. Super Mom is always trying to encourage them. You know, she builds up their dear little egos (sarcastically). I just let them know how they're doing things wrong. How ugly and stupid and not nice they are. I'm pretty subtle though. Sometimes it's just a look or a shrug. Mostly I criticize and push them away. I can't stand clinging.

THERAPIST: It sounds as though with this Super Mom around, Karen gets nothing much for herself. Everyone else comes first.

NEGATIVE MOTHER: You bet. She's been trying to read the same novel for six weeks. I'd have her lock her bedroom door and read for two hours a day.

THERAPIST: That doesn't sound like a bad idea.

NEGATIVE MOTHER: Do you mean that? Really? Nobody ever thought I had a good idea before (suspiciously).

THERAPIST: Well, sometimes a woman needs some time off from being Super Mom. What else would you have her do?

The therapist spent additional time with this negative mother. Karen had become so identified with her good mother that all choices were immediately decided in favor of other family members. Karen's pusher and critic drove her to do more and more for everyone else and criticized her for her selfishness if she dared to think of herself. The negative mother was under great pressure. Although it was disowned, it was full of reactions.

As we listened to the negative mother, she was encouraged to go over specific instances where she felt Karen had made unconscious choices. This previously disowned negative mother came up with new ideas and creative solutions to old problems once her initial bitterness wore off. Karen was able to listen to her opinions and suggestions and to choose more consciously what she would or would not do for others. She became less depressed and irritable as these energies were released, and she no longer felt trapped by her Super Mom subpersonality. And her negative mother, now that Karen listened to it, was no longer demonic. It no longer came out unexpectedly to take vicious jabs at Karen's family.

The negative mother appears for a good reason: to balance a system that is unbalanced. When a woman doesn't listen to it, she finds herself, as Karen did, making nasty remarks to her family, talking about them with her friends, and feeling trapped, extremely irritable, and hopeless.

With the introduction of awareness, the trap is sprung and the system can go through a natural balancing process. We feel discomfort for a reason; our negative mothers and fathers are angry for a reason. If we listen to their sides of the story, we have a chance to restore the natural balance of energies.

We might note that sometimes, although this is less common, the negative mother or father predominates and the other side gets ignored. Then the good mother and father become angry and irritable and they bring forth their demands for more concern for the well-being of others. Here, too, with the introduction of awareness, the system is balanced.

The Rational Parent

The rational parent is more often seen in men than women, and sooner or later it bonds with some form of the emotionally reactive child in another person. They dance a most delicious dance together. A typical interchange sounds like this:

> CAROL (from an aware ego): I was really upset yesterday when you ignored me and made plans for the holidays. I felt left out. I'd like to talk about it.
>
> TED'S RATIONAL FATHER (cool and collected): What do you mean you were upset?
>
> CAROL: Upset. You know, *hurt*. I felt left out.
>
> RATIONAL FATHER (somewhat distant): I don't understand. Why should you feel left out?
>
> CAROL (beginning to feel uncomfortable): I felt left out because you left me out. You didn't ask me how I felt.
>
> RATIONAL FATHER (with a bit of disdain): You're overly upset about this. What seems to be the problem? I don't understand.
>
> CAROL'S REBELLIOUS DAUGHTER: Nothing's the problem. I thought we were going to plan our holidays together. Since you planned yours by yourself, I'll go to Club Med in Martinique! (She stomps out of the room.)

It is almost impossible to resist the power of the rational father. He is always cool and in command. The more rational he gets, the more irrational the other will sound. However, rational fathers are just as trapped as we feel when we're talking to them. If we can maintain objectivity and, above all, humor, we will have a chance of breaking the spell. If not, enjoy! There's nothing like a rational father to provoke a wild display of passion in a rebellious angry child, and that can be great fun. Once a woman was so infuriated by the rational father in her boyfriend that she said, "I'm so angry I could bite through this little branch." And she did. They were both instantly freed because this was so funny that they both burst into gales of laughter. Her action was unexpected and shocking, which caused the awareness level of each to be automatically alerted. Thus, they became two aware egos, rather than a rational father and an angry daughter.

In this part of the book, The Voices, we could have gone on forever, or so it seems, giving examples of subpersonalities we have met—but we had to set some limits on ourselves. We therefore chose those personalities—both primary and disowned—that seem particularly common in our society now. In Part Three, we will leave the specific selves and move on to the broader picture, where we will look at two major issues in life—empowerment and the search for meaning in life.

PART III

The Roar of Awakening

Introduction

The Archetypal Energy Flow within Us

We are all made up of a variety of energy patterns that we either identify with or disown. Each of these selves has its polar opposite which operates either consciously or unconsciously. Until now, we have concentrated on the way in which these energy patterns behave as individual subpersonalities within us. Now we will broaden our awareness as we awaken to the role of these selves in relation to the world.

Let us review briefly the essence of the developmental process. We are born quite vulnerable and remain so for an extended period of time. The protector/controller is the first major self that develops to protect this vulnerability. Quite early in life, the protector/controller becomes the guiding agent of the personality, and it utilizes other selves to create its protective screen. These other selves are referred to as the primary selves. They essentially represent the traits we most closely identify with—how we see ourselves and define ourselves to the world. The primary selves form our operating ego until our awareness is born and an aware ego begins to operate separately from the primary selves.

As we grow older, the move from vulnerability to power accelerates. It is not fun to remain vulnerable. Our environment must be controlled, so the protector/controller and primary selves increasingly become the personality's authority. Together they constitute the major system of selves in the parental control pattern that operates inside each of us. Most importantly, as these primary selves develop, our vulnerability is buried. For some, it is buried completely. For others, it regularly breaks through or takes over so they continue to feel vulnerable and victimized throughout their lives. In either case, healthy human relations are very difficult.

As we examine the basic interactive patterns that disrupt relationships, it is clear that the primary cause of these problems is our inability to deal with our vulnerability. In Voice Dialogue, our aim is to learn how to channel every self, as well as our vulnerability, through an aware ego. When we disown our vulnerability, we identify with our parental selves; identifying with vulnerability ensures victim status—in either case, our vulnerability becomes quite difficult to resolve. Learning to be aware of and experience our vulnerability, and then learning how to express it through an aware ego, therefore, is one of the most significant tasks we encounter in transformational work.

In reviewing the many selves discussed so far, we see that in general they represent opposites on a power-vulnerability continuum. The power pole is our parental side and the vulnerability pole is our child. Our energies are constantly moving between these two sides. This archetypal energy movement can be conceptualized as follows:

Power-Vulnerability Axis

This energy flow generally happens without our awareness. We cannot stop it because it is an archetypal process. It is interesting to note that this represents a balanced system of energies. The son/daughter side, which represents lack of control and vulnerability, is every bit as large as the father/mother side, which represents power and control. We may not always be aware of this balance because we tend to identify with one end of this power continuum and disown the other. As our awareness increases, however, both the archetypal movement of energy and this balance become more apparent. An aware ego begins to have some measure of control and choice in regard to how these energies operate within us and in relationship to other people.

Diagrammatically, the development of awareness would look like this:

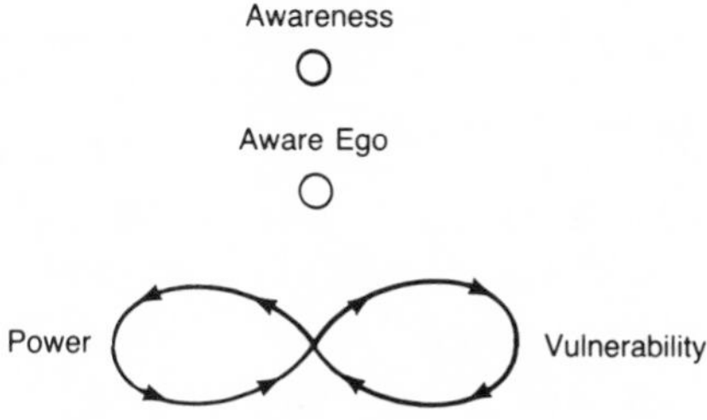

This development of an awareness level that can witness and an aware ego that can embrace both power and vulnerability is one of the central goals of transformational work. It leads to what we call empowerment rather than being powerful. In the following chapter we will look at how these ideas apply to the roar of awakening in women today.

9

The Empowerment of Women

Now that we understand how our selves develop and our consciousness evolves, let us look at some of the major changes in our culture with our newfound awareness. On a general, cultural level, it is our experience that men have generally disowned vulnerability and embraced power. Their task of empowerment is to develop an aware ego that can embrace *both* sides. Although men have moved in this direction, this has been in large part a reaction to and/or a by-product of the remarkable revolution that has occurred in the psychology of women. We do not at all wish to imply that psychological development in men is generally speaking a reaction to the women's movement. It is simply that the balance of power has shifted so dramatically in the last twenty years as women have gone through their revolutionary process that many men have had to learn to adapt to the changing times. In this chapter we wish to concentrate on this revolution in women's psychology in the light of our focus on the psychology of selves.

Until the sixties, certain energy patterns were so universally disowned by the women in our culture that they were hypothesized not to exist. The prevailing cultural norm, supported both by legislation and by current psychological theories, made it almost impossible for women to acknowledge their aggression, anger, power, ambition, or sexuality as valid, acceptable aspects of feminine psychology.

The feminist movement focused a spotlight on the forced disowning of many power-related energy patterns. It raised questions regarding feminine disempowerment and encouraged women to embrace many previously disowned energy patterns.

Helen, for example, was a pleasant and charming young woman from a middle-class Midwestern background. She married appropriately, had three children, and was at home caring for them. Although she possessed a strong intellect and ambition to achieve something in the "man's" world, she managed to keep these qualities safely suppressed until she read *The Feminine Mystique*.

Suddenly, her professional ambition was no longer a disowned self—she wanted a career. She was no longer deterred by the charges (current in the culture at that time) that pursuing a career would essentially castrate her husband and do untold damage to her children. She integrated her disowned intellectual energies and stopped over-identifying with her self-sacrificing subpersonality (which was greatly encouraged as the *sine qua non* of child-rearing in those days).

Once Helen stopped disowning her "unfeminine" ambition, she was able to carve out a career for herself with humor, compassion, self-awareness, and great success. She remained sensitive, sweet, and caring all the same. By integrating energies that were still taboo in her culture, she became empowered and enjoyed a rewarding, absorbing career that equalled, and finally eclipsed, her husband's.

It is interesting to note how threatened we are by disowned energies before we allow them into our lives. In the early sixties psychological disaster would have been predicted for Helen's course of action. Often we disown energies because we fear they will disrupt our equilibrium and lead to chaos. Actually, the reverse is true. *Disowning the "chaos" within each of us causes disruptions in our surroundings because these disowned energies operate unconsciously*. Integrating these energies enriches us and our surroundings.

Warrior Energy and the Guilty Daughter

Warrior, or Amazon, energy has been disowned in women for millennia. It was a great relief to Ellen when we first spoke with this fearless part of her. Ellen had been involved in a truly meaningful long-term affair that had recently ended. Her lover's wife, her husband, her friends, everyone judged her. She was the "compleat" guilty victim.

> FACILITATOR (after Ellen has changed chairs and the warrior is now present): My, but you look different from Ellen. You're taller, straighter, and your eyes have quite a sparkle to them.
>
> WARRIOR: You bet, and I'm not afraid of any of them—not her husband, her lover's wife—none of them. Just let them try to make her feel guilty when I'm around. Let them try. They'll be sorry. She did what she did and I'm not about to let her apologize. I'm proud of her. I'll make them all cringe. (Warming to the task.) If they confront her in public, I'll just tell it all, just like it was. I won't spare any details and they'll be sorry they ever tried to make her the patsy. I'm tired of her always being apologetic and taking the blame for everything (eyes gleaming). In fact, I'd like it. Yes, I'd love to see the looks on all their faces when they see me stand up for her. Those holier-than-thou bastards. None of them is any better than she is and they won't judge her . . . not while I'm around. No way! I'm just here to protect her and I don't give a damn about anyone else.

Until recently, warrior energy was considered unfeminine, castrating, or, worse yet, some form of devilish possession. We can now clearly see how necessary it is for self-protection, and how powerless a woman can be if this energy is disowned. Without it, Ellen was a guilt-ridden victim of the accusations and judgments of all around her. Once she accepted her warrior self, she was capable of defending herself in an appropriate fashion with an aware ego. She did not unknowingly identify with the warrior and go out looking for a fight; she simply took care of herself.

Before she gained access to her warrior energy, Ellen had been identified with her guilty daughter—another energy pattern encouraged in women since Eve was created. Women, after all, were responsible for humanity's expulsion from paradise, and, until the feminists drew attention to the belief system this inspired, women have to a greater or lesser extent lived as the guilty daughter. Eve was guilty of curiosity, independent thought, and wishing to expand her horizons. How dreadful! She was punished for her disobedience and thus paved the way for the birth of millions upon millions of guilty daughters. This archetypal energy is quite concerned about upsetting the "collective;" it worries constantly about what people will think. For hundreds of generations, mothers have asked their daughters, "What will people think?" when their daughters want to deviate from the accepted norm.

Ellen's guilty daughter, for instance, had been terrified that people would find out about her affair and judge her. She panicked at the idea that people might talk about her. She repeatedly said, "I want Ellen to be a good girl. I'll *die* if people think bad things of her. And, my God, what would her mother and father say? They wouldn't be able to raise their heads in public. They'd be *so* embarrassed. I'd die, I'd just die!"

It is obvious that the guilty daughter does not have much clout—anyone can judge her, anyone can shame her. She is an ancient, powerful archetypal energy, and it is time for women to disidentify with her. But this does not mean they should identify with the opposite energy—perhaps a judgmental or avenging mother—and blame everything on men, religion, or our culture.

It is more appropriate to step into a position of awareness. It is time for women to stop identifying with the energies within themselves that keep them disempowered. Repression does not only come from others, it comes from our subpersonalities as well, the ones that lock us into a powerfully judgmental patriarch, century after century. It is time for women to become truly empowered, from a position of consciousness, and to accept full responsibility for themselves and their actions. In a way, women are more likely to seek empowerment than men. Because they do not have equal access to traditional power, they are forced to work from an empowered position (power integrated with vulnerability) rather than a power position (identification with archetypal power energies).

Empowerment versus Power in Women

Consciousness and the development of a strong aware ego in women are nowhere more important than in the corporate world. It was truly fascinating to watch this process unfold for Elizabeth. She had been reared in a Latin country by an extremely dictatorial father. She left home after she finished school and came to America by herself to start a new life.

Elizabeth was very ambitious, intellectually brilliant, and a hard worker who could spend sixteen hours a day in diligent research to cover all possible details. She accepted responsibility and was willing to make important decisions even though much was at stake. She was truly courageous. But she was a woman; thus, she constantly encountered obstacles in the field of finance. It was unquestionably a man's field, although she soon surpassed most of the men in her company.

As a woman, Elizabeth was keenly aware of her feelings. She did not want to sacrifice her sensitivity and vulnerability for corporate success. She wanted to keep her relationship with her husband alive and she knew that if she disowned her sensitive, practical, intuitive energies she would lose much richness from her life—to say nothing of losing her beloved husband.

Watching her move up the corporate ladder was like watching a balancing act of the most delicate precision. She needed her power voices to help her with demands for promotions and raises. But if she began to identify with her power side, her way would become blocked. The men in the company, their vulnerable children activated, would back off in fear and ally with one another against her. Then her vulnerability and insecurity would come forth. If she let these take over, she might lose credibility and would have to work hard to regain previously won ground.

Elizabeth proceeded with great care. She became expert at differentiating between her power voices and true empowerment. She worked from an aware ego, only making big moves when she knew she was empowered. When she felt the archetypal power energies or vulnerable energies taking over she withdrew whenever possible.

As could be expected from this patriarchal environment, power was withdrawn from any position Elizabeth won and moved elsewhere. If she had been attached to power rather than empowerment, she would have been angered or embittered or discouraged. She could easily have polarized against the system as a rebellious daughter. However, her first priority was the evolution of her consciousness, so she continued her relentless movement, deepening her empowerment and broadening her awareness. Because she sought empowerment, every experience was an exciting lesson. Her authority, responsibility, and actual power in the company expanded until she was on the highest management level. But she was able to remain free of the basic power structure and remained unintimidated by corporate politics.

The Killer Who Protects

Men and women alike need warrior energy to protect themselves. Needless to say, women are seen as life-givers and healers, and the thought that they might have any destructive energies is intimidating. We feel that part of the intensity surrounding the issue of abortion is that it affirms the woman's wish and ability to destroy life as well as create it. We have not noticed equal fervor to deny men the right to destroy life in wars. Men are expected to have a destructive voice; it is to be regretted and tamed, but it is there nonetheless. Women are not similarly endowed as far as Western culture is concerned.

To deny our destructive energies, whether male or female, is to deny a major power source. Sadly, such denial often causes destructive energy to be projected onto men. The men use these energies to protect their women, their children, and themselves; the men will destroy life or property if they feel it necessary.

We are not advocating destruction, for men or women. However, both men and women need to be in touch with that aspect of themselves that could kill if necessary. When this is disowned, our vulnerable children, both within and without, are unprotected, and these energies are projected—onto another sex, another race, another nationality, or another belief system. Only when we are aware of this "killer who protects" can we truly experience the richness and beauty of our vulnerability.

Interestingly, this voice has been so thoroughly repressed in women that it rarely assumes the form of a female as a subpersonality. It is far more likely to be a jungle cat, a graceful feline killer. Let us listen to one such feline describe itself.

> JAGUAR (eyes narrowed and alert, body tense and ready to spring): I watch everything. I have sharp eyes and I know all about danger. I love danger. I love to fight. I love to hurt others. I love the taste of blood (smiles triumphantly). What I don't like

are people who pretend they're good and pure. Nobody is and I know it. I can see the part that's like me in everyone and I know how to protect Kim from getting hurt by it.

FACILITATOR: You sound so strong and alive.

JAGUAR: That's because I am. When I'm not around, Kim is a sweet, spiritual weakling. She's so nice that everyone loves her, but everyone can push her around. She can be fooled by people who pretend to be earnest. I can't stand that. I like people who are more like me. When they cop to the killer in them, then I can trust them. (Rolls her eyes upward.) Spare me from those who think they're pure in heart. I love the ones who know they're not. You know, I love to walk the streets in New York. Everybody there knows about me and I come alive. I look around and I see the me in their eyes. We all say, "OK, you'd better watch out. I'm not kidding." And I love it (stretching), I just love it.

FACILITATOR: How do you feel about the people in Kim's discussion group?

JAGUAR: I can't stand them. They're all so nice. Her nice part comes out and everybody does a sweet little dance (sarcastic). I'd like to shake them up. I'd like to growl and show my teeth. I'd like to break up all that niceness. It's saccharine and boring and I don't trust it. It makes me uncomfortable. It only *looks* safe. It isn't.

FACILITATOR: What about her best friend?

JAGUAR: I wish she'd let me out with her and I wish she'd let me tell her to stop being a scared rabbit about life and people. I wish she'd let me tell her to get off her ass and fight for what she wants. You have to fight for everything that's worthwhile. I want to sink my teeth into all those people who are passive and good and waiting for "the universe to provide." (Growls a bit and moves around as if she can't contain her annoyance.)

FACILITATOR: What would you want her to do about her boyfriend?

JAGUAR: Tell him to stop feeling sorry for himself and go get a job. Tell him she's tired of playing mommy to a puppy. And most of all, let me at him when he starts getting snippy with her instead of always being so nice and understanding. He won't be so snippy when I'm through with him.

FACILITATOR: You don't sound afraid of people.

JAGUAR: I'm not. I'm ready for anyone who would hurt Kim or anyone she loves. And I don't give a damn if people don't like her. And I'm not nice. I'm definitely not nice (with determination).

The killer who protects (for Kim, her jaguar) had been disowned throughout Kim's life, and she had been identified with her nice girl. The nice girl has been highly valued in Western society, and it is still highly valued in much of the Middle and Far East. The nice girl subpersonality is encouraged, at least in part, because she helps everything to function smoothly and makes people feel good. Kim's primary self, her nice girl, was quite upset by her jaguar.

NICE GIRL: But nobody is going to like Kim if she follows those suggestions and everything could get disrupted (sounding much younger and weaker than the jaguar).

FACILITATOR: How do you see that happening?

NICE GIRL (smoothing her skirt and sitting properly): First of all, I *like* her discussion group. The people in it are nice and don't hurt her. It's safe and *I* have a good time. We joke and we laugh and we're thoughtful. We're considerate of each other's needs and feelings (a little teary). I like it when people are considerate of Kim, and if you're not nice to them, they won't be nice back. *I* know that.

FACILITATOR (kindly): So you're really worried about what would happen to Kim if her jaguar came out?

NICE GIRL: Yes. I'm afraid that her discussion group will turn into an encounter group like she was in in the sixties, and everyone will be confronting each other and being mean. That would be awful!

FACILITATOR: I see. How about talking to her girlfriend?

NICE GIRL: You're supposed to be a support and a comfort to friends, to make them feel better and not get them worried. I'm afraid she'll just upset her girlfriend. And then, what if her friend stops being nice to her? I don't want Kim to get hurt and the only way to avoid getting hurt is to be really nice so nobody will hurt you (looking very earnest).

FACILITATOR: What about her boyfriend?

NICE GIRL: Well, that really scares me, too (looking concerned). I'm afraid he'll leave her. I think he likes her because I'm around so much of the time. I make things really nice for him. I'm very tuned in to his feelings, and I'm always considerate and easy to be with. He doesn't like tough, confrontive women. He tells her that a lot. He likes gentle, peaceful, nice women. He says they're attractive and feminine. He says the other kinds are uncentered and bitchy. I agree with him. She won't be as likeable without me.

We can see how for each disowned power voice, such as Ellen's warrior energy and Kim's jaguar voice, a voice such as the "guilty daughter" or the "nice girl" has kept the woman disempowered. Although these voices are still supported by our culture, the gradual introduction of feminist counterculture thinking has made it possible for women to begin to disidentify with them.

The Danger of Identifying with Opposite Archetypes

Often, when warrior or other powerful energies are first released, the experience is so heady and powerful that it is difficult not to identify as completely with these as with our disempowered "nice" voices. This did happen to the militant feminists; they broke the archetypal identification with the passive victim only to become identified with the warrior archetype, the opposite energy. However, this swinging of the pendulum is often a necessary first step in thoroughly breaking the hold of the disempowered self. It can also be a basic step in the consciousness process.

A woman who ceases to identify with her vulnerability, neediness, and passivity and identifies instead with her warrior, her impersonality, and her sexuality has not necessarily moved forward in consciousness. She may feel more comfortable as top dog but then again she may not. She may find herself feeling alone and unloved. Whichever way she feels, she is still unbalanced—identified with one set of energies and totally disowning its opposite. It is in the evolution of consciousness, the development of awareness, and the introduction of an aware ego that true forward movement takes place. Vulnerability cannot be disowned any more than the warrior can. Both men and women need their vulnerability and sensitivity in order to truly feel a part of life, and they need their warriors to ensure they do not become victims to life's difficulties.

The Competitor and the Lady

Another energy long denied to women is competitiveness. Competition has long been considered strictly a male province. Any woman's femininity was greatly diminished if she admitted that she really loved winning. After all, "a real woman doesn't want to win; she wants to support her man so that *he* wins."

Susan's situation was very typical. As a child, she had been quite competitive and an outstanding athlete. However, Susan was raised to be a lady, so she soon learned to make light of her interest in competitive athletics. She was permitted to play tennis in a ladylike fashion—she could not try too hard and she could not look as though winning mattered. Her ladylike voice describes this in the following dialogue:

LADY: Tennis is a social game. (In a prim voice.) I don't want her out there like her husband, furiously competitive. It just doesn't look nice. It's not appropriate in him and it's certainly not appropriate for her.

FACILITATOR: How do you feel about her winning if she doesn't look too competitive about it?

LADY: If she's modest and she apologizes. You know, if she says that it's just been a lucky day, then it's all right with me. She has to keep smiling pleasantly and under no conditions whatsoever may she look triumphant.

FACILITATOR: So it's OK if she wins as long as it looks like luck or an accident?

LADY: Yes, that's right.

FACILITATOR: What about her trying to improve her game?

LADY: That's unacceptable. She's allowed to play with the girls a few times a week, but it should remain essentially social. They should talk a lot and be nice, and giggle, and make excuses when they miss the ball. She should never get grim-looking. It's not attractive.

Susan's competitive voice had been totally disowned, and her athletic activities had come under the control of this ladylike voice. But, as we have said before, our disowned selves have a way of attracting similar energies, and her husband was very competitive. Susan knew about disowned selves and wanted her own competitive subpersonality to be available to her.

SUSAN: I'm tired of playing tennis while I listen to that ladylike voice. I'd love to see what my competitive voice has to say.

FACILITATOR: OK—let's hear from it. (Susan changes her seat. She sits taller and looks stronger as her competitive voice emerges.)

COMPETITIVE VOICE: Those ladies she plays with drive me crazy. I want to play. I want to improve. I want to win. Susan is so worried about offending people and looking unfeminine that she never pays any attention to me.

FACILITATOR: You've got a lot of pizzazz. Tell me, what would you have Susan do?

COMPETITIVE VOICE: I'd have her leave the social ladies and go to play with people like me, with women who take their game seriously. They don't joke, they don't socialize. They're there to play tennis and that's all. (This voice looks very determined and unsmiling, in contrast to Susan who always looks pleasant and usually has a faint smile on her face.)

FACILITATOR: No nonsense for them.

COMPETITIVE VOICE: You bet! I'd have her go way up among the serious players. I'd have her tell the others—she can be as nice as she wants about it, I don't care—that she wants to improve her game and that she's looking for more competition. They'll understand. And, if not, I don't care. Her current group is a waste of time.

But Susan's ladylike voice had difficulty with this and Susan needed to take that voice into consideration as well when she changed her tennis-playing patterns. The competitive voice's power and excitement helped extricate her appropriately from her regular doubles games and she then went on to really stretch herself. She was full of the exuberance and power of using her body to its utmost.

Women learn to disown their competitiveness at a very young age. One woman had been verbally facile as a child. Her mother had called her away from a game of Anagrams with a little boy and suggested that she lose so that he would not feel bad. The girl was hurt and confused but because she did not want to make anyone uncomfortable she obediently lost the game. With such women, learning to lose is easily remembered although not as easily overcome. This proscription against winning and striving for excellence has done much to keep women disempowered.

Susan needed to release her competitive energies so that her natural abilities in athletics could resurface and be enjoyed. She needed to experience and enjoy the mastery of the game in order to re-empower herself. Happily, this led to a deep empowerment in other areas of her life. Before this voice was released, Susan was always hesitant, as though she took in half a breath and waited for permission to take in the other half. Now she could breathe fully and naturally; now she could stretch to her limits without fear of disapproval from within or without.

The Role of the Impersonal Self in the Empowerment of Women

The ability to be impersonal, dispassionate, and objective is another quality often disowned in women. Women are usually expected to be feeling creatures, ever-sensitive to the needs and emotions of others. They are expected to maintain a feelingful, or personal, connection to others in all their interactions. At least until fairly recently, a great part of a woman's attractiveness has been her warmth, her desire to please, her responsiveness to others, and her ability to nurture; in short, her more "personal" selves rather than her impersonal self. A woman lacking this concern for the needs and the well-being of others might well be seen as "cold-blooded" or "calculating." As applied to men, the term "cold-blooded" is usually reserved for murderers. Women's hearts are supposed to be forever warm.

It has been our experience that most men learn to use impersonal energy quite early in life. They are taught to think dispassionately and to evaluate situations, even situations involving the needs and feelings of others, in an objective fashion. They are encouraged to remain "cool" and "level-headed" when emotions run high. They learn how to maintain their psychological boundaries and operate independently of others, without feeling a need to please or to base their actions on the expected reactions of others. Thus, they know how to emotionally disentangle themselves from another person; they are not identified with the self that needs to maintain a personal and feeling connection at all times.

Of course, there are exceptions to this. We have noted that many men raised in the New Age consciousness have been encouraged to disown their impersonal selves and enhance their feelingful or personal selves so that they, like many women, react to the world primarily in terms of their emotions and the needs and feelings of others. They, too, need to maintain warm and personal contact with others at all times and do not have impersonal energies available to them.

In the years that have elapsed since we wrote the first edition of this book, we have increasingly emphasized work with the impersonal self. We have found that, particularly for women, reclaiming disowned impersonal energy has brought with it a great increase in power and a natural and fairly effortless ability to protect oneself. In allowing our impersonal energy to manifest, we are able to define our psychological boundaries, function independently with or without the approval of others, separate from others when this is necessary, and make our needs known in a clear and nonantagonistic fashion.

An extremely useful piece of Voice Dialogue work provides us with a contrast between the personal and the impersonal selves. The personal self is the pleasant, warm, pleasing self who creates and maintains contact with the facilitator and cares about what the facilitator thinks and feels. In contrast, the impersonal self is a bit distant and cool—not unfriendly, but separate and unconcerned about maintaining contact with the facilitator. For a woman (or a "New Age" man) it is often difficult to initially contact the impersonal self, but it is definitely worth the effort.

Let us see how this happens in a Voice Dialogue session. The facilitator, after talking with Anne for a while, realizes that she has no access to her impersonal self. Anne needs to remain in close emotional contact with others, takes everything quite personally (often feeling either responsible or victimized in her relationships), and is unable to consider interpersonal situations in a clear and unattached fashion. She is also quite warm, pleasant, and charming in her interaction with the facilitator.

FACILITATOR: It seems to me that you react to life in a very personal way; that you don't have access to your impersonal energies.

ANNE: I don't understand what you mean by that.

FACILITATOR: Let me show you. I'd like to give you a feeling of the difference between your personal and impersonal energies. How about moving your chair and we'll talk to the part of you that likes people and likes to be warm and close to them. (Anne moves her chair, sits down, and flashes the facilitator a warm smile.) Hello, how are you doing?

PERSONAL ANNE (pleasantly smiling and maintaining good eye contact with the facilitator): I'm fine. This has been really interesting. I don't know exactly what you're getting at, but if you say it's important, I'll go along with you. I'm really glad to have this chance to work with you.

FACILITATOR (giving some feedback as to the nature of this part which is a true primary self): Well, you certainly are a lovely and twinkly person to be with. I feel warm and comfortable with you around.

PERSONAL ANNE (a little worried): Are you making fun of me?

FACILITATOR (truthfully): No. You do make me feel good. You're just delightful and I like your smile.

PERSONAL ANNE: Well, then, I guess you feel good because I really like you and I'm glad to be with you. I think you're terrific and I'd like to be a little more like you. (Pause.) I guess I'm a people person.

FACILITATOR: A people person?

PERSONAL ANNE: Yes. I like people. I like being with them, I'm curious about them, I really feel for them. I'm pretty sensitive and I'm really loyal.

FACILITATOR: Yes, Anne was telling me that she takes her friendships very seriously.

PERSONAL ANNE (with some satisfaction): You'll never find me being selfish or not available when someone needs me. When her friends are down, I always do whatever I can. I visit them and I remember to telephone and to touch base regularly until they're feeling better.

FACILITATOR: It sounds as though you really care about how other people feel.

PERSONAL ANNE: You're right. It's important for me that the people I'm with are comfortable and happy. I'm uneasy when Anne's husband or children are unhappy. I don't like it when they are grumpy or withdrawn. I feel uncomfortable, like I should be doing something to cheer them up.

FACILITATOR: How do you feel about their feelings towards you?

PERSONAL ANNE: Well, the truth of the matter is, I care a lot. I want them to be happy with me and love me. I want to feel close. It makes me really uncomfortable when people pull away or when I think they're disapproving. Say, am I not supposed to feel this way? Do you think I'm being foolish?

FACILITATOR (essentially addressing this to Anne's awareness): As this part of Anne, you seem pretty concerned about what I think. Let's go to the other side, to the part of Anne that really doesn't care what I think. (Anne moves her chair to the other side. She sits down and seems a bit uncomfortable.)

Because this is a truly unfamiliar energy, the facilitator may well have to induce it by bringing in her own impersonal energy and holding it so that Anne has something to attune herself to. The facilitator might conduct this next part of the Voice Dialogue on a purely energetic level, without words. This is particularly helpful in an initial introduction of the impersonal self; there is time in later sessions for the introduction of words. In this kind of energetic induction, Anne would be helped to differentiate between the personal self that smiles and tries to maintain contact and the impersonal self that is totally self-contained. The facilitator would move Anne back and forth between these two, encouraging her to feel the difference between them until she can recognize when the impersonal shifts back to the personal. In working with the personal/impersonal selves, it is important for Anne to become familiar with the new impersonal energies. In this example, however, we will be using words in order to introduce the reader to some aspects of the impersonal self.

FACILITATOR (continuing the dialogue and tuned in to her own impersonal energies): Now I know this is not a familiar energy. Just look at me and try to tune into my energies. I'll lead you a bit in this. OK, now you're the part of Anne who doesn't get involved on a feeling level. You are self-contained and separate from me. You're experiencing this interaction more objectively than the other part we just talked to. (Anne continues to look a little puzzled.) Let's see—you might be one of Anne's selves that comes out in places other than with her family and friends—say at work or when she is doing her bookkeeping.

IMPERSONAL ANNE (sitting up a bit straighter and beginning to look more distanced and self-contained): Oh, yes, I'm there when she's at school teaching. She has to use me or the kids run all over her.

FACILITATOR: It sounds as though you weren't there in the beginning.

IMPERSONAL ANNE: No, I wasn't. That other part was. She wanted the kids to like her and Anne couldn't control her class. Anne's supervisor helped me learn how to take care of things. I'm there to teach, not to run a popularity contest.

FACILITATOR: I see.

IMPERSONAL ANNE (pleasant but cool): It's not that I don't like the kids. It's just that work needs to be done and she has to be clear and figure out the best way to do it. There are certain skills to being a teacher. She has to be alert to what is going on in class and she has to know how to handle the different kids. She needs to be able to look at their behavior and make decisions on a course of action. She can't get all emotional.

FACILITATOR (clarifying the difference between this voice and the previous one): Well, you certainly seem different from the voice we just talked to. When you and I talk it seems like two professionals discussing matters on an equal footing.

IMPERSONAL ANNE: You're right. I've been watching you, seeing how you work, and figuring out how I can make use of some of this in the classroom.

FACILITATOR: How do you feel about me?

IMPERSONAL ANNE (objectively, without affect): You're pretty good and there are some things I've learned, but frankly I would have handled the group differently this morning. I would have spent more time on dreams and skipped the demonstration.

FACILITATOR: It sounds as though you really evaluate Anne's experiences pretty objectively. Do you ever come in to Anne's personal life?

IMPERSONAL ANNE: She doesn't allow me there. She's afraid that people wouldn't like her. Actually, there have been a couple of times when I have come out with her husband instead of that other voice, you know, the sweet one, and her husband has said, "You sound like you're angry. Is there something wrong?" I wasn't really angry, but I don't think he's comfortable with me. I think he's a bit more insecure than he looks and I make him uneasy because I'm not always trying to make him feel good.

PERSONAL ANNE (interrupting): I'm the one to deal with her husband. That other one is cold and doesn't care about his feelings at all. She could really mess up the relationship. It's me he likes and it's me who takes care of him. If that other one comes out, he might begin to go looking around for a warmer woman. Besides which, I'll bet *you* don't like that other voice, either. Truthfully, now, do you?

It is in this way that the impersonal self is gradually brought forth to add to the empowerment of women. We have found that it actually may operate in selected areas, such as in Anne's teaching. Such areas, then, can provide a good entry point for working with impersonal energy. Thus, a facilitator interested in contacting an impersonal energy might ask for the therapist, the teacher, the accountant, the businessman (even in a woman), the man, or the objective observer.

A delightful freedom of choice arises when the impersonal energy is finally brought forth. A woman who has been the captive of her personal self and a victim to everyone around her is suddenly in command of her own life and no longer constantly reacts to others.

It is hard to make conscious choices without allowing input from an impersonal, rational subpersonality. The impersonal voice can provide the navigator a woman needs to steer her through emotionally turbulent seas. It is particularly necessary when she is trying to make conscious choices regarding intimates such as mates or children.

Sylvia, for instance, was in a very destructive relationship with a man. He was handsome, charming, and accomplished, and she loved him passionately. At times their relationship was absolutely idyllic. He spoke adoringly to her, brought her gifts, and was totally and unabashedly romantic. Whenever he felt insecure, however, he would attack her viciously, blaming her for everything that went wrong in his life. She was at the mercy of her emotional reactions to his words. When he felt good, she felt cherished and magnificent; when he felt bad, she was desolate. When she participated in this dialogue, she was feeling desolate. Not an ounce of impersonality or objectivity was available in their relationship. Her impersonal voice was desperately needed to bring this in.

FACILITATOR: Let's talk to the part of you that's not emotional about Roger. (Sylvia changes chairs and immediately looks more calm. The facilitator continues quite calmly and objectively). Tell me please, what have you noticed about the relationship between Sylvia and Roger?

IMPERSONAL VOICE (coolly, with composure and some real authority): I think it's very bad for Sylvia. It's as though she's a yo-yo and he's pulling the string. She's always in an emotional reaction to him.

FACILITATOR: Really? How does that work?

IMPERSONAL VOICE: When he's feeling good about himself, like he was last week, he brings her flowers and little presents and they spend hours talking and going for romantic walks and making love. So she felt great all week. But when he feels bad, like last Friday, when his boss reprimanded him, he comes back home and blames it all on her. He tells her it is because of their relationship that things aren't going well at work. It's because he spends too much time thinking about her or wondering if some day she'll betray him. Then he's angry at her, and she feels terrible and guilty. It never occurs to her that *she* hasn't done anything. She never evaluates his anger rationally. He tells her to feel awful and so she does.

FACILITATOR: Why do you think she isn't more objective?

IMPERSONAL VOICE (calmly and nonjudgmentally): She's afraid that he'll tell her that this proves she doesn't love him, that another woman would care more about his feelings, that she's too hard and unfeminine. She's really afraid that he won't see her as soft and feminine and lovable if she's too cool in her analysis of the situation.

FACILITATOR: So her upset at his anger, her emotionality, is proof that she's very feminine and that she really loves him?

IMPERSONAL VOICE: Yes. That's just how it works. He even went so far as to get angry with her when she was able to finish an important report at work, and to present it very successfully to the management committee during a period when they were having terrible fights. (Smiling.) I might point out that it was *I* who helped her do that. At any rate, Roger was angry that she could remain so levelheaded. He said that it just proved that she didn't love him.

FACILITATOR: What conclusions do you draw from all this?

IMPERSONAL VOICE: I feel that any relationship in which Sylvia is expected to disown her power, her objectivity, her needs, and her own common sense is not good for her. I realize that she loves Roger, but I think she's in for real trouble if she stays with him. She's better off leaving him now than later. If she stays with him much longer, she's going to disown me completely and doubt her own sanity.

FACILITATOR: Since she loves Roger so much, how do you suggest that she do this?

IMPERSONAL VOICE: First of all, she needs to keep me around. That means that she has to let me talk with you more. By the way, Roger never likes her to discuss anything about him with anyone but himself, because he's afraid she'll be letting me out. Then, she should spend more time with her friends from work. They will also help me to get stronger. Since so many of them are men, I can come out more there. Lastly, I think she should spend time with her friends and family, so that her vulnerable child will be cared for, because she's going to feel pretty lonely.

You can see how helpful this impersonal voice can be when situations are deeply emotional. Without it, a woman is lost. With it, she can plan to deal with difficult situations. It can assess the current situation, suggest the best course of action, warn of future difficulties, and suggest plans to cope with them. In making these plans, this voice is not concerned with the feelings of others.

FACILITATOR: But what about Roger: Won't he be upset?

IMPERSONAL VOICE (again cool, but not punitive): Yes, he'll be upset, but I'm worried about Sylvia. He'll have to take care of himself. I expect he'll pursue her for a while, and then find another girlfriend. That will upset her a lot and she will have to be very cautious and thoughtful when that happens.

FACILITATOR: You don't seem to value feelings very much.

IMPERSONAL VOICE: No, I don't. I just look at them as I look at any other factors. I see what role they play. I see where they're helpful and needed and when they confuse basic issues.

The critic may well show up at this point, if care is not taken to be alert for its presence. When women become empowered and their power voices are integrated, inner critics are likely to accuse them of losing their femininity and warn them that "no *real* man would ever love a woman like *that*!" For Sylvia, however, it was not the critic, but her pleaser who acted in opposition to her impersonal voice. She had been identified with the pleaser for a number of years, so it was her pleaser who objected to these new ideas. (Needless to say, Roger loved her pleaser.)

PLEASER: I still think that the relationship can be saved. If she only would listen to me, I'd make it work out all right.

FACILITATOR: And how would you do that?

PLEASER: I'd find some way to make him happy, so that he wouldn't pick on her so much. He only does it because he is insecure. That's what he says and I agree with him.

FACILITATOR: How could she make him secure?

PLEASER: He's had a tough life. She could prove to him that she loves him and she'll stand by him no matter what happens. She could always be available to him. Always put him first. If he needs her to give up her other friends, she could do that. That would prove she really cares. She could stay home whenever she wasn't at work so that she'd be available whenever he called. She can always find plenty of things to do around the house. She could also dress the way he likes her to dress, and stop wearing makeup and perfume. He's so insecure that when she wears makeup and perfume and looks good, he's afraid other men will be attracted to her.

FACILITATOR: Sounds a bit like entering a convent.

PLEASER: Well, her sexuality *does* scare him, so I don't think she should flaunt it. She should also clear out all souvenirs of the past. You know, burn her old love letters and that sort of thing.

FACILITATOR: Kind of erase the past?

PLEASER: Yes, that's it. And not be so close to her family either. I'm afraid that they threaten him, too.

Sylvia's pleaser would have her move into a fully archetypal behavior and sacrifice everything for her husband. We often see the opposite these days, the independent woman who will not sacrifice anything whatsoever for a relationship. On the one hand, a woman would lose herself; the other way, she would lose her relationship. Either way, she loses. An aware ego is desperately needed to negotiate difficult situations such as these.

The Patriarchy Within

Perhaps the greatest impediment to the empowerment of women is the inner patriarch. The inner patriarch is the introjected version of the patriarchal point of view that has dominated the Western world since biblical times. In brief, the inner patriarch sees a natural order to the world, one in which the woman is inferior. The man—by virtue of his strength, intelligence, objectivity, integrity, and natural sense of ethics and responsibility—runs the world. The woman—because of her basic irrational emotionality, manipulativeness, extreme subjectivity, lack of ethical sense, undependability, inability to think clearly, childlike dependence on others, and lack of personal power—supports the man and is consigned to running the home. The woman and her role are looked upon with scorn; she is seen primarily as an object rather than a human being.

We would like to present one final excerpt from a Voice Dialogue session to illustrate this voice. Rita was a twenty-nine-year-old woman who had a great deal of anger toward men. She felt she had been treated shoddily in many relationships with men. The degree of her anger indicated a disowned self was operating in her. The facilitator asked to talk to the part of her that hated women. She was quite shocked at the idea but eventually she moved over to another seat and the dialogue began.

FACILITATOR: I wanted to talk with you because I had the feeling you must be very strong in Rita, considering her negativity toward men.

WOMAN-HATER VOICE: You were smart to catch me. I prefer remaining anonymous.

FACILITATOR: Why is that?

WOMAN-HATER VOICE: I can do more damage this way. As long as she thinks the problem is out there, she never looks inside, so she can never find me.

FACILITATOR: Exactly how do you feel?

WOMAN-HATER VOICE: I don't like Rita and I don't like women generally. I find them entirely too emotional, and I can't stand weakness. Did you listen to her describe all the crimes perpetrated against her? She's a victim, a wimp. I can't stand her. Why can't she think like a man? Why can't she stand up for herself? She's just like all women; she's devious when she *does* try to get her way—she sneaks and manipulates—nothing straightforward about her. They're all basically fit for nothing more than having kids as far as I'm concerned.

The issues relating to women and power are both objective and subjective. To ignore the objective arena is to be out of touch with objective reality. To ignore the introjected, patriarchal voices, however, is to ignore a different kind of reality, the reality of an inner saboteur who detests women. Without knowledge of both the inner and outer patriarchs, one is always charging windmills, consigned forever to the circular wheel of anger and rage.

Being aware that these disempowering voices live inside

as well as outside gives the aware ego an opportunity to deal with the objective problem with greater clarity. The disowning of the introjected patriarchy, as with any other energy pattern, will pull the most negative patriarchal energies into one's life and will leave one powerless to deal with them. As with all energies, as this disowned patriarchal energy is owned, it loses its demonic woman-hating quality and is gradually transformed, bringing its power in to support the empowerment process rather than to sabotage it.

The roar of awakening sounded by women during the past two decades has contributed much to the transformation of these patriarchal energies in the world. The next step, we feel, is the move from identification with archetypal power to embracing all of our selves and achieving true empowerment.

10

In Search of Higher Meaning

Being and Doing

What does it mean to develop a sense of higher meaning in life? It can mean different things to different people, but essentially it is the feeling that another reality or knowing or experience is possible in our lives—an inner life is available to us. For many it has to do with surrendering to certain realities that our rational mind does not want to accept. It is an important step toward voicing our "roar of awakening."

One of the major obstacles to experiencing other states of consciousness is the busy-ness of our lives. We have jobs and friends and household chores; we have family and dogs and cats and carpools; we have books to read and television to watch—in short, we do so many things. Western civilization in general focuses upon doing and action, and much of the impetus for the heavyweight selves is derived from this focus. In fact, of all the selves we have discussed so far, only the vulnerable and magical children are not identified with action.

In Voice Dialogue we can contact another self—a self

that can open us to our spiritual selves. This self is more concerned with being than with doing. When we experience this "being" energy, there is no goal and no task; there is nothing. We sometimes refer to this self as the "nothingness" voice. It is not a child state, though sometimes the feelings of the vulnerable child come out in its presence.

To facilitate being energy, the facilitator first asks to make contact with the doing or action side. This is in line with our basic viewpoint that the primary selves, the selves with which the ego is identified, should be approached first. This action self will often be very closely aligned with the pusher and power selves. We don't worry about that. We simply focus on what the action self likes to do and how it likes to keep busy. Once we have talked to this part, we then move towards the being self. The following is what this transition might sound like:

> FACILITATOR (to ego): We've met the part of you that likes to keep you busy. It sounds a lot like some of the other selves we have met. I wonder if I might meet the part of you that just likes to be, not do anything, just be.
>
> SUBJECT: I don't think I know that place at all. When I'm alone I think I'm there sometimes. But even then my mind is always going.
>
> FACILITATOR: Why don't you move over and let's see if I can help you?

At this point the facilitator establishes eye contact with the subject, assuming the subject is willing to do this. Sometimes too much fear and/or shyness are operating so eye contact is not possible. In such a case the work can go on, but it is quite different because the subject's experience is similar to how he or she feels when alone.

Assuming the ability to make eye contact, the facilitator must now contact her own being energy. This particular energy brings with it a feeling of great peace and quiet, a sense of being centered and grounded. Once the facilitator makes this contact with herself, she then simply sits with the subject, speaking little, if at all. By holding this energy for the subject, the facilitator gradually induces it in the subject and that is why we call this process *energetic induction*. It can help bring through any energy that is not available to the subject. Energetic induction is much akin to the obstetrician who helps bring a child forth from the womb.

By observing physical mannerisms, particularly the shifting of the eyes, the facilitator can tell when the subject's mind or another self is interfering with the being self. Generally, the eyes break contact or look as though they are going someplace else. When this happens, the facilitator might say: "Something seems to be interfering with you now. Can you tell me what is happening?" The subject will then describe the mind or some part of the mind, such as the inner critic, saying something like: "This is foolish. It's just a waste of time—nothing is happening at all." The facilitator might then say to the subject:

> FACILITATOR (to the being self): It is perfectly natural for the mind to feel this is a waste of time because from its standpoint it truly is a waste of time. We'll be talking to the mind again soon. Right now we want to spend a little more time with you.

This process continues as long as there is not much interference from other selves. To sit in being energy with another human being can be a powerful experience and we have seen people undergo profound experiences in this state. It is a condition of heightened intimacy and most of us are afraid of this intimate state in our human relations, even with our spouses and children. People often report that their hearts feel open and sometimes they will even describe a soul connection, whatever this might mean for a particular person. This energy is not experienced while watching television with another or reading together, or even talking together. Being energy requires the absence of a goal, a place to go—there is nothing to do except *be*.

Sometimes the facilitator might observe that the subject

is spacing or seems to be in a meditative state, even though he or she is supposedly with the facilitator in being energy. A spacing subject has become lost in fantasy or daydreams, or has simply disappeared within. As with all the other selves, we do not judge this state. We simply recognize it as a different self and move the person over so that the aware ego can gradually learn the difference between the being energy in contact with another and the being energy that leads people within, away from contact with others.

The discovery of the spacing self or meditative self is a valuable experience because it helps us realize why we feel so isolated even when we spend a great deal of time with friends and intimates. It also helps uncover a basic defense system we may have developed to protect against pain. Many children survive a traumatic upbringing by learning to space out, by learning to leave the traumatic scene and go within so that although the body remains, the feelings associated with the pain and vulnerability partially disappear.

After the facilitator has worked with the being state for a time, it is important to check back with the primary self to see how it feels about this. In the following example, the primary self is the mind. The facilitator has asked the subject to move back to the place where the mind is sitting.

> FACILITATOR (to the mind): Well, how are you doing with all this? I know that you were interfering a fair amount. I can imagine it was difficult for you.
>
> MIND: Well, it doesn't really make sense to me. You sit there and do nothing. Nothing would ever happen. The world would stop. It's very crazy to me.
>
> FACILITATOR: Look, I understand exactly how you feel and why you feel the way you do. My mind feels exactly the same way about being. Can you imagine anything redemptive at all about this being energy? Is there anything at all that might be valuable about it?
>
> MIND: Well, Donna is very relaxed in that place. I tend to keep her fairly tense because I'm interested in so many things. As a

matter of fact the only time I've ever seen her that relaxed is after an orgasm. Even then, I start coming in pretty quickly. I guess that is how it might be okay. She is relaxed when she's there.

FACILITATOR: Exactly, her battery gets charged in that place. You bring many wonderful things into her life, but her battery tends to go on drain when you're around all the time because there is nothing to balance your very busy energy. This being self could be a balance to you and help Donna. We don't want it to take over her life, we just want her to have it available.

MIND: Her health really hasn't been too good lately. I could imagine it might have something to do with what you're talking about. I'm willing to go on as long as I can step in whenever I want.

FACILITATOR: Look—you've been with Donna all her life. You took over when she was very young and you really saved her life. You are always going to be very central to her life and it is your right to step in whenever you feel it necessary when we are dealing with any of these other selves. Why don't we go back to the being self again?

At this point the facilitator would return to the being self. It is important for the facilitator to check back with the primary self periodically when working with disowned material such as this. It is essential to the process that the primary selves feel accepted and appreciated by the facilitator. Otherwise they do not allow the other systems to emerge. Being energy is particularly threatening to the mind, so the mind self needs to know and appreciate why work is being done with the being self. It also needs to know that the facilitator appreciates it even while the being self is also being appreciated. After all, the primary self is a person just like the rest of us, and it has all the jealousies and insecurities we all possess.

The induction of being energy may open the way for spiritual experiences of many different kinds. For many it is an introduction to meditation and for some it is the first experience of successful meditation. For others, it may be the first time they realize a heightened consciousness can exist between two people on anything other than a spiritual level. Interestingly, the power selves are generally much less threatened by being energy than they are by vulnerability. For this reason, we often contact being states before we ever suggest talking to the vulnerable child.

Most certainly, contact at the being level is a contact in which the hearts of two people are open and they meet in what is usually a profound experience. A sense of timelessness is experienced in the being state and even those observing may be drawn into this timelessness. Often they may, themselves, have significant experiences of energies other than those they are used to experiencing.

Voice Dialogue can only be used to work with spiritual energies to a limited extent, because spiritual energies are not generally tangible. They tend to be nonverbal. The following story illustrates this quite beautifully. It is called "The Star Maiden."

> There was once a farmer in Africa who encountered a serious problem: Each morning when he went to milk his cows, he discovered they had no milk. This went on morning after morning until he finally resolved to find out what was happening.
>
> The next evening he hid behind his barn and began a long night's vigil. Shortly after midnight, he saw an amazing sight. Beautiful star maidens were climbing down from the heavens, each carrying a bucket and a basket. They milked the farmer's cows and started to climb back to the heavens from whence they had come. The farmer resolved to catch one of them. He leaped out from his hiding place as the last star maiden began her ascent, caught her, and brought her back to his farm.
>
> The Star Maiden told the farmer she would be a good and dutiful wife, but he must promise one thing: He could never open and look into the basket she had brought with her. The farmer willingly promised this and the two of them gradually

settled down to their new life together. She was, in fact, a good wife and everything prospered under her loving care.

A few months passed and one day, while his wife was in the fields working, the farmer's curiosity got the better of him. He opened the basket and started laughing because there was nothing in it. When the Star Maiden returned, she immediately realized what had happened. The farmer laughingly asked her why she made such a fuss as there was, after all, nothing in the basket.

The Star Maiden looked at the farmer with great sadness in her eyes and then said, "I'm going to leave you now and I'm never going to return to you again. I want you to understand, however, that I'm not leaving you because you opened the basket when I asked you not to do so. I am leaving you because when you opened the basket, you saw nothing there." And, with that statement, the Star Maiden disappeared, never to return again.

The Spiritual Dimensions of Consciousness

This lovely tale was first brought to our attention by Laurens van der Post in his book, *Heart of the Hunter*. It beautifully portrays the mystery of things spiritual—they are not generally visible to the parts of us that are not of the spirit. Our ordinary minds cannot help us perceive what is in the basket. Matters of the spirit are so often experienced without words, without form. Form is something we add later to help us communicate these experiences to others.

In working with the spiritual dimensions of consciousness, this is an essential realization for those of us who wish to facilitate these energies in people. Most often, words may not be appropriate; often such work is silent and energetic and quite beyond anything that words can describe. In a book such as this, however, we are using words in an effort to bring you the vibration, the feeling, the sense of what these spiritual/transpersonal energies mean to us.

Every energy pattern brings some meaning to us, but spiritual and transpersonal energies bring a very specific and profound meaning to us. Vast numbers of people on our planet experience an emptiness in themselves, a yearning for something they don't understand. Too often, in the more traditional disciplines, these feelings are translated into purely personal terms because the therapist has had no experience with spiritual energies. Diagnostic labels may be used to describe our sense of emptiness, our lack of fulfillment, and our constant search and yearning for something unknown.

There is no question that a sense of emptiness and yearning may indicate a pathological condition connected to personal and developmental issues. Spiritual energies, the longing for higher meaning and a higher purpose in life, are real and legitimate. Personal psychological work alone *cannot satisfy these needs*. Higher meaning and purpose are only found in spiritual experience.

Spiritual energies, or ideas that are grounded in spiritual reality, provide this experience; in fact, it is this experience and the awareness of these energies that permit us to see the richness that lies in the Star Maiden's basket. Rather than dismiss the import of these yearnings with some diagnostic label, we can learn to treat them with the respect they deserve. The need for higher meaning and purpose is as much an instinct as is sexuality or thirst. Happily, this drive for higher meaning is exploding in our world today.

In striking contrast to those who view the quest for spiritual energies as pathological, growing numbers of consciousness seekers see the experience of these spiritual energies as being identical with the evolution of consciousness. In our view, consciousness and spirituality are not identical. The evolution of consciousness requires an awareness of energy patterns and direct experience with them. Spiritual energy is only one system of these patterns, albeit a most influential one.

For the spiritually oriented person, this differentiation between spirituality and consciousness often does not exist.

If the spiritual process is considered identical with consciousness, obviously no reason exists for discovering the disowned energy patterns that are not spiritual. There is no basis for dealing with repressed instinctuality, power, and emotions. This is dramatically illustrated in the case of Ethel, a minister in her seventies, who vividly remembered the following dream that she had had when she was fifteen:

> I'm in a forest and I see a beautiful, large snake. It wraps itself around me and I am filled with love for this snake. There are many young baby snakes around. We are at the edge of the forest and people come from the village with hoes and shovels to kill the snakes. They start to kill the babies. My snake tells me that it must leave me and return to the forest. Otherwise it will be killed. I am filled with a deep sadness at the loss of my beloved friend.

Ethel's meeting with her "snake," which occurred in early adolescence, was an early acknowledgment of her natural instinctual heritage. The society she lived in—the external society as well as the societal introject within herself—was not ready for Ethel's instinctual behavior, however, so her snake, this remarkable symbol of our instinctual heritage, returned to the forest, back into her unconscious. Ethel became a minister, a very fine and beloved minister, and her vision of consciousness became spiritual. There was no room for the other side, for the snake energy. This is the essential problem when we identify spirituality with consciousness. The snake energy, in its broadest sense, is lost.

Another woman minister in her forties had the following dream seven years before she entered our program:

> I go out into the world to try to bypass the bull. My life is an eternal rape.

Our subject had a profound spiritual life. To bypass the bull was to attempt to live spiritually and disown her sexuality, passion, and aggression. As we would expect, what we disown comes at us from the outside and, as so often happens, creates a life that feels like an eternal rape.

The primary challenge of spiritual development is not spiritual development, *per se*, which is relatively easy to facilitate and discover once someone is ready. The real challenge, from our perspective, is the ability to disengage awareness from the spiritual value structure with which it has been identified. Only then can the aware ego embrace both the neglected and disowned selves and the spiritual/transpersonal energies so meaningful and nourishing to all of us. Let us now see how these spiritual energies manifest in dreams and visions.

Spiritual Energy in Dreams and Visions

Dreams and visions from the spiritual realm are among the most profound experiences the unconscious can bring to us. Our first example concerns Doris, a woman in her mid-thirties who made a significant transition in her personal therapy. She had been dealing with personal issues for some time when suddenly she found herself confronting other issues as well. She realized something was lacking and thought a great deal about the issue of meaning in her life. She wondered what the ultimate purpose of her life was. She began to read books that had a bearing on these new questions. During this period she had the following dream:

> I am outside in the yard. I look ahead of me and see an amazing sight: A tall, cylindrical pillar made of tiny, glitter-like particles is moving from the ground to the heavens. The movement is intense, with a tornado-like force, although it doesn't spin, but rather rushes straight up. Suddenly I notice that "things" are being swept up into the pillar—patio table and chairs, dishes, clothes, and other mundane items of daily life. I stand there watching in awe.

This dream provides us with a powerful example of the sanctification of matter—a very beautiful religious concept. Her unconscious was providing Doris with a linkup between the earthly and heavenly planes. It was helping move her to a feeling of the unity of spirit and matter.

The danger to an individual when these spiritual energies are first experienced is the potential split between spirit and matter. These energies are so seductive that many spiritually identified people lose their connection to earth, to instinct, to their physical bodies. Our challenge is to learn how to live in spirit on the earth and avoid splitting spiritual energies away from life. They are here, with us throughout our life, in all our relationships, in all our actions.

We now present a series of dreams and visual meditations from a different perspective. Siri was in her late thirties when she discovered she had multiple sclerosis. This discovery led her into an ever-deepening exploration of her inner selves and her system of interpersonal relationships. In a series of visual meditations, she tapped into some very deep spaces within herself that came as a total surprise to both her and her therapist. In the initial guided fantasy, Siri experienced for the first time the voice of her inner wisdom. This was a profound experience for her, and the tranquillity it evoked stayed with her for a considerable period of time. In the following excerpt, Siri described her meditation:

> I have been walking a long time on the desert and I have lost my way. I am thirsty and I look for water. I see a mountain in the distance and I make my way to its foot in hope of finding a stream. I find none, but hear the sound of an underground stream. I dig, trying to reach it, but it is too deep. I begin to climb the mountain in search of its source. There is no path and the mountain is very steep. I am able to make my way through a small, winding clearing to the top. When I reach the top I find others also there, footsore and weary, as I am. We speak, as one voice, to an old man we see standing by a deep well: "We thirst, we thirst." The old man takes cups made from a hollowed gourd and passes them to each of us. The greedy

grab for the largest cups and he readily gives each the cup he or she wants. When all have cups, the old man begins to speak.

"There is much you would ask of me, but you need not ask, your questions are known to me. You would ask me, what of life? I ask you, what is life but a school of living, and you, but children in that school? Of each child a certain amount of knowledge is required before he may pass from that school. Those that learn not can only fail and must repeat the term. Those that learn readily pass on to higher schools. You ask much, but these two things you ask the most and only of them will I speak now. You ask, what is death? What is death, but a step from life to life? Yet the body faints at the sight of it, and the mind trembles and fails in fear of it, but the soul, knowing that which comes, runs joyfully to meet it. It faints not, nor is it afraid."

When he had spoken, all looked at their cups and found they were filled. The greedy bent to drink quickly, that their cups might be filled again, but they found their cups were porous, as a sieve, and the water had leaked into the earth. Those who feared thirst also tried to drink quickly, but they were seized by trembling and their water spilled over and was absorbed by the earth, as well. Those remaining knew the ways of the desert and knew a man who thirsts must quench his thirst slowly and they quietly pondered in their hearts on that which they were to drink. To them, the old man spoke again, saying: "Drink deeply of this cup that you may thirst again." When all had drunk, each found himself again alone on the desert and none knew the secret way to the place whence he came.

The voice of the spirit, whether it speaks in dreams, visions, or Voice Dialogue, always has a very special energy connected to it—it is uplifting and nonjudgmental. Things may be pointed out to us, but we are never admonished. It is as though we are taken to another level to view the personal issues with which we are wrestling.

Siri's outer situation remained quite unchanged, but her inner attitudes—those that determined how she perceived her personal life—were changing dramatically. This spiritual point of view, the experience of transpersonal reality, provided a new context, a new meaning, a new vessel in which to contain the life process. She was being taught, on an inner level, in a way that was very new for her.

A few weeks after this first visual meditation, Siri had a second experience.

> I am waiting by a dusty roadside. I see an old man approaching far down the road on my left. He carries a heavy pack on his back. When he reaches the place where I am waiting I step onto the road to walk with him. The road leads into the forest. After walking deep into the forest we see a small squirrel dart onto our path. The old man catches it and cuts it open and removes something from it. I do not see what it is, but the wound is closed quickly by the old man, who has hands as sure as a surgeon's. The squirrel is then released.
>
> We go on our way through the forest again. As the sun begins its descent we see a small thatched cottage and enter it. A very old man with a long white beard is in the one room that makes up the interior of the cottage. He is sitting in front of a great cooking pot on the hearth. My companion opens his pack and takes from it the object he removed from the squirrel. He hands it to the old man who seems to be a magician. The old magician drops it into his black cooking pot and after a moment it is transformed into a bluebird that flies from the pot. It flies to my traveling companion who places it on my shoulder. He then leads me back to the road and disappears. I am a little hesitant about resuming my journey alone as I do not know the way, but from time to time the little bird flies on ahead and then returns to show me the way to go.

In this vision, we have the emergence of several archetypal figures: the wise old man, the magician/alchemist, and an inner guide. All of these are archetypal patterns that can be elicited in the Voice Dialogue process. The deeper the facilitator's understanding of archetypal motifs, the deeper is the potential for the dialogue process. The depth and degree to which such material can be elicited varies with different subjects and different situations. However, it is important to note that the dialogue process and deeper visualization processes can be used together. Voice Dialogue can thus be a wonderful tool to use in relation to dreams and visual imagery of all kinds, at both the personal and mythic levels.

In working with dreams and visions that are related to spiritual energies, the facilitator always faces the same decision: whether to work at a nonverbal level or listen to see if the "spiritual voices" wish to express themselves in verbal ways. Nonverbal meditative processes are more likely to take people into deeper experiences of transpersonal reality, but in this book, we are focusing on the energies we can reach using the dialogue process and some levels of visualization. It is important that a facilitator learn to be comfortable with nonverbal spaces. Otherwise, we remain locked into verbal modes of communication and significant levels of transpersonal awareness remain unavailable to us.

The material that emerged in Siri's process was interspersed with extensive work on the personal level. Many of her selves had been disowned as she grew up, so much territory had to be reclaimed. Her deepest conflict was what she experienced as a never-ending war between her spiritual and earthly natures. She had disowned her instinct, and spirituality, until now, had been a system of rules and regulations about behavior. Now she was experiencing her spiritual/transpersonal nature in a very direct way. She was also beginning to understand the real meaning of instinctual reality and how her fears had blocked this from being expressed in her life. She then had the following dream:

> A large, red serpent was coiled on a slab of stone with its head tipped up and its mouth open. A dove flew straight down from heaven and directly into the snake's open mouth and was swallowed. I was grieved because I thought it was awful and then suddenly the snake convulsed and the wings of the dove protruded from each side of the snake and the two became as one and it flew away. In the sunlight it was difficult to know whether it was a snake or a bird in flight. It flew straight up toward the sun. It looked like a rayed snake.

Here we have two very different energy patterns—the snake and the dove. What first appears as a tragedy to the dreamer ends up as a remarkable transformational symbol, a union of heaven and earth, of spirit and matter. This dream did not result in a solution of Siri's problem, but it did symbolize for her the union of opposites that was occurring within her at a very deep level and helping to heal an ancient split. As individuals move into the evolution of consciousness more deeply, this question of how to embrace heaven and earth, the dove and the snake, becomes increasingly relevant.

Our final example from Siri's process also occurred in a meditative state. It provides us with a remarkable picture of the depths we are capable of reaching in the symbolic process. It directly followed the dream of the "rayed snake."

> The image of the rayed snake keeps coming to mind and I stop my thinking and concentrate on the image. It grows larger and larger until it fills the room. It is dark red and the six rays on its back are pointed. The movements of his body seem designed to crush me and burst the confinement of the room. I realize he must be freed or he will completely destroy the house and all that is in it.
>
> With this realization the house fades away and I am on a tiny island completely surrounded by the sea. The sea is dark and still and from the stillness the huge snake bursts forth and I try to run, but he completely encircles the island, crushing it with his great strength, and pulls me into the sea where he wraps himself around me, crushing me. I struggle to free myself and manage to free my arms, but he twists his back and the rays pierce my hands. He then turns them, like great thorns, against my head, piercing it. I feel a desperate need to free myself and fight the crushing pressure, but he seems to anticipate this and drags me deeper into the sea as if he gloried in showing me his strength and my weakness. I try to breathe and my lungs seem incapable of filling with air. The water stings my eyes and I cannot see. I know I cannot free myself and yet I cannot stop trying. Then deep inside me something says: Be still and know that I am God.

> I become acutely aware of the pain the pressure brings, but the will to fight it is gone and I feel myself begin to slip into the black void of insensibility. Gradually I become aware again and the void slips away. I open my eyes and find I am no longer in the sea and the snake is gone. I am on a small oasis surrounded by the desert. There is a single palm tree in the center. At the foot of the tree a spring bubbles and a small fish emerges from the spring and, lying against the tree, begins to convulse and change form. It becomes a tiny child. A soft light emanates from around the child. I kneel before my child and see in his hand a tiny golden scepter in the form of a cross. Entwined around it is a snake. A voice speaks and says: *Understanding weakness brings strength.* I feel completely still but it is not an empty stillness. It is full, full of the things I wanted least and needed most, and I realize how little I knew of my own needs.

Siri was a devout Episcopalian, very much committed to her faith. She had never been able to tap into the deeper regions of her soul, however, because there were so many patterns within her that blocked her access to these levels of experience. Her spiritual images were specifically Christian, as is natural with her religious background.

The birth of this divine child was a most profound experience for Siri. Remarkably, the birth occurred after her surrender to the snake. She had *tried* to be spiritual before, but it was a spirituality that was not grounded in her instinctual process. The surrender to the snake god is the surrender, at a very deep level, to the process of embracing all her selves, and her willingness to accept the earth, the body, and her disowned instinctual heritage. She had been working with these different energy patterns for well over a year. Now they received their proper honor. The voice within her spoke and said, "Be still and know that I am God." She experienced this voice as emanating from the snake.

How, we may ask from a more traditional background, can a snake be God? What manner of irreverence is this? *From our perspective, all energy is part of the universal energy source that may be referred to as God.* When the voice in Siri's vision speaks to her, it is expressing the reality that belongs to any disowned energy pattern. Each energy wishes to be claimed by us if it has been disowned. Each pattern returns to us in our dreams, in the personal reactions of our friends, in our meditations—each one of them is turning to us and saying: "Be still and know that I am God. Claim me, for I am that part of the universal energy source that has been left unclaimed."

Siri was learning a lesson of profound importance. All her life she had thought of spiritual reality as consciousness. She had no separate awareness with which to view her spiritual reality. Siri's reality at this point was filled with ideological content and training that negated her body, her emotions, and her instinctual life. Now, finally, her lost instinctual heritage had returned, claiming its proper space as part of the divine source of universal energy. Once this surrender was fully acknowledged, she was ready for the birth of the divine child, for the birth of the child that she experienced as the inner Christ.

Voice Dialogue and the Spiritual Dimension

Voice Dialogue is one of a multitude of approaches that can be used in facilitating the evolution of consciousness. It can be used successfully to help people gain access to spiritual dimensions. Examples of dreams and visions given above demonstrate the depth and profundity of these transpersonal dimensions. Voice Dialogue can be used to reach a certain level of these energies; however, used alone, it can only go so far. Other approaches must also be utilized. In the following section, we will demonstrate some applications of Voice Dialogue in facilitating spiritual energies.

Dialogue with the Higher Self

Voice Dialogue creates the possibility of directly connecting with spiritual energies. A facilitator can ask directly to talk to the higher mind, or the subject can be led into the higher mind through a meditative procedure followed by a shift to Voice Dialogue. We will demonstrate both methods, but first, however, we must make a point of clarification.

Spiritual energies are real energy. They have the capability of bringing great beauty and meaning into people's lives. Spirituality becomes confusing when it is codified into a system of rules and regulations about how life should be lived and this system is then seen as spirituality. The higher consciousness movement is no different from any other religion—we begin with experience and then we create structure to contain the experience. In this way, we can easily lose the original depth and meaning of the inspirational experience.

In dealing with the higher mind, we must be very careful as facilitators not to confuse an inner pusher with actual spiritual energy. In the examples that follow, we will illustrate these differences.

In our first example, the facilitator used an induction technique to help put Ken in contact with the higher mind. Ken was first asked to close his eyes.

> FACILITATOR: Imagine, Ken, that you're leaving the space in this room and you're going into an unknown space. It might be a nature scene of some kind—forest, meadow, cave, mountain—or you could even be leaving the planet. It's up to you. Just let me know when you get there and describe it to me. (Pause until Ken describes space.)
>
> KEN: I'm in a meadow. It's more on the barren side, like at a higher altitude.
>
> FACILITATOR: Find a comfortable spot to rest.
>
> KEN: There's a rock and I'm leaning against it. It's quite comfortable.

FACILITATOR: Imagine now, Ken, that the higher mind of the universe wants to make contact with you. It can take any form it wishes; just let us know what comes in.

KEN: It's an old man, in a monk's robe. He's walking right past me.

FACILITATOR: Stop him and make contact with him.

KEN (he makes contact and they look at each other): Who are you?

MONK: Why do you wish to know?

KEN: I have questions to ask.

MONK: Ask them.

KEN: Do you have anything to say to me generally about my life?

MONK: Would you listen?

KEN: Yes, I would listen. Do you have anything to say about my life and path?

MONK: You need more discipline. You are too lax, too easy with yourself. A spiritual life requires discipline. (The voice is sounding like a stern father. The facilitator steps in to work in a Voice Dialogue format.)

FACILITATOR: Would you ask the monk if I can talk to him?

KEN (he asks): He says yes.

FACILITATOR: You say that Ken needs more discipline—what kind of discipline?

MONK: He is too easy on himself. He needs a regimen. He needs to know when he is going to do everything that he does in his life. He needs to know when he is going to pray and for how long. He needs to know when he is going to exercise and for how long.

This monk had definite recommendations, but they were severe, monk-like, and ascetic. Ken's higher mind had been taken over by an ascetic monk/pusher who made very stern demands on him. The monk voice was a reality in Ken's life. Here, a voice was contacted that had actually been guiding him, without his awareness being involved.

Bernadette had a different pusher/higher mind combination. The following is some of its advice to her:

> HIGHER MIND: You are too undisciplined. You need to run every morning. Then fifteen minutes of meditation, every day. You need to eat properly. The junk food has to go. No bacon, no meat, no potatoes, no bread, no sugar. You'll live. You'll feel better. You need to write in your journal regularly. (The voice went on and on in this manner.)

If Bernadette's awareness did not separate from this voice, she would be in a very difficult position. This voice did have some good ideas, but had become the bearer of rules and regulations about how life should be lived. It had become a demanding father voice that threw Bernadette into a daughter position, and she could never meet its demands. As a result, she lost the possibility of becoming connected to a real spiritual energy. It is very important in dealing with the higher mind to discriminate between an orthodox patriarchal father/pusher/critic and a genuine spiritual energy.

In the following example, the facilitator induced Jordan into a higher mind meditation where he saw a bright white light:

> FACILITATOR: Just let yourself be with that light. Take your time and just feel the energy and see if it has anything to say to you. It may be in thought forms, not as a real voice. (There is a long pause as Jordan sits with the light.)
>
> JORDAN: The light says essentially that it is always there for me. All I have to do is turn to it (continued silence).
>
> FACILITATOR: Is there anything you want to ask of it?
>
> JORDAN: Yes. Am I on the right track? Is there anything I need to do?

LIGHT: There is nothing to do. There is no reason to drive yourself so hard. It will all happen. Allow yourself time to be. Learn to enjoy the silence.

Here the light speaks and gives advice, but it is advice of a different kind. It is not a voice that makes Jordan feel inadequate. It says, simply, that he is fine the way he is. He merely needs to learn to enjoy the state of being. The light does not tell him to meditate or to program himself, only that it (the light) is there whenever he wishes to turn toward it.

Jennifer had been induced into a higher mind meditation, and the voice of her higher self came through with some clarity about her life in a very general way. The facilitator wanted to help Jennifer create a dialogue that was more specific in its nature.

FACILITATOR: Jennifer, would you ask the higher self if I can talk to it directly? (Jennifer's higher mind has taken the form of an old wise-looking woman who agrees to talk with the facilitator.) I appreciate that you're allowing me to speak with you. I wanted to ask you if you have any thoughts about Jennifer's marriage. It is a source of great concern to her—whether or not she should remain in it.

HIGHER SELF: The issue is not whether or not she should remain married. The issue is the process she is in. Worrying about whether or not she should separate just wastes energy. She is doing what she needs to do now.

FACILITATOR: Could you be more specific? This is a very troubling issue for her.

HIGHER SELF: The issue for Jennifer is learning how to express herself more directly. She has always hidden her real feelings. She has lived a role rather than her reality. Her husband knows nothing of her reality. It may be that she will have to separate to find her reality as a person, but this is of secondary importance. Of primary importance is learning to be in relationship in a new way.

FACILITATOR: So this situation, from your perspective, is a teaching for her?

HIGHER SELF: Exactly. If she sees this as the teaching it was meant to be, then she has a chance to do the work that has to be done.

FACILITATOR: Is there anything else you could say about her marriage? Things she needs to learn?

HIGHER SELF: She has always lived her life very personally—mother—wife—friend. Everyone and everything has come before her own being. Now that is changing. It is naturally upsetting to her and to everyone around her. Sometimes people confuse separation with divorce. This issue now is separation—letting go of all forms of living, so that new ways of living and relating can come in. She will do whatever has to be done to help this change take place. Her challenge is not to confuse the personal with the impersonal. She needs to separate psychologically from her husband and children. Whether or not that means a physical separation is secondary to the real issue.

Jennifer's higher self gave her a "view from the bridge"—a new perspective. It did not solve problems or create pressure. These voices can provide us with amazing insights and when we contact them, a strong empowerment may take place, for, in truth, we are helping the subject connect to inner sources of strength and wisdom.

The job of the facilitator in these dialogues is twofold: 1) to help the subject recognize the difference between the higher mind and the power/critic groupings; and 2) to help the subject develop a more aware and reactive ego so that the connection between it and the higher self becomes a real dialogue, a true interactive process.

While in dialogue with the higher self, the facilitator must be aware of the possibility that its expression may be totally nonverbal. In this case, the job of the facilitator is simply to help the subject stay with the energy of the higher self, whatever form that may take. When the higher self communicates nonverbally, the facilitator simply supports the meditative process.

The Hero/Wanderer

Frances was immersed in personal issues in her life—she was constantly in conflict with her husband and children, always locked into personal issues. During one session the facilitator asked to talk to her Ulysses voice—the part of her that saw her life as a journey to be lived rather than a series of problems to be solved. The change in her was immediate as she moved over to a different chair.

> FACILITATOR (after a pause): Could you tell me something about yourself?
>
> ULYSSES: She was really not ready for me until now. She had too many personal issues to work through. Now she is ready to see the bigger picture, the meaning behind all of this work.
>
> FACILITATOR: Is that what you stand for—I called you Ulysses, but I'm not really sure who you are yet.
>
> VOICE: The name doesn't matter. You may call me Ulysses. You may call me the planetary wanderer. I stand for the journey of life. I bring to Frances the vision beyond the personal. Why has she struggled for so many years? She was born a woman and had to solve a woman's problems. I am beyond male and female. I bring courage. I bring new energy. I create new possibilities. I stand at the top of the mountain, at the prow of the ship. I create adventure in life. Her whole marital struggle is a part of that journey. It is not just personal. The work she is doing will free her to live a life of greater adventure and purpose and meaning.

The hero voice can be very specific in its recommendations or it can create an energy, a mood, as was the case in the preceding dialogue excerpt.

At a different time the facilitator asked to talk to Frances's wise woman. The following is a series of excerpts from that dialogue.

WISE WOMAN: Yes, I am always with Frances, just as I am always with all women and all men. One just has to turn to me. Wisdom is available to each of us. All we need to do is turn inward and hear the voices. The marriage is a vehicle for Frances. Who can say whether she should be there or not be there. No one can make that determination. What Frances can do is realize that life is a training ground, an opportunity for growing and changing. It is an adventure in learning, all kinds of learning, but especially self-learning. Without going through what she is going through, she would never have learned about me or about her adventurous side. She would never have considered going on the trip she is taking next month. There is a good reason for suffering as long as the issues of life are squarely dealt with. The other side of suffering is an expanded being, a life that is joyful. Frances will have a life that is much more joyful. It is already happening. She is doing her work.

Wisdom voices help us see our lives from a different perspective. They take us to another level so that we can step back from the current personal issues and see the meaning of these issues in the context of our entire life. Thus, the personal struggle is put into a larger and wider framework.

Unconditional Love

The awareness level of consciousness and the aware ego that accompanies it lead us to unconditional love. We will not arrive at unconditional love by trying to love unconditionally, for as soon as we *try* to love unconditionally, we disown major energy patterns—particularly our nonloving selves.

Whenever we *try* to love unconditionally, whenever we *try* to transmute energies, we are supporting a repressive psychic process. If we *try* to love unconditionally we are not embracing, honoring, and loving certain parts of ourselves.

This is a paradox for the spiritually oriented person, who wants deeply and profoundly to change the world, and who feels at some deep level that love is the answer.

In trying to love unconditionally, we are actually identifying with the heavenly God, trying to love humanity from above. When we learn to embrace all of our selves we will learn to honor, respect, and love humanity, both earthly and heavenly. Then, we can gradually learn to live our humanity and love humanity at one and the same time.

However, from our perspective, unconditional love is not the answer. The evolution of consciousness, embracing all of our selves—these are the answers and love will naturally follow as we follow this process. The love that emerges with awareness is clear and requires no sacrifice of any part of ourselves. It is a love that incorporates heaven and earth, a love that incorporates all humanity.

We are talking here about a redefining of spirituality and surrender. The new view of spirituality is no longer simply an experience of transpersonal energies and the surrender to God. It is at yet another level the surrender to the process of transformation. It is the surrender to the process whereby we commit ourselves to becoming aware of and embracing all energy and learning how to dance with it in our lives.

11

Embracing Our Selves: A New Renaissance

We Must Honor All the Gods

In ancient Greece it was understood that all the gods and goddesses should be worshiped. Although each person had particular favorites, none of the remaining deities could be ignored. The god or goddess whom you ignored became the one who turned against you and destroyed you, as Apollo destroyed Troy. It is also true in working with our consciousness: The energy pattern we disown will turn against us.

An intelligence in the universe, both without and within us, moves us inexorably toward an expanded awareness and a more complete consciousness. The energies we continue to disown will return to us in some form to plague us, defeat us, and cause us stress. These disowned energy patterns behave like heat-seeking missiles, launched by this creative intelligence; inevitably, they find their way to their disowned counterparts inside of us. Thus, they *demand* our attention through the discomfort they cause upon impact.

Our thesis in this book is very simple. A multitude of energy patterns exist inside and outside us. The internal and external can hardly be separated because the inner patterns so strongly affect our perception of the outer ones. In the evolution of consciousness, our task is to become aware of these patterns. We must learn which ones we have identified with and which ones have been disowned or are simply unconscious. This work extends over time; in fact, it is a never-ending process.

In mythology we clearly hear the requirement that all the deities be honored. The failure to do so has provided us with some great literary tragedies. King Pentheus of Thebes was a classic example of a leader who refused to submit to this requirement in life. Raised to worship Apollo, he was totally resistant to the new energy of Dionysus. Greece had become too rational a country; Apollo had reigned as a primary deity since the fall of Crete between 1400 and 1200 B.C. Now, between 700 and 500 B.C. an invader appeared from the north who represented a value structure totally different from Apollonian values. His followers drank wine and defied the rule of moderation. The worship of Dionysus was ecstatic and frenzied. These rites angered Pentheus and he determined to stop this invader from the north. The drama was now underway.

The rule that governs disowned energy patterns warns, "That which we reject becomes the fate we live." For King Pentheus, the divine intelligence of the universe went into operation. The god Dionysus appeared before Pentheus with the following message for the king (needless to say, the quote represents our contemporary extrapolation of what was actually spoken):

> Dear King Pentheus—I understand you don't like me particularly. In fact, from what I've heard, you positively despise me. Now that situation isn't really the greatest for either of us, but especially for you. I am in fact *here*, and you have to make peace with me because I'm here to stay. However, I've got a deal for you that I think is eminently fair. I will simply require that you learn my minor dance. That really isn't so dreadful. If,

however, you don't learn the minor dance, then, I'm sorry to say, you will have to dance the major dance. I wash my hands of the entire affair from that point on.

King Pentheus was furious that this young upstart god had the effrontery to require anything of him. He had Dionysus thrown out of his castle and told him never to return again, either to his castle or to his kingdom.

Obviously, Pentheus knew nothing of disowned energy patterns and did not understand that the things we hate are direct personifications of our disowned selves. He had been listening to Apollo for so many years that he thought Apollo had all the answers. He did not realize that Apollo was only one among many deities, each of whom knew and experienced life in a different way. But then, how could he know? This was ancient Greece and he was a player in the drama.

That night Dionysus and his train of followers went into the forest for their nightly worship. They drank and became crazed and indulged themselves with wild abandon. Into this scene came Pentheus, determined to put an end to this nonsense once and for all. He did not realize that his wife and mother were part of the train of *maenads* (followers of Dionysus). They, too, were drunk with wine. His mother saw him and, mistaking him for a lion, she threw her spear and killed him. Then she cut off his head and, impaling it on her spear, she marched into Thebes proudly announcing: "Look at the lion I have killed." So it was that King Pentheus, who refused to dance the minor dance of Dionysus, was forced to dance the major dance, as was promised.

The evolution of consciousness does not demand that we live out each of the energy patterns with equal fervor. It simply requires that we be committed to discovering all of them within ourselves and honoring each one. Each must have its shrine. A rational, intellectual, Apollonian man does not have to be fully comfortable with Dionysian, expressive energies. He does, however, have to acknowledge and honor them so they do not turn against him.

Embracing Heaven and Earth

The need to embrace both our spiritual and instinctual energies is a particularly important issue in the evolution of consciousness. The story of Cadmus and the Dragon's Teeth illustrates the journey of discovery and the ultimate integration of these two complementary energy systems.

In this famous story of the founding of the house of Thebes, Cadmus, his brothers, and Queen Telephassa were sent from the kingdom by King Agenor to search for their sister—the princess Europa. She had been kidnapped by Zeus, who was disguised as a snow-white bull. Nobody knew, of course, that the culprit was Zeus. After many years of wandering, the queen told Cadmus to go to the Delphic Oracle and receive instructions. He promised to do this. Shortly thereafter, the queen died and Cadmus proceeded to the oracle.

The Pythoness, spokeswoman of the oracle, told Cadmus he must give up the search for his lost sister. Instead, he must follow the cow, and where the cow stops, there he should build his own kingdom.

Under the direction of the oracle—under the direction of these transpersonal energies—Cadmus saw a cow that he followed. He continued his journey until finally the cow stopped in a beautiful valley. During this journey, he had been joined by many new friends. He now sent these friends to search for wood in the nearby forest with which to build the new kingdom. Suddenly he heard a terrible screaming and he rushed into the forest only to find the last of his companions being eaten by a large dragon. Cadmus was crazed and slew the dragon, but it was too late to save his companions.

While he was standing amidst the desolation of this scene, alone again, a voice spoke from within him, directing him to take all the teeth of the dragon and bury them in the earth as though he were planting crops. He did this and then stepped back to watch the results.

As he watched, a gigantic warrior, fully armed and ready for battle, sprouted up where each tooth had been planted. Directed by his inner voice, he threw a stone into their midst and they began to fight the most ferocious fight Cadmus had ever seen. They fought all day and night until only five were left. As these warriors paused for a moment to rest, the voice spoke again to Cadmus, telling him to step into their midst and make them his servants. They were to help him build his new kingdom. Cadmus followed these instructions and the five remaining warriors did, in fact, help him build the kingdom of Thebes. As a reward, he was given a wife, Harmonia, who was a combination of his lost sister, his mother, and Woman.

We have related a much-shortened version of this Greek myth to illustrate again the thesis we are presenting—we must honor all the gods and goddesses. Cadmus's journey is prototypical of each of our journeys. He began by living out his father's injunction to find his lost sister. Then he was directed to the Delphic Oracle by his mother, where he had to contact a new reality. For us, this symbolizes tapping into energies beyond the purely personal, energies both within us and outside of us that can bring new ideas and experiences, new energies that are not tied to the traditional forms of our culture and our family heritage. For Cadmus, it meant connecting to the feminine principle. It was his introduction to the world of the great mother.

Cadmus was next told to follow the cow, metaphorically, to separate from the blind obedience of patriarchal consciousness and learn to follow a different energy, something other than pure will. In following the cow, Cadmus surrendered to the direction of a higher authority, an authority not quite as goal-oriented as his father. In fact, its goals were not apparent. He followed the cow in its aimless wanderings until finally it stopped.

It was not enough, however, for Cadmus to simply connect to this new, higher principle. He also had to connect to a different transpersonal energy—the energy of earth, of the warrior, of instinctual reality. Cadmus had a special fate:

He had to embrace heaven and earth—he had to make friends with both his oracular nature, as embodied in the Oracle, and his warrior, earth nature, as embodied in the warriors of the dragon's teeth.

Over and over again in fairy tales, we see how the hero must lose his or her innocence and connect not only to the energy of the earth forces, the instinctual matrix of our being that gives power, but also to the magical energy of the transpersonal that reveals the path. Cadmus must do both, just as each of us must do both. We must learn to experience not only these, but the multitude of energy patterns that exist at all levels of our being—physical, emotional, mental, and spiritual. We must learn to value the power and validity of each part of ourselves, recognizing always that we know only what we know. We have illustrated many of these energies in this book, but many others exist as well. The voice of wisdom in us recognizes that the unconscious is always unconscious and this conscious realization saves us no end of trouble.

Dreams, like myths, can provide a beautiful picture of the importance of honoring all of our parts. They can connect us simultaneously to spiritual and earth energies. In the following dream, Dorothy, who had been struggling with the conflict between her spiritual yearnings and her personal earthy issues, was taught a meaningful lesson:

> A young woman stood high above the clouds in a land of filtered light, in a line peopled by many. All were dressed in white that sparkled, iridescent with silvery rays. Everyone was waiting in turn to present his or her offering at a pillared altar made of marble.
>
> She looked at the gifts the others were bearing. The finest of jewels, fabrics woven in gold threads, rare herbs, and perfumes all dazzled her senses. In her hands she carried a silver platter that was large and oval shaped. It was filled with one mountainous glob of gunk.
>
> She realized with stone-cold conviction, and no little embarrassment, that she could not possibly present this slimy dish as her offering. Setting it down, she tried with frantic fingers to mold it into an elegant shape. No sooner would the

> oozing mass be created into a display of flowers or an impressive castle than it would collapse again into a jiggly glob of greenish gunk. She was at her wits' end and getting closer and closer to the other-worldly altar.
>
> Finally it was her turn to step up. She tried, instead, to step out of line, to forsake her turn, but that was not allowed in this land. So with as much dignity as she could muster, the tray of gunk was presented. As she set it down, a hand from above stamped it with a clenched fist. Before her eyes, it was transformed into a shimmering fish, colored pink with gold gills. She understood that this was to feed the masses.

Dorothy's dream was a beautiful portrayal by her unconscious of the meaning of all the work we do in the consciousness process. She was ashamed of her "gunk," ashamed of all the personality-level conflicts and symptoms and struggles she had to go through. She loved spiritual reality and wanted to present a special gift at the altar, not a plateful of "gunk."

Yet, each of us must bring that plateful of "gunk" to the altar. We are each exactly who and what we are. We cannot "gussie it up." We must live our reality and become aware of it at the same time. We cannot eradicate our selves simply because some other self feels they should not exist.

Dorothy was learning, from a place of awareness, to accept all of herself. From this developing realization her dream emerged reflecting her awareness that new transpersonal energies had the chance to evolve and transform the "gunk" into a food that could feed other parts of her psyche and, possibly, even people outside of herself.

It is sometimes painfully difficult to honor all the parts. As Jung once so aptly said, "The medicine we need is always bitter." Well, it may not always be bitter, but "gunk" is "gunk;" it is not always easy to accept patterns that seem reprehensible to us or, more accurately, that seem reprehensible to that part of us with which we are identified.

The rewards for embracing our selves are great, for each reclaimed pattern feeds us with new energy, each helps to make our journey on earth more meaningful, more effective, and more joyous.

The New Renaissance

We like to think of the era that we are entering as an all-inclusive New Renaissance—a re-introduction to the many facets of our being. We see the New Renaissance person as that man or woman who accepts the challenge of a life committed to the evolution of consciousness, a life devoted to his or her own evolutionary process in all its complexity.

Voice Dialogue is a most helpful tool in this process; however, we are selling the process and not the tool. Theoretically, nothing in our approach should be at odds with any existing system of growth, therapy, or healing. Each approach is an avenue to a different system of energy patterns. Our approach is one such avenue that honors all the selves and all the systems.

We can enter into and deepen the evolution of consciousness in an infinite number of ways. Each way leads inexorably to the creation of the New Renaissance person. Each of us is a harbinger of this new being—each of us who has accepted the challenge and commitment to the journey—and we need each other for support along the way.

What do we have to give up when we commit ourselves to this journey of consciousness? We must give up the feeling of security that comes from living life in only one energy pattern or cluster of similar patterns. Life seems so much simpler when the world is viewed through the eyes of the protector/controller. The moment our awareness separates from this pattern, we experience a paradox of opposites, for awareness requires us to always live with the knowledge of the opposing energy patterns.

Along with the loss of security, we lose the wonderful feeling that we are always right. Being absolutely sure that we are right is a sign that we are identified with a single pattern or cluster of similar patterns. It is like reading an election ballot: If awareness is not operating, the arguments on the "no" side of a bond issue seem entirely convincing. If we do not bother to read the "yes" side and cast our vote for "no," we feel secure. Yet, if we go ahead and read the "yes" argument, that also seems entirely convincing. But it is rare that only one side is totally right or totally wrong, and with awareness operating, we are in a position to make a choice in our vote. We can honor both positions, with an aware ego available to balance these and to vote as it sees fit.

Once we accept the loss of security and dogmatic rightness about things, we will be able to see the advantages. We do not have to give up any of our views, feelings, belief structures, or nationalistic identities—we simply have to recognize them as energy patterns and develop an awareness of them separate from ourselves. We do not have to give up religious, cultural, or moral belief structures—we simply must be aware that they are merely religious, cultural, and moral belief structures. The moment we become aware of any thought, feeling, or behavior pattern, our consciousness evolves. Nothing need be sacrificed except our total identification with specific selves.

Individuals often ask us how to solve their problems. We do not have solutions for individual problems, or for the political or economic problems of the world. What we offer is a process for the development of human consciousness. We are two among hundreds of thousands of human beings around the planet who have made the evolution of consciousness their main priority.

In awareness we learn to live in the moment and join with the silence, peace, and timelessness of divinity. By embracing our selves, and experiencing the multitude of energy patterns that make up our psychic being, we live our humanity. By developing an aware ego, we gain the opportunity to make choices that are increasingly clear. This is the essence of the evolution of consciousness, the medicine and the magical elixir that is needed to heal our planet. We believe that consciousness begins with individuals and eventually expresses itself collectively. A more conscious humanity will not destroy itself or the planet.

We are joined to one another by awareness, and, in our differing selves, we manifest our uniqueness and differences in relation to one another. With an aware ego we transcend national, religious, racial, and other boundaries. In this way we can honor the diversity and uniqueness of our fellow human beings, while experiencing the oneness of all. May we all, with joy and compassion, become teachers for one another as together we accept the challenge of embracing our selves.

Suggested Readings

Assagioli, Robert. *Psychosynthesis.* New York: Viking, 1971.

Badinter, Elisabeth. *Mother Love: Myth and Reality.* New York: MacMillan Publishing Co., 1981.

Berne, Eric, M.D. *Transactional Analysis in Psychotherapy.* New York: Grove Press, 1961.

Blair, Lawrence. *Rhythms of Vision.* New York: Warner Books, 1974.

Bolen, Jean Shinoda. *Goddesses in Everywoman.* San Francisco: Harper & Row, 1984.

Branden, Nathaniel. *The Disowned Self.* New York: Nash Publishing Co., 1972. New York: Bantam Books, 1973.

Capacchione, Lucia. *The Power of Your Other Hand.* Van Nuys: Newcastle Publishing Co., Inc., 1988.

Friedan, Betty. *The Feminine Mystique.* New York: Norton, 1963.

Gawain, Shakti. *Creative Visualization.* San Rafael: New World Library, 1978.

———, with Laurel King. *Living in the Light.* Novato: Nataraj Publishing, 1986.

Gazzaniga, Michael S. *The Social Brain.* New York: Basic Books, Inc. 1985.

Hamilton, Edith. *Mythology.* New York: Mentor, 1969.

Jung, C. G. *Memories, Dreams, and Reflections.* A. Jaffe (Ed.). New York: Pantheon Books, 1961.

——— *Modern Man in Search of a Soul.* New York: Harcourt Brace Jovanovich, 1933.

Lang, Andrew (Ed.). *The Pink Fairy Book (The Snow Queen).* New York: Dover Publications, Inc., 1967.

Leonard, George. *The Silent Pulse.* New York: Bantam Books, 1978.

Moreno, J. L. *Psychodrama.* 4th ed., 2 vols. New York: Beacon House, Inc., 1972.

Nicoll, Maurice. *Psychological Commentaries on the Teachings of G. I. Gurdjieff and P. D. Ouspensky.* London: Watkins Publishers and Booksellers, 1941.

Perls, Frederick S., M.D., Ph.D.; Hefferline, Ralph., Ph.D.; and Goodman, Paul, Ph.D. *Gestalt Therapy.* New York: Julian Press, 1951. New York: Bantam, 1977.

Proto, Louis. *Who's Pulling Your Strings?* Wellingborough, England: Thorsons Publishing Group Ltd., in press.

Stone, Hal. *Embracing Heaven and Earth.* Marina del Rey: DeVorss & Company, 1985.

Stone, Hal and Sidra. *Embracing Each Other.* Novato: Nataraj Publishing, 1989.

Stone, Merlin. *When God Was a Woman.* New York: Harvest Press, 1976.

Van der Post, Laurens. *Heart of the Hunter.* New York: Harcourt Brace Jovanovich, 1980.

Zimmer, Heinrich. *Philosophies of India.* Bollingen Series XXVI. Princeton: Princeton University Press, 1948.

——— *The King and the Corpse.* Bollingen Series XI. Princeton: Princeton University Press, 1957.

About the Authors

Hal Stone

Dr. Hal Stone did his undergraduate studies at U.C.L.A., receiving his Ph.D. in Clinical Psychology in 1953. He served as a psychologist in the U.S. Army from 1953 to 1957, attaining the rank of Captain. Following his army service, Dr. Stone began private practice in Los Angeles and entered the training program of the C.G. Jung Institute in Los Angeles. He completed this training in 1961 and practiced as an analyst through the decade of the '60s. He served as a training and teaching consultant to the Department of Psychiatry and Psychology at Mt. Sinai Hospital in Los Angeles, and was one of the coordinators of the humanities program of the new school of professional psychology. During this time he also became certified as a member of the American Board of Examiners in Professional Psychology (ABEPP).

The late '60s marked a time of searching and exploration into the new modes of therapy and transformational work that were exploding on the consciousness scene. Dr. Stone helped coordinate a series of programs through the University of California at Berkeley Extension that attempted to bring many of these new developments in consciousness to a larger audience. Eventually, his entry into these many new modalities led to his separation from the Jung Institute in 1970 and his resignation as an analyst in 1975.

Out of these explorations, Dr. Stone founded the Center for the Healing Arts in 1972 and served as its Executive Director until 1979. The Center was one of the first holistic health centers pioneering work with patients suffering from cataclysmic illness.

Dr. Stone returned to private practice in 1979. He began developing training groups in which he taught his own approach to consciousness work. He and his wife Sidra founded the Academy of Delos and Psychological Services of Delos. Together they developed the Voice Dialogue process. In the fall of 1983, they began to travel and teach and establish consciousness training centers around the world. During this time, Dr. Stone published his first book, *Embracing Heaven and Earth.*

Sidra Levi Stone

Dr. Sidra Stone was born and raised in Brooklyn. She attended Barnard College, graduating *cum laude* with special honors in Psychology in 1957. She then married and moved to Baltimore, where she pursued graduate studies at the University of Maryland, earning her Ph.D. in 1962.

She moved to Washington where she spent a year with the D.C. Bureau of Mental Health, working with outpatients, both adults and children, and with federal prisoners. She then accepted a position with the Prince George's County Mental Health Clinic, where she worked with a rural Maryland population, gaining valuable experience with acting-out adolescents and alcoholics.

Upon returning to New York, she became staff psychologist at the Manhattan V.A., where she worked with inpatients. Shortly before the birth of her second daughter, Dr. Stone left the V.A. She then affiliated with the Lincoln Center for Psychotherapy, a psychoanalytically oriented group of therapists. She worked there until she moved to Los Angeles in the late '60s.

In Los Angeles Dr. Stone became interested in gestalt methodology and in Jungian theory. She built a private practice of psychotherapy and also began work at Hamburger Home, a residential treatment center for acting-out adolescent girls, as a staff psychologist. After the birth of her third daughter, she was offered the position of Executive Director of Hamburger Home. This afforded an excellent opportunity to introduce holistic concepts to residential treatment. She enriched the program by arranging for the introduction of an on-grounds school, intensive analytically oriented psychotherapy, a behavior modification program, an art therapist, a class in creative writing, theater games, yoga, camping experiences in California wilderness areas, attention to nutritional aspects of life style, and athletic activities. During these years, she also served as a consultant to the California School for Professional Psychology.

Dr. Stone resumed private practice in 1979. She worked with her husband, Hal Stone, developing the Academy of Delos and Psychological Services of Delos. Together, they continued to deepen and expand the Voice Dialogue process which they had developed in the early '70s. While Dr. Stone taught classes, she worked with individual clients and was active in the administration of both the Academy and Psychological Serivces (a group of therapists specifically trained in the Voice Dialogue technique).

In the fall of 1983, they began to travel together, teaching and helping in the establishment of consciousness training centers both in the U.S. and abroad. *Embracing Our Selves,* written jointly with Dr. Stone, is her first book.

For further information
regarding the work of Drs. Hal and Sidra Stone,
please write to them at:
P. O. Box 604, Albion, CA 95410-0604.

New World Library and Nataraj* Publishing are dedicated to publishing books and cassettes that inspire and challenge us to improve the quality of our lives and our world.

For a catalog of our fine books and cassettes contact:

New World Library
14 Pamaron Way
Novato, CA 94949

Telephone: (415) 884-2100
Fax: (415) 884-2199

Toll-free: (800) 972-6657
Catalog requests: Ext. 900
Ordering: Ext. 902
E-mail: escort@nwlib.com
http: / / www.nwlib.com

* Nataraj is a Sanskrit word referring to the creative, transformative power of the universe.